Foundation Website Creation with HTML5, CSS3, and JavaScript

Jonathan Lane, Tom Barker, Joseph R. Lewis, and Meitar Moscovitz

friendsof

DESIGNER TO DESIGNER™

an Apress® company

FOUNDATION WEBSITE CREATION WITH HTML5, CSS3, AND JAVASCRIPT

ISBN-13 (pbk): 978-1-4302-3789-1

ISBN-13 (electronic): 978-1-4302-3790-7

Distributed to the book trade worldwide by Springer Science+Business Media New York, 233 Spring Street, 6th Floor, New York, NY 10013. Phone 1-800-SPRINGER, fax (201) 348-4505, e-mail orders-ny@springer-sbm.com, or visit www.springeronline.com.

For information on translations, please e-mail rights@apress.com or visit www.apress.com.

Apress and friends of ED books may be purchased in bulk for academic, corporate, or promotional use. eBook versions and licenses are also available for most titles. For more information, reference our Special Bulk Sales– eBook Licensing web page at www.apress.com/bulk-sales.

Any source code or other supplementary materials referenced by the author in this text is available to readers at www.apress.com. For detailed information about how to locate your book's source code, go to www.apress.com/source-code.

Credits

President and Publisher:
Paul Manning

Lead Editor:
Ben Renow-Clarke

Technical Reviewers:
Heather Wallace

Editorial Board:
Steve Anglin, Ewan Buckingham, Gary Cornell, Louise Corrigan, Morgan Ertel, Jonathan Gennick, Jonathan Hassell, Robert Hutchinson, Michelle Lowman, James Markham, Matthew Moodie, Jeff Olson, Jeffrey Pepper, Douglas Pundick, Ben Renow-Clarke, Dominic Shakeshaft, Gwenan Spearing, Matt Wade, Tom Welsh

Coordinating Editor:
Debra Kelly

Copy Editor:
Patrick Meader

Compositor:
SPi Global

Proof Reader:
SPi Global

Indexer:
SPi Global

Artist:
SPi Global

Cover Image Artist:
Corné van Dooren

Cover Designer:
Anna Ishchenko

For my beautiful Rachel.
You are amazing in so many ways, and I absolutely adore you.
—Jonathan Lane

For my beautiful Rabbit.
—Tom Barker

To my beautiful wife, whom I love beyond measure.
—Joseph R. Lewis

For Aba, whom most of my work on this book is really for.

Hopefully you'll now feel comfortable using your editor's Source view.
—Meitar Moscovitz

Contents at a Glance

Contents

About the Authors

Jonathan Lane works for Harvest (GetHarvest.com) and is the sole employee of Industry Interactive, Inc. He does design and development for a range of clients in Canada and the US, and he produces a few of his own side-projects (like Mailmanagr—www.mailmanagr.com). Jonathan has been working with the Web for more than a decade now in varying capacities.

Jonathan is married and has three kids, Reilly, Parker, and Serenity, which pretty much occupies all of his nonworking time.

Tom Barker has been a software engineer since the late '90s, focusing on the full stack of web development. Currently he is the Senior Manager of Web Development at Comcast, an Adjunct Professor at Philadelphia University, a husband, a father, an amateur power lifter, and an armchair philosopher. On his team at Comcast are the craftsmen that create and maintain xfinity.com, and xfinitytv.com. At Philadelphia University, he teaches undergraduate and graduate classes on HTML, JavaScript, ActionScript, PHP, and MySQL. He is obsessed with elegant software solutions, continual improvement, refining process, data analysis and visualization.

Joseph R. Lewis is the Chief Web Architect at Sandia National Laboratories, where his activities include research, development, and instruction of semantic web, social media, and mobile technologies for scientific collaboration and national security applications.

Prior to the computer science career, Joe was a professional classical musician with a masters degree in performance from the New England Conservatory of Music, and he still plays and teaches the double bass when he can.

Born and raised in New York City, **Meitar Moscovitz** first touched a computer when he was an infant in 1986 (an Apple Macintosh Plus). At his father's prompting, he created his first website at the age of 12 and through it created the first online community for teenagers and young adults with bipolar disorder. Out of school by 16, he officially joined the workforce as a junior network administrator; and at 18, he started freelancing full time as a web developer. After brief excursions into corporate IT with such companies as Apple and Opsware (now HP), he returned to professional web development and worked on websites for clients including Oxygen Media, Inc., and the Institute of Electrical and Electronics Engineers (IEEE).

He now lives in Sydney, Australia, with his brilliant girlfriend of three years, Sara Hames, and works as the senior front-end web developer and IT director for Digital Eskimo, Pty Ltd. In his rapidly diminishing spare time, Meitar enjoys volunteering his technical talents to nonprofit organizations and other small groups. He's also an avid blogger and juggler, and he has way too many profiles on social networking sites.

About the Technical Reviewer

Heather R. Wallace is the author of several bestselling titles on a variety of subjects. Her most recent technology related title is *WordPress 3 Site Blueprints* (Packt Publishing, 2010), which shows readers how to build various websites using WordPress along with the right combination of either free or premium themes and/or plugins. Heather has also managed several successful websites and blogs, which she developed using a combination of HTML, CSS, and WordPress.

About the Cover Image Designer

Corné van Dooren designed the front cover image for this book. After taking a break from friends of ED to create a new design for the Foundation series, he worked at combining technological and organic forms, with the results now appearing on the cover of this and other books.

Corné spent his childhood drawing on everything at hand and then began exploring the infinite world of multimedia—and his journey of discovery hasn't stopped since. His mantra has always been "the only limit to multimedia is the imagination," a saying that keeps him moving forward constantly.

Corné works for many international clients, writes features for multimedia magazines, reviews and tests software, authors multimedia studies, and works on many other friends of ED books. If you like Corné's work, be sure to check out his chapter in New Masters of Photoshop: Volume 2 (friends of ED, 2004). You can see more of his work (and contact him) at his website, www.cornevandooren.com.

Acknowledgments

Not a lot of technical books reach a second edition! I was overjoyed to hear that the wonderful folks at Apress wanted to keep the "Foundation Website Creation" train running! Thank you to Ben Renow-Clarke, Matthew Moodie, and Debra Kelly for ushering me through the process for a second round. Thanks to Heather Wallace for all of her excellent and thoughtful feedback in editing this book. Thanks to Tom Barker for seemingly seamlessly filling in all of the gaps in my knowledge and really kicking this edition up a notch. You're a fantastic writer Tom. Thank you Patrick Meader for dotting our i's and crossing our t's. Your feedback was extremely valuable.

Thanks to my co-workers at Harvest, every single one of whom has taught me a lot during my tenure there. I'm honored to get to work with such a fantastic group of people.

Thanks to my wonderful wife, Rachel, for giving me the time and support to write again, and to my kids, Reilly, Parker, and Serenity, for once again keeping the noise level to a dull roar (some of the time). Thanks also to my parents: my mom, Cynthia, for the writing genes, and my father, Rick, for that "get it done" attitude. I'm not sure which was used more on this project.

Jonathan Lane

I want to thank my amazing wife, Lynn, and our beautiful children, Lukas and Paloma, for their patience and understanding while I would write every night until late in the night.

I want to thank Ben Renow-Clarke for thinking of me for this great project. I want to thank Matthew Moodie and Debra Kelly and the rest of the team at Apress for their guidance and direction. And I want to thank Jonathan Lane for being an incredible collaborator.

I want to thank my team at Comcast, every one of you is amazing and I am made better by being a part of such an incredible team.

Tom Barker

To the memory of my teacher, neighbor, mentor, and friend Lester M. Henderson, who taught me that most any problem can be solved with a pencil, a sheet of blank paper, and plenty of determination.

Joseph R. Lewis

First of all, I'd like to acknowledge the web standards giants who came before me, such as Eric Meyer, Molly Holzschlag, Peter-Paul Koch, Jeffrey Zeldman, and others too numerous to mention, without whom I'd have no shoulders to stand on. I hope my contributions to this book have added some real value to the work they produced before me.

I also want to thank all the people who worked with me on this book: my coauthors and technical reviewers, Jonathan Lane, Joe Lewis, and Tom Barker, for their very astute observations and suggestions while I was drafting my contributions; and the staff at Apress/friends of ED.

Thanks also to the wonderful people with whom I work on website projects every day—the staff of Digital Eskimo in Sydney, Australia, for allowing me to take the time off I needed to focus on this work. Even more important, thanks for providing a really great working environment where I can feel like I'm doing the things I want to do instead of the things I need to do to earn a living.

Acknowledgments

I would also like to thank my girlfriend, Sara Hames, the writer. Not only does she deserve thanks for helping proofread all of my work before the copy editor saw any of it and for not being upset with me in spite of getting published before her, but also for her immense support and encouragement in many more important ways than words can ever describe.

Finally, I'd like to thank my family for their support years before I knew I'd ever write a book: my brother, Shir, for being the single most resilient, methodical, and authentic person I know; my mom, Rina, for teaching my brother and I how to be the stalwart people we are (whether we make the choices she'd prefer we make or not); and my father, without whose inspiration, insight, and guidance I may never have found the path that led me to where I want to be today.

Meitar Moscovitz

Introduction

Coming to web development with a blank slate can be pretty intimidating. There are a lot of things to learn about the proper construction of a website, and the most successful websites have a great deal of thought and work put into thembefore they're even put into production

Although it can be scary, there has never been a better time to get started than the present. Web browsers are finally starting to reach a point where they all follow web standards (more or less). You have to do less fiddling with things to get them working properly now than ever before. We don't want to jinx it, but we think we can finally start letting our guard down a bit and start trusting browser manufacturers more (yes, even Microsoft).

Who is this book for?

This book is intended for people who are new to developing for the Web and those who are interested in overhauling their current work to be standards-compliant. It is relevant to individuals working within companies and institutions, as well as for those who freelance.

How is this book structured?

This book offers a brief history of the World Wide Web and then walks the reader through several chapters on each of the areas relevant to developing a website. Each chapter covers a separate process or technology relevant to working with the Web today.

Readers learn about planning a website, managing the design and development process, and development using web standards; we also provide an overview of server-based technologies and share sample projects along the way.

Conventions used in this book

To keep this book as clear and easy to follow as possible, the following text conventions are used throughout.

Important words or concepts are normally highlighted on the first appearance in *italic type*.

Code is presented in fixed-width font.

New or changed code is normally presented in **bold fixed-width font.**

Pseudo-code and variable input are written in *italic fixed-width font.*

Menu commands are written in the form Menu ➤ Submenu ➤ Submenu.

Where we want to draw your attention to something, we've highlighted it like this:

> *Ahem, don't say we didn't warn you.*

Sometimes code won't fit on a single line in a book. Where this happens, we use an arrow like this:➥

```
This is a very, very, very long section of code that should be written all on the same line
without ➥ a break.
```

Prerequisites

Have you heard of the Web? Ever used Facebook? How about searched for something on Google? Prerequisites passed, this book provides a great introduction to standards-based development for a novice audience. It doesn't stop there, however. Intermediate and advanced readers will also learn new concepts they'll be able to apply to their professional practice.

Chapter 1

Introducing the Past, Present, and Future of the Web

Believe it or not, when we were kids the standard way to send a message to a friend or family member was by mail. Not e-mail, mind you, but the physical kind requiring a stamp on the envelope. Fax machines came blazing onto the scene and revolutionized communications because, all of a sudden, you could send a document across the country in a matter of minutes, rather than a number of days. Personal computers were starting to show up in houses, but they generally cost an arm and a leg, and they certainly did not have any sort of way of communicating with the outside world. For the most part, assignments in school were handwritten, unless you had a typewriter at home! It was just the standard.

Most people in their twenties today will have a hard time believing that the Internet is a reasonably new invention, and the World Wide Web is even newer. Yet both have had as profound an impact on civilization as the printing press, the steam engine, or the light bulb. When we were growing up, we had an impossible time finding good video games for our PCs. Computers were all about business then. It was easy to find six different word processors, but nearly impossible to find the latest release from Sierra Online (which is owned by Electronic Arts now). These days, if you are looking for a video game, where do you go? The average person will head over to Amazon and preorder their copy of the latest title for next-day shipping. E-commerce has become so ubiquitous that, for certain products, it is preferred over a trip to the local store.

Even between the time that the first edition of this book was written and now, big changes have taken place (and that was just three years ago!). For example, there is now a really good chance that you are not even reading this book in a paper format! You might be using a tablet like an iPad or Playbook, an eReader like Amazon's Kindle, a PDF on your notebook or desktop computer, or even reading this on your cell phone. I have to tell you, it is really an experience to step back and think that in my lifetime, I have gone from a place where 1 in 1,000 households had access to a computer to now, where computer ownership may have peaked and people are moving to simpler, easier devices.

The standard way of doing things

Because of its highly technical childhood, the World Wide Web has a lot of "hacker baggage." When we say that, we don't mean that it's a dangerous place where people roam the wires trying to steal your credit card information (although there is some of that, too). We're using the term *hacker* in the classic sense of someone who has a curiosity about technology and tries to find her own way of solving problems. The Web started off very much from a position of trying to solve a problem: distributing research information. It evolved and gained features out of necessity—people needed to be able to add images and tables to their documents. In the early days of mainstream adoption, when businesses started to move online, there wasn't always a perfect way of doing things, so people came up with their own solutions.

A classic example of this is using a table on a web page to lay it out. At one point, we were guilty of this; but at that point we had no choice. Using a table was the only way we could get two columns of text to display on a page side by side. Things are vastly different today, and most would agree that the layout of a page is something better handled in the style information, rather than in the page's markup itself. Web standards have evolved; this isn't 1995 anymore, nor is it even 2005. Things have changed—and, dare we say—improved!

Every journey starts with a single step: the Web past

It is hard to find a book about Hypertext Markup Language (HTML) and the Web these days that doesn't start off with a history section. We used to wonder why that was the case. To understand why the web standards approach to building websites is the best way to go, you have to know about the progression of the World Wide Web and how it evolved to become what it is today. The World Wide Web has very technical roots, and the trouble (or charm) with most techies is that they like to customize and change things until those things are perfect in their minds. They cannot follow what everyone else is doing; they need to add their own flavor to it.

The Web started its life as a research project at CERN (the European Organization for Nuclear Research) in Geneva, Switzerland. At the time, a researcher there by the name of Tim Berners-Lee was looking for a way to quickly and easily share research findings with his peers and organize information in such a way that it would be easy to archive and retrieve. Although the process was started in the early 1980s, it wasn't until 1990 that Berners-Lee produced the first web server and web browser (which was called WorldWideWeb, the origin of the name).

In 1992, the Web began to hit the mainstream when the National Center for Supercomputing Applications (NCSA) in the United States released Mosaic, which was capable of displaying text and graphics simultaneously. Mosaic gave nonscientists easy access over the Internet to documents created using HTML, what we now call *web pages.* Encouraged by this early success, one of Mosaic's creators, Marc Andreesen, left the NCSA and started Mosaic Communications Corporation. This later became Netscape Communications Corporation, which created Netscape Navigator, the first commercial browser and the web standard-bearer through most of the 1990s.

A company called Spyglass licensed NCSA's source code and eventually released Spyglass Mosaic (although on a newly developed code base). This became the basis for Microsoft Internet Explorer, and it set the stage for the battle for browser supremacy between Netscape and Microsoft.

Just prior to the start of the "browser wars" of the 1990s, Berners-Lee recognized that, without some sort of governance, the World Wide Web would experience great challenges as competing web browsers introduced new features. One of the ways to get someone to pick your product over your competition was to offer a bunch of really cool features that the other guy didn't offer. He foresaw compatibility problems emerging as competing companies introduced their own tags in order to add features to the World Wide Web. HTML was the glue binding the Web together, and some central body would need to oversee its evolution in order to maintain a high level of interoperability.

Microsoft gave away Internet Explorer as part of Microsoft Office, bundled it with Windows, and made it available as a free download for all its various operating systems, as well as for Macs. Microsoft was a late starter in the browser market; and by the time it entered the game in 1995, Netscape had an estimated 80 percent market share. The tides rapidly turned, however. By the time Netscape was acquired by America Online in 1998, Microsoft had approximately half of the web browser market. By 2002, Internet Explorer reached its peak with an estimated 96 percent of web surfers using Internet Explorer. In fact, Microsoft so thoroughly thrashed Netscape in the browser wars that the companies ended up in a contracted lawsuit. Eventually, this led to a finding that Microsoft had abused its monopoly power in the marketplace. Figure 1-1 shows a timeline of major browser releases, starting in the early 1990s.

The browser wars were an incredibly difficult time for web developers as manufacturers raced to do their own thing. Versions 3 and 4 of the major browsers often had developers coding two entirely separate versions of their websites in order to ensure compatibility with both Internet Explorer and Netscape. Although web standards existed, most browsers only really supported the basics and relied on competing (and incompatible) technology to do anything advanced, which is what web developers wanted to do.

Netscape, although owned by a fairly major company, started to stagnate. Netscape open sourced its code base, and the Mozilla project was born. The Mozilla community took off with the code and started to really implement standards support in a new way through a complete rewrite of the rendering engine. Although Mozilla was initially based on Netscape Navigator, the tables rapidly turned, and subsequent releases of Netscape became based on Mozilla.

The Mozilla project has forked into a number of new browsers, most notably Firefox, which has sparked a new browser war with Microsoft. Yet this time, the battle has had a positive effect. Microsoft had all but stopped working on Internet Explorer once it released version 6. When Firefox hit the scene with near-perfect support for web standards, it became an immediate hit and gained a great deal of popularity with both

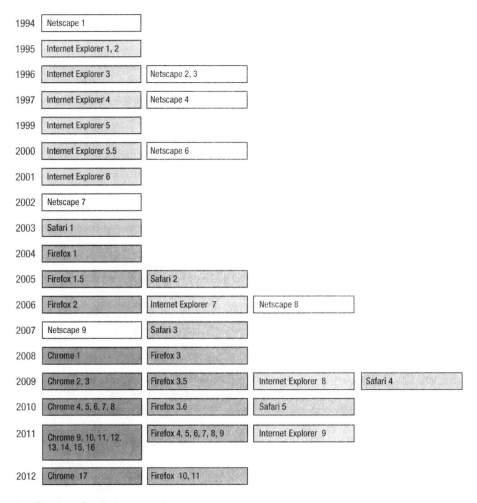

1994	Netscape 1		
1995	Internet Explorer 1, 2		
1996	Internet Explorer 3	Netscape 2, 3	
1997	Internet Explorer 4	Netscape 4	
1999	Internet Explorer 5		
2000	Internet Explorer 5.5	Netscape 6	
2001	Internet Explorer 6		
2002	Netscape 7		
2003	Safari 1		
2004	Firefox 1		
2005	Firefox 1.5	Safari 2	
2006	Firefox 2	Internet Explorer 7	Netscape 8
2007	Netscape 9	Safari 3	
2008	Chrome 1	Firefox 3	
2009	Chrome 2, 3	Firefox 3.5	Internet Explorer 8	Safari 4
2010	Chrome 4, 5, 6, 7, 8	Firefox 3.6	Safari 5
2011	Chrome 9, 10, 11, 12, 13, 14, 15, 16	Firefox 4, 5, 6, 7, 8, 9	Internet Explorer 9
2012	Chrome 17	Firefox 10, 11	

Figure 1-1. Timeline of major browser releases

the web cognoscenti and the general public. It seems as though Microsoft had no choice but to improve its web browser, and the result is Internet Explorer 7.

A number of other players emerged in the web browser marketplace, offering competition to the major players. Notably, Opera has always touted excellent support for web standards as one of its major selling features. It has caught on to some degree (2.4 percent as of January 2012), and it is also focusing in large part on mobile devices.

Safari by Apple Computer hit the scene in 2003, and it quickly became one of the most popular choices for Mac users because it integrates well with the operating system and is generally faster than competing browsers on the Mac. Apple introduced a Windows version in 2007. One of the most unique qualities of Safari is that, even with its minor updates (so-called point releases), the browser has improved its support of web standards. This is something that is often relegated to major releases among other browser manufacturers.

Another 800 pound gorilla joined the browser race when Google came on the scene with Chrome in 2008. Chrome took things in a completely different direction and has really shaken up the web browser scene. For the first time since the late nineties, a web browser was created that focused on speed, stability, and security, putting features on the backburner. Sure, Chrome has great standards support and is usually even ahead of the curve when it comes to supporting emerging standards; however, the folks at Google (at least at first) ignored the race to add more to their browser, and instead focused on delivering a blazing fast experience, something that has really resonated with a number of people.

Then there were standards: the Web now

Imagine if each TV channel was broadcast in either PAL or NTSC in each country, requiring viewers to use a different TV set, depending on what they wanted to watch. Or, imagine writing a research paper, running a search on Google, and then having to open each of the results returned in a different web browser. For example, you would open the first link is Internet Explorer, but the second and third links in Netscape. And for the next link, you would be back to Internet Explorer. Yet, this is pretty much how things worked in the late 1990s. Developers either produced parallel versions of their sites or designed for one specific browser. One of the most common sights on the Web was these wonderful (heavy sarcasm here) graphic badges telling visitors that a given website was "Optimized for Internet Explorer" or "Best Viewed with Netscape Navigator" (see Figure 1-2).

Figure 1-2. The "get it now" buttons for Netscape Navigator and Internet Explorer

When we talk about web standards, we're generally referring to the big three players on the Web: HTML (or XHTML), Cascading Style Sheets (CSS), and JavaScript. The World Wide Web Consortium (W3C) maintains many other standards, such as Scalable Vector Graphics (SVG) for vector graphic display, Portable Network Graphics (PNG) as a way to compress bitmap graphics, and Extensible Markup Language (XML), which is another markup language that is similar in a lot of ways to HTML.

While HTML/XHTML is all about structuring your document, CSS handles enhancing the user experience through formatting and some interactivity. Because they're two separate pieces of technology, you can physically separate them (by keeping your markup in one file and your style declarations separately in another). The early versions of HTML (prior to the release of CSS) were intended to be everything to everyone. The ability to specify colors and fonts was built right in by specifying the attributes of various tags. As sites began to grow in size, however, the limitations of going this route quickly became apparent.

Imagine that you have put together a website to promote this book. Throughout the site, which covers all the chapters in detail, there are quotes from the book. To really make these quotes jump off the screen, you decide to put them in red and make them a size bigger. In the good old days, your code would look something like this:

```
<font size="+1" color="red">In the good old days,
➤ your code would look something like this:</font>
```

With a little HTML and CSS, the code could look like this (note we said "could" because there are multiple ways of doing things—including the old way—but this is a good, structurally relevant example):

```
<blockquote>In the good old days,
➤ your code would look something like this:</blockquote>
```

And then, in a separate CSS file (or at the top of your HTML document—but again, that's just another option), you could import/link to pages of your website, which would look something like this:

```
blockquote { font-size: 1.5em; color: red; }
```

So what? They both do the same thing. Web browsers will display the quotes in red and make them nice and big. One of the immediate advantages, however, is in making updates. As we mentioned previously, you are liberally quoting the book throughout the entire website, chapter by chapter. By the end of the project, you discover that you have used more than 300 quotes! The only problem is that we, as the authors (and your client), absolutely hate red text. It makes us so angry. So, we're going to ask you to change it everywhere.

What would you rather do: update one line in the CSS file or open every page on the site and change the color attribute to blue? (Blue is much more calming.) Three hundred quotes—you're billing by the hour—so that's not so bad. It's maybe an extra half day of work. Now extrapolate this example to something like the *New York Times* where there are quite likely millions of quotes throughout the entire website. Are you still keen to go change every font tag on every page?

You might be thinking to yourself, "My software can do search and replace." This is true. We were once asked to update a department website at an organization where we worked. The website had about 16,000 pages; and by the end of a week, our search and replace still hadn't finished. We're not that patient. Are you?

Ease of updating aside, separating content from presentation in this way will help you to maintain consistency across a site. Did you have those quotes set at 1.5em, or 1.2em? It can be hard to remember day after day, week after week, just what sort of formatting parameters you have set up for every bit of text on your web site—so why not remove your memory from the equation? It's far easier to define a set of style options that can be applied to your document.

Additionally, CSS has evolved and is still evolving, allowing designers and developers to do more and more in terms of the layout and appearance of their pages. Using CSS3, you can position any element anywhere you like on a page and set the opacity of that element (if you have ever used layers in Photoshop, I think you can quickly see the possibilities with this). Although you could probably accomplish the same thing with a table-based layout and transparent graphics, it would probably require you to write a considerable chunk of code in which you would need to set absolute heights and widths of table cells, not to mention all of the time needed to generate and regenerate the graphics as you work through a design.

CSS3 has even more formatting options baked in. It lets you specify multiple background images for an element, set the transparency of colors, allow certain elements to be resized on the fly, and even to add drop shadows to text and other elements on the fly. CSS3 takes things one step further by branching out from simple formatting into the "experience" layer. CSS3 lets you perform transforms and transitions on elements; for example, you can rotate and scale them dynamically. Check out the W3C website for more information; or, for a slightly easier to follow format (that includes examples), visit www.CSS3.info for more information.

The example described previously is a pretty simple representation of what you can do using HTML and CSS. If you head over to the CSS Zen Garden (http://CSSzengarden.com/) and click through some of the examples there, you can gain an appreciation for the level of control you can achieve by tweaking the CSS for a website. CSS Zen Garden uses the same markup for every example (the XHTML part stays the same on every page). The only thing that is different on each page is the CSS file that is included, as well as any supporting graphics (see Figure 1-3, Figure 1-4, and Figure 1-5).

Figure 1-3. An example from CSS Zen Garden (Make 'em Proud), which you can find at www.CSSzengarden.com. It uses the same XHTML markup as Figures 1-4 and 1-5, but each page is styled using different CSS style sheets and images.

Imagine not having to touch a single page of markup when redesigning a website and still getting a completely different end result. Properly structured, standards-based pages will let you do that. This could be a major advantage for companies building large-scale content management systems: simply change the style sheet, and the CMS has been tailored to a new customer. Some companies are doing this, but others haven't caught on to this, yet.

Figure 1-4. This is the same page as shown in Figure 1-3, but styled using an alternate style sheet (Orchid Beauty) at the CSS Zen Garden.

Figure 1-5. A final example (CSS Co., Ltd.) that shows just how powerful CSS can be for changing the look of a page.

A crystal ball: the Web future

The Web is a cool place in many ways, not least because we don't need to be a fortune-teller to see into the future. Because standards take time to develop, we already have an idea of what the future holds. HTML5 is the new hotness, but it is still an evolving standard in the world of markup. The majority of the specification has now been defined with the goal of tying up a lot of the loose ends from HTML 4 and bridging the gap with the world of XHTML.

The W3C process for standards approval goes through numerous steps, and it can easily span several years. The final product of this process is a W3C Recommendation. Because the W3C isn't a governing body, all it can do is make a recommendation that software companies can then choose to follow. There are no "laws" of the Web; so if Apple were to decide it wants to drop HTML support in Safari in favor of its own markup language, it could. As you can see from our previous history lesson, this wouldn't have been completely out of the question in the 1990s; but today, it would probably be very self-defeating. The culture of the Web is all about interoperability; and when companies attempt to limit interoperability to gain some sort of competitive advantage, we all lose.

This has led to somewhat mixed results. On one hand, you can go to almost any website and have it work in almost any web browser. There are still some companies that are pulling the old "Please download Internet Explorer" trick, but those companies are few and far between (my bank just pulled this the other day on me, and I am now looking for a new bank). The fact of the matter is that interoperability, for businesses, means a larger potential customer base. For most Mac users, if they visit a website that is "Internet Explorer–only," they're dead in the water. This is true for mobile users, the fastest-growing segment of Internet users, as well. Sure, they could all buy a Windows machine or run some virtualization software to make it work; but chances are, if they have the choice (and the Web is all about choices), they just won't bother. They'll go find a competitor that supports Chrome, Safari, or Firefox.

The consultation process for developing new standards and revising old ones is very thorough, and it involves a lot of consultation with the community. Several drafts are developed, a great deal of feedback is collected, and eventually a Recommendation is put forth. We've presented HTML and XHTML almost interchangeably in this first chapter. And while both HTML and XHTML are valid web standards, in this book we'll focus on HTML5, the latest in a long line of markup language recommendations.

HTML5 was originally targeted at web applications with an eye to improving speed, compatibility, and the ease with which you can construct them. It introduces a number of new elements and relaxes some of the strict rules around markup in XHTML, making it easier to learn than its predecessors. HTML5 also attempts to minimize the need for a lot of third-party plugins for displaying content.

What's inside this book?

Our goal is to take this book beyond web standards to cover the entire process of developing a website based on standards. Believe it or not, there is more to putting together a great website than just knowing a little HTML and CSS. This introduction will expose you to different techniques and technologies, and we hope it will encourage you to pursue those areas you find most compelling.

The publishing industry as a whole is changing and evolving. Websites, and other electronic publishing media are becoming more and more prominent as they drive costs down, facilitate and speed up the process of creating content, and allow instant delivery of that content. This is having a profound effect in a number of related industries as advertising dollars are shifted out of newspapers and magazines toward online venues.

Technologies come and go or—as in the case of HTML—evolve. Three years ago, we wrote that "Two years from now, we may have to completely rewrite sections of this book." That has proven itself true! While everything in the original edition of this book will still work, the techniques presented there are not the fastest, easiest, or best ways to do things anymore. It's exciting to be working with ever-changing Internet and web technologies. When the original edition was written, the mobile web was just on the horizon and hadn't fully developed. There's no telling what we'll find around the next corner.

Chapter 2

Keeping a Project on Track

Project management doesn't have to be rocket science. Sure, there are libraries full of books on the topic that make managing projects sound like PhD-worthy material. Trust us, though: when you're starting out, keeping things simple is the best advice we can offer you! Chances are that the project that you're currently staring down isn't overly complex, so don't let it jump in complexity in your mind. We're going to take a quick look at a few different ways of managing projects and the three things you should always keep in mind: time, money, and *scope* (what needs to get done).

The process of web design and development is a unique one. The old-school method of managing projects isn't necessarily the best approach in an industry where new competitors and technologies can emerge during the course of a three-month project. It's often reasonably cheap and easy to make changes at any stage of a project. Even though we made the direct comparison of construction work to web work in Chapter 1, we framed it like that in order to give you an idea of what the various roles are on a web project. In reality, building a website isn't like building a house at all; you're not tied to particular dimensions after pouring the foundation. The materials used are all digital; and for that reason, they are easy to work with and make changes to after the fact. Deleting something doesn't involve a wrecking ball, and adding something new doesn't require materials to be purchased and brought in from off-site. If you're five days into the project and your client suddenly decides that she would, in fact, like to accept orders online instead of only telephone orders, then all you have to do is hand the client a revised cost estimate and timeline (if even this). After a website has launched, you might start hearing from visitors that they need to be able to import data in a certain format. If so, you can develop and push that revision out near-instantly by publishing it to the server. No jackhammers, no demolition crew, and no need to make three million duplicates. So, why then should you plan everything up front and set it in stone on day one?

The project manager on a web project doesn't have to be fluent in all development languages, database systems, and server setups (it doesn't hurt to know a little about each, though, just so you can tell whether someone is pulling your leg). The project manager has to know how to deal with people, keep everyone happy (or at least productive), and assure everyone involved that the project is moving forward. The main goals are to remove any roadblocks to project completion. If your developers' office is under renovation and they can't get any code written because someone is always hammering, then find somewhere quieter for them to work. If your designers' computers are constantly crashing, causing them to have to revisit the same work over and over again, get them new machines.

The traditional approach to project management

Project management, in the traditional sense, is often very complex. This single chapter definitely couldn't cover all aspects of it, but we are hoping to share with you some tips and things to look out for along the way. We're strong believers in developing project-management skills, if for no other reason than to improve your skills in estimating. Since everyone has his own way of dealing with things and no two projects are the same, we can't give you the perfect road map for getting from x to y to z in every case. Our best advice is to go with your experience; and if you really don't know the answer, admit it and then find the answer. Although it's possible that you may be the only person working on any given project, more often than not you will be part of a team. There will always be someone to turn to for advice (or at least an opinion) if you get stuck. If the worst comes to pass, there's always the Internet—we hear you can always find someone willing to give you their opinion there, right or wrong!

The traditional approach to project management has its roots in the construction industry. In fact, the U.S. Navy first conceived of this project-management process in order to get a better handle on the process of building ships. When materials need to be ordered, parts manufactured off-site, and specialized labor brought in, there is a big advantage in trying to plan things in advance. Having software specialists sitting around before the computers used for targeting enemies have been installed is a huge waste of time and money. Having a master plan that lets you see, in advance, whether things are ahead of or behind schedule gives you that ability to contact subcontractors in advance and either delay or move up their participation in a project.

When we mention the traditional approach to project management, we're referring to the formal process taught by the Project Management Institute (www.pmi.org). This process is sometimes referred to as the *Waterfall model*; with this method, a project is planned as much as possible up front. Planning continues until a consensus on "perfection" is reached, and then work commences. There is a lot of criticism of this way of doing things, particularly in software and web development projects, because there is no feedback and evaluation built in until the end of the project. Instead of building something small, checking in with your client (and possibly end users) to validate your assumptions, and then continuing, you're instead deciding how the end result will look on day one. That removes a great deal of flexibility from a project; or, at the very least, it wastes a great deal of time as things need to get planned and replanned. This method does have its place in certain industries, however. For example, in large-scale construction projects, you need to have a plan in place before you start. It would be foolish to start building a high-rise floor-by-floor, without knowing how many stories it will have until you're done. You can't just leave some "feature" of the building (such as electricity) until the last minute. But you can do precisely that in web development projects.

The rigidity and linear nature of the Waterfall model just doesn't suit web development. The upfront costs in both time and money associated with this type of planning are out of scale with most web work.

Another consideration is that, with the pace at which various technologies progress, taking three months to plan a project up front may in fact put you three months behind the curve in terms of the technology available. A different way to think about this is the following: say you're spending a week at the beginning of the planning stage of your project to do an analysis of the various database systems available, so you can determine which one is fastest for implementing a new short text-messaging application. You look at three different products and decide on Product A because it's definitely the fastest in database inserts (adding records) and selects (querying data out of the database). You finish planning and begin development. After one week of developing your application, Product B releases a new version that is 100 times faster at doing selects (which makes it about 20 times faster than Product A, which you're currently using). Do you switch? Well, you're already falling down the waterfall; there's no turning back now. Your entire timeline will fall apart, and things will need to be replanned if you switch at this stage.

The nine knowledge areas

Even though the methodology may not be the most fitting, it's worthwhile drawing from the experience of the Project Management Institute to gain some guidance in how we should proceed. Nine knowledge areas are covered in the Project Management Body of Knowledge (PMBOK), which is published by the Project Management Institute (see Figure 2-1). These nine areas cover every possible aspect of project planning and management. We have space in this book only for a quick overview of each; but if you want to learn more, we encourage you to take a look at some of the publications put out by the Project Management Institute.

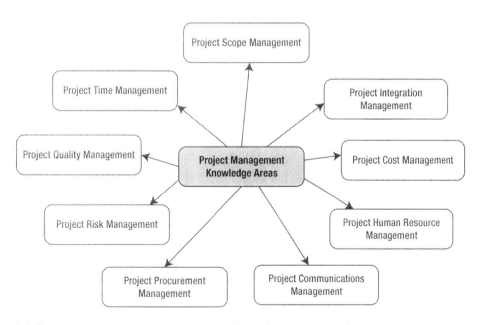

Figure 2-1. The nine knowledge areas covered by the Project Management Institute

Here is a brief description of each of the areas:

- *Project Integration Management*: This area looks at planning and integrating all the various parts of the project. It talks about developing a project charter (a document that summarizes what the project will accomplish and why it's needed), developing a plan for the project (how you're going to do what you've outlined in the charter), and how everything is going to be communicated between the team and the client or stakeholder(s).

- *Project Scope Management*: This area outlines, specifically, what work has to be done to complete the project and how that work is going to be broken down between the various "resources." It also identifies how any changes will be handled during the project.

- *Project Time Management*: This area defines how long a project is going to take and identifies how many people, including the specific skills and at what times, will be needed to complete the defined project.

- *Project Cost Management*: Money is another important factor. This area defines the budget for the project and how things will be controlled to stay within that budget.

- *Project Quality Management*: How will you make sure that what you produce works and does what it's supposed to do? What kind of testing will be done, and what test results are acceptable?

- *Project Human Resource Management*: Where are you going to get your team members? What skills do they need? Do you need to train anyone? How will the team be managed?

- *Project Communications Management*: This area covers how things will be shared amongst the project team and the stakeholder(s), how progress will be communicated and tracked, and how things will be documented.

- *Project Risk Management*: This area looks mostly at the risks involved if the project fails (or succeeds; there may be risks either way). It attempts to anticipate any problems that may emerge at various points in the project and to plan ways to minimize or eliminate those risks.

- *Project Procurement Management*: How/where will products or services be acquired when needed, and how will subcontractors be managed (if applicable)?

Although we don't advocate going the PMI route on web development projects, your client/employer may have different ideas (and hey, it's their money!). If you're required to go this route, do yourself a favor and find somebody with the project management professional (PMP) designation to bring on board. It's a fairly expensive process, in both time and money, to obtain this designation; however, if your client is a stickler for the Waterfall method, having a PMI-accredited project manager on board will save you hours of time. Be aware, however, that a PMP doesn't come cheap. You will want to contact him at the very start of a project, before the budget is set, so that he can get involved immediately.

Web project management: the power of iteration

As we mentioned previously, the web is an inexpensive medium. Making mistakes during development is OK, and they are usually easy to fix. Because of this, web-project management can be more relaxed, allowing for feedback and change at any stage. The heavy-handed scope-management system imposed in the traditional method of project management can be relaxed, and a more collaborative development process can be pursued. The gist of this approach goes like this: "Let's just start building this thing; we can make changes as we discover the need for changes. You've got a fixed timeline and budget, that's fine. I'll do my best to give you updates on how we're progressing through each of those as we go along."

The reason this is the opposite of traditional project management is that the traditional approach aims to control change very tightly (some might say discourage change, but that's not necessarily true). This approach encourages it (within the limits of time and budget), so that all parties are happy with the end product because they've all been deeply involved in shaping it from the beginning. While the end result may look nothing like what was originally talked about, the end result will still meet a need.

When it comes to developing web projects, you'll hear a lot of different terms thrown around. *Agile development* is commonly used, and it describes a number of development processes that involve multiple iterations and working closely with stakeholders until everybody agrees that an end result has been reached. If you were working for a client, you would build something and show it to her at a very early stage. The client could try it, react to it, and tell you that changes need to be made or that something is missing. You could then take that feedback and make those changes right away. Working this way, you would step, piece-by-piece, through a project adding all of the functionality that is necessary.

An agile example of planning

Agile project management is better illustrated through example. Say you're building a news website for a client, a television network launching an on-air news program incorporating citizen journalism. The client tells you he needs a site that will allow its viewers to submit news stories and categorize them. Site visitors should then be able to vote on which stories they like the best, and those will be the stories that make it on air. The client wants the entire program to be about news as it happens from the perspective of those who are "at ground zero." You chat a bit with the client, and you both throw together a one-page document that outlines the general idea of what you're going to try to accomplish. You work through a schedule and a budget for the project, and then you get started on building a submission page.

The news website absolutely cannot exist without a place for viewers to submit stories and a place for those stories to be displayed. It's always a good idea to identify the core of a website (or most "inner" page of a website) and start there, because the only thing limiting your work is time and money. Think about it: if your time runs out and you've spent all of it developing a viewer-to-viewer messaging system, then the website doesn't accomplish what it needs to be able to do.

The submission page asks the visitor to enter her e-mail address, enter a link to the story, select which categories it belongs to, and enter a brief synopsis. You then build a news display page that groups everything by category (picture something similar to Digg.com or Slashdot.org). Your designer puts together a mock-up, and you paste in the graphics and CSS so that your client can get an idea of what the end product will look like.

Your client takes a look at what you've done so far, and he comments that the station can't have people submitting news stories with only an e-mail address. The station needs to know more about the source of the story. We've discovered an addition; we'll need to flush this part out into a user management piece with usernames and passwords (who wants to reenter all her contact information every time she submits a story?). You throw together a few more pages exhibiting this functionality, and you have your client take a new look.

At this point, the client remarks that the news network has finished developing the "look" of the show: the set design is complete, and the show's introduction is done. Understandably, he wants the website to have a similar aesthetic. You get your designer in contact with the network's in-house marketing and design staff, and they begin working through revising the visual details of the website. Meanwhile, you continue with development.

The client thinks the site looks great and functions really well so far. The network's sales staff has decided that the website is going to need to make money and support itself by selling advertising targeted toward each of the different categories of news. So, if there's a food category, restaurants or specialty food shops might be approached to advertise. You start building a component that displays ads based on the category, as well as some reporting on how many times those ads are being clicked and viewed; this will enable the site to bill the advertisers fairly. You think it would be pretty neat to build a "this section sponsored by" function, so that each category can have a major advertiser. You throw together a quick mock-up of how this would look and again have your client visit. The client is completely thrilled with the idea.

Development continues back and forth like this until something is produced that's good enough to make public. At that point, it may be released with the word *beta* attached to it, and news junkies (AKA early adopters) are invited to come participate. Changes continue to be made (RSS feeds are added a day after the site goes into beta, user comments two weeks later, and so on) until the client calls it quits and declares the project complete. The on-air show premieres a month later and is a huge success because its content is extremely timely.

Taking the agile approach here allowed the requirements of the project to be discovered based on the best and most up-to-date information as the project progressed. If you had taken the traditional approach, you may have missed certain pieces of functionality that became apparent while you were using and interacting with early versions of your news website. You may have missed the user management part altogether; and then, once you launched, had a flood of junk stories by people promoting various "performance enhancement" products. You might have missed the opportunity for the additional revenue stream from on-site advertising or missed the user comments section, which is something that has contributed greatly to the website's success by building an online community around the show.

Achieving the goal: identifying doneness

If there's a single practical bone in your body, you're probably thinking to yourself: "Boy, that sounds great, but how do you really know when it's done and when to call it quits?" As we hinted at it in the previous example, you can keep an eye on three elements to determine when a project is done and when it's time to stop working. Usually it's a combination of all three; however, occasionally one factor will override the others.

These three things relate to the traditional approach to project management. The success of all projects boils down to time, budget, and scope; and a project manager's job is to balance these three qualities to produce a high-quality product within the time and budget allotted. These three factors are often represented as the points of a triangle, and your goal is to try to get each of the sides to be the same length (to achieve balance). More often than not, if you're doing client work, the client will have a deadline for when she wants to (or has to) launch her website. Most clients will have a budget, which is some amount of money that they've allocated to complete the project. Usually there will be some definition of what is needed functionally (e.g., they need a website to show off their new line of hair care products).

best bet at this point is to identify the single most important thing to do and to do that first. What would a news website be without a news page? What's a search engine without a database to search? How good is a financial management application without the ability to track expenses? Everything else is peripheral to the project and can be added if time permits, or even in a later version.

Finally, there is the debate over hourly and fixed-price quotes. Most clients want you to commit to doing some piece of work for some set cost. They're trying to minimize their exposure on a project and prevent it from going over budget. Most freelancers aren't completely comfortable with that approach because they know that changes can happen throughout a project, and committing to a fixed price limits what they can and can't do. They'll either push for hourly billing or give a fixed-price quote with a lot of contingency built in.

It's pretty easy to see that this situation puts you at odds with your client right out of the gate. It seems like you're fighting a struggle to make money vs. the client's attempt to save money. Again, why not try to work with your client and tell him that you're billing for the time you put in? You think that what he has budgeted is realistic, and you won't leave him high and dry (that's why you always start with the core of the project); however, if he starts to ask for bells and whistles at the end of the project when time is running out, he may have to come up with additional funds.

That might be a little vague, so suggest to your client that you'll give him weekly updates on time and money; and when there are only 10 hours left in the budget (adjust accordingly based on length/complexity), you'll have a quick conversation about wrapping things up.

Focus on scope

And that leads us into our final factor: scope. In casual conversation, you'll frequently hear the term *scope creep* thrown around when people are discussing project management. Scope creep is a dirty term in traditional project management; it means that the "perfect" project plan conceived at the outset is flawed and that the expectations are changing. Something has either changed or wasn't thought about at the outset.

With an agile approach, though, you could make the argument that scope creep is, in fact, the single greatest thing that can happen on a web project (within reason). As long as you have the time and the budget for it, you want change. You want your client to point out the deficiencies in your design, so that you can fix them early on. You want your client to tell you where she became confused by your interface. Why do you want this? The answer is easy: if your client is laying it out for you, then the eventual end user of your website is not. This means you're producing a better, more intuitive product. That's a good thing!

On the other hand, scope has a funny way of creeping out in a different direction, such as your client coming back to you midway through the project and telling you about how she was at this great website the other day. This site let people chat with each other in real time and share photos, and third parties could even develop little applications that would plug into the website and do different things. "Can we make our news site work like that?" she asks.

There is a bit of an assumption being made here that, between you and your client, you can come up with what's best for the end user. Because of that assumption, make sure that you're never just accepting things because your client asks for them—the requests have to make sense. If there's ever conflict, go to a neutral third party (ask an end user). This can be a formal process involving in-depth user testing and focus groups, or it can be as simple as asking somebody else, whether a friend or colleague (assuming this person is the target audience of the website). You can do this at any stage of a project life cycle, whenever you're not sure what the answer is (or you just want to make sure you're heading in the right direction). If you're considering adding a new feature to an existing website, but you're just not sure if it's the right idea, ask your current users (run a short survey).

Let's hope that, at this point in your project, you're comfortable speaking frankly with your client. Chances are, the client has been involved in the project from day one and has bought in to what the vision is. Sure, what he's describing sounds great, but it's not what you're working toward. Websites don't need to remain static once they've launched (in fact, it's better if they don't!), and you would be pleased to work with the client to develop these features for "version 2" of the site. However, if your client has decided that this website just won't be as good without all this other stuff, feel free to take an hour, sit down, and work through the numbers with him. Tell him that you need to finish the project core first, and then you'll be happy to move onto some of these other features. Live chat? That sounds great! It will take 150 hours and will push the launch back two weeks. Third-party apps? That's a great idea, too: 300 hours on your end and probably a couple of months. Don't overinflate these numbers—just be honest and ask the client whether he's willing to increase the budget and push back the launch date. Pragmatism is important when it comes to project management.

One of our favorite quotes—one that tends to surface at times like this—comes from a company based in Chicago called 37signals (you'll hear more about the company later in this chapter). It likes to say that it's always better to build half a product than a half-assed product. This means that it's better to build something that's really simple but doesn't have a ton of features when the features that it does have are really well implemented. Spend a little extra time on your forms to figure out whether what you're asking makes sense. Take the extra time to implement Ajax where it makes sense. Your customers will thank you for it, and it's less likely that you'll hear, "Gee, this news site is really informative and well built. Too bad I can't use it because it doesn't have live, real-time chat." On the other hand, if you rush through building things, you're likely to hear about how ugly, how complicated, or how many errors people are getting.

"But the PMI covers nine areas; you've talked about only three!"

Hey, we warned you that the PMI approach to project management is more complex than what's necessary in your average web project. That said, there are a few more lessons to extract from the traditional approach to project management.

Communication is paramount

Clients love to see progress. If you could e-mail them every day showing them some really cool new piece of functionality or some neat new design element, you would probably have the happiest client in the world. The flip side is true, too: if you've run into some major roadblock, it's better to get it out in the open early and explain how you're going to handle it.

The agile approach is very powerful, if everyone is along for the ride. One of the reasons the traditional approach is still hanging in there is that a whole pile of documentation is created at the outset and then handed to the client to sign off on. The client feels good about things because she knows what the plan is and can see how it's going to go off without a hitch (and then reality sets in). If you take the agile approach, you must be diligent about talking with your client, forwarding changes to her, and actively seeking her feedback. With the agile approach, you can't just accept a project, walk away for two weeks, and then come back saying, "Here you go!" It's a very interactive process.

Chances are, you'll won't hear many complaints if you're overcommunicating with your client, within reason. (Remember, he has a job to do, too!) From our experience, however, the single greatest factor leading to a project's failure is a breakdown in communication. If one party stops talking to the other, you have a serious problem that needs to be resolved immediately. If your client fails to tell you until the very last minute that the design you've come up with makes his stomach churn, then that's not fair to you, and it will likely result in an 11th hour redesign. If you're running out of budget and you don't get in touch with your client until you only have an hour left, then that's not fair to the client, and it could potentially leave him with an unfinished product.

Here's an excellent strategy: as soon as you can, give your client access to your development (staging) server, so she can see the project progressing and start working with it immediately. Put some sort of informal policy in place about how she is looking at a work in progress and how things may break for a short period of time as things change (if the client is constantly checking out the project, then don't send an e-mail every time something breaks, unless it remains broken for 48 hours). Also, be sure to send the client messages periodically that highlight various features and areas you want her to play with in depth. Finally, encourage the client to send you her impressions and information about any bugs she might find.

Quality and testing

As we touched on earlier, your goal on any project should be to build as high a quality product as possible. If you have the option of adding just one more feature or spending the time getting the existing features working perfectly, do the latter. It's pretty hard to launch a product and have absolutely no problems with it, whether the problems are technical, functional, or even a pesky cross-browser bug or two. Try to allocate at least 10 % of the time you spend on a project to testing it and using it yourself. Encourage as many other people as possible on your team to do the same. Different people look at problems in unique ways; although you may have absolutely no trouble filling in that news submission form in the previous example, a different visitor may look at it and freeze because he doesn't have a URL to submit with the news story. Or, maybe the story is something he saw on TV or read in a magazine—what does he do then?

The issue of quality also brings up another concern: who will be responsible for maintaining the website once it's launched? If a bug is discovered, do you and your team fix it, or does your client have someone in-house do so? How will that cost be handled? Is there a separate budget for maintenance, or is that included in the overall project budget (if the latter, hold back at least 10 % of the budget to fix things post-launch).

Procurement and contracting

A lot of projects will require you to seek external service providers. Chances are you aren't a project manager, designer, developer, database administrator, information architect, and systems administrator all rolled into one. Unless your client plans to host the app on her own servers or already has a host in place, it may fall to you to at least find secure hosting for the project.

Although outsourcing parts of the project can be a life-saver, you need to keep a few things in mind. First, be sure you know how much it's going to cost you up front. If you don't know how much that hotshot designer is going to run and you quote some hourly amount to your client, you might find yourself working quite a few hours for free. Second, make sure you know the quality of the outsider's work and that you're comfortable handing control of a certain part over to him. If there is some highly technical aspect to your project that falls outside your skill set, it's OK to admit it and find someone else who can do it. Your strong preference here should be for someone you've worked with before or someone you know by reputation. If the entire project hinges on a specific function, you need to consider how comfortable you are having that function outside of your control.

The next thing to consider is that a subcontractor is just that: he works for you, not for your client. You don't need to worry about whether you let him communicate with your client (in fact, I'd encourage you to allow that); however, you do have to establish that any major changes to the scope of the work he is going to do has to run through you. Also, you're on the hook to pay this person. This subcontractor isn't your partner; he's more like your employee. If your client fails to pay you, you're still on the hook to pay your subcontractors, so plan your payment structure accordingly.

Last, but certainly not least, you're on the hook for the quality of the subcontractor's work/service. One of the most common requests during new site development is for you to handle the logistics of where the website will be hosted. This is a positive thing in that you have control over what host you choose and what features the host offers, enabling you to get exactly what's needed. The downside is that you will likely be the point of contact for both your client and the host. So, if the host suffers a major outage, you can count on getting angry phone calls from your client. Just as you wouldn't hire a designer who has never done web design before, you shouldn't engage a hosting company unless you're sure about the quality of the service it offers. Do your research here: hosting is a very competitive field, and all players definitely aren't equal. Because you're on the hook, check out a potential host's support in advance. For example, does it take you 24 hours to get a response? If so, would you be comfortable with that when your client is breathing down your neck?

Tools available

We're quite fortunate, for this part, because it has been only in the past five years or so that the tools in the project management space have evolved to the point where they're usable by mere mortals. Imagine what kind of a tool professional project managers (PMI-trained) use. If you guessed a complex application that involves a great deal of abstract lines and symbols, you're right!

The old toolbox

Up until a few years ago, your choices for managing projects were either to use Microsoft Project, as shown in Figure 2-3 (or a similar product), or to just fly by the seat of your pants and handle everything with a calendar and e-mail.

We don't mean to come down on Microsoft Project; it's a brilliant tool for managing Waterfall projects. It will automatically calculate dates and schedules based on the parameters you lay out. But, like the Waterfall model in general, it's just not appropriate for a web project. Planning a project using a Gantt chart locks you into a number of things up front when you have the least amount of information with which to make an informed decision. Gantt charts plot out the sequence and dependencies between tasks. They also remove a lot of flexibility from your scheduling, so you might wonder why you would use them.

Again, we'll issue the same words of warning we used before: some organizations will be using Microsoft Project and require you to do the same. If that's the case, go register yourself in a course (yes, there are entire courses on how to use Microsoft Project); or, at the very least, go buy yourself a good book on the topic. It's a pretty complex piece of software, and it really pays off to know how to use it properly.

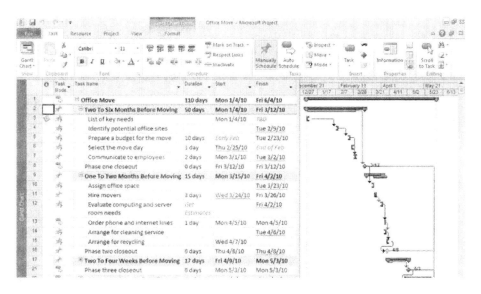

Figure 2-3. A Gantt chart view in Microsoft Project. Sure, there's a lot of information packed in there, but is any of it really useful?

The alternatives

This section started off hinting that there are some much better alternatives that definitely bear consideration. A lot of the innovation in this field is happening online, in the web-based software world. We've talked about the Waterfall approach, as well as something called the agile approach—but in all honesty, there is no formal "agile" approach. Instead, there are several different methodologies that can be classified as agile, and there are several different tools that work well for the various approaches. Here are a few of our favorites:

Basecamp

The trailblazer in this arena of simpler management tools is a service called Basecamp (www.basecamp. com), which is shown in Figure 2-4. It's a web-based, hosted application that you subscribe to (this is often referred to as "software as a service"). There's nothing to install, and Basecamp offers a free trial that gives you access to the majority of its features.

What makes Basecamp different from Microsoft Project? Basecamp represents a fundamental shift in thinking about project management. Similar to the earlier discussion about agile development, Basecamp takes the stance that project management is more about communication and collaboration than it is about reporting and control. Basecamp provides a simple set of tools, including Messages, Todos, a Calendar, and file sharing. You use these tools to work with your clients and to communicate a project's progress to them. Instead of producing a complex chart at the beginning of the project, you identify a series of milestones to work toward and share updates through messages. Prior to Basecamp's arrival, a lot of these types of activities would have been handled through e-mail and a calendar.

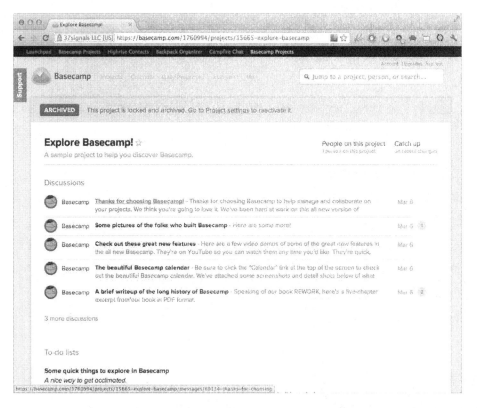

Figure 2-4. Basecamp is a web-based (no software to install) management tool that provides a clean, easy-to-use interface.

With its easy-to-use tools and clear interface, Basecamp is something we strongly recommend you take a look at to help you keep on top of client projects. 37signals has recently launched a new version of Basecamp that is even easier to use than the last. Your projects are represented by a single page, but most of the same great communication tools are still present.

Trac

Trac (http://trac.edgewall.org) is an open source project-management application. It's a little more technical than Basecamp because you need to download and install it on a server of your own; however, the advantage is that you don't have to pay a monthly fee to use it. Trac is another simple tool that enables you to centralize the communications of your project team. Most notably, it integrates well with Subversion (see Figure 2-5), which is open source version control software that keeps a record of changes you make to files. If you make a mistake, Subversion lets you easily "roll back" to a previous version of a file (to learn more about Subversion and version control in general, check out the book *Foundation Version Control for Web Developers* by Chris Kemper and Ian Oxley (friendsofEd, 2012).

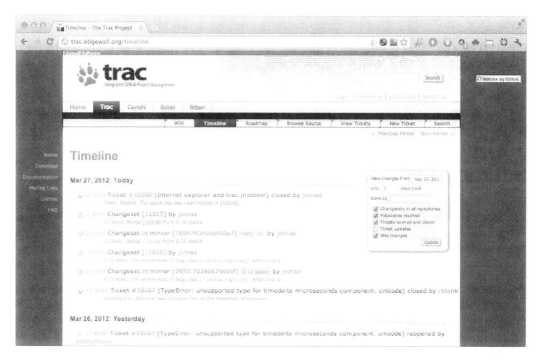

Figure 2-5. Trac is also web-based, but it must be installed on your own server. It's a little more technical than Basecamp, so unless your client is a technical individual/organization, you might be best saving this tool for internal team collaboration.

Trac also provides a great wiki that is extremely helpful in making notes for yourself and other team members as the project progresses. The interface for Trac isn't as simple as the one for Basecamp. Therefore, we use Trac as an internal tool among the technical team members, and we use Basecamp to collaborate with our clients.

If you're looking for something similar to Trac, but in a hosted format (like Basecamp), check out github. This tool excels at software development (including web development) projects. It uses git as a version-control system, and it offers a lot of documentation tools similar to those in Trac; however, there is nothing to install. Git can take a little getting used to, so if github sounds like it's up your alley, do a Google search for git and github tutorials to ensure you're setting things up right.

Harvest

Harvest (www.getharvest.com) is a time-tracking and reporting application. It can help you keep a handle on how much time and money you've already spent on a project, and how close you are to the total budget. If finances are one of your hard and fast constraints (aren't they always?), then you'll need some way to track how much money you've spent and how much is left in your budget. Harvest provides a great way to do that, and it features a very simple interface (full disclosure: the author, Jonathan, is an employee of Harvest).

Others

There are a million (give or take a few hundred thousand) project-management applications out there. Some are web-based, and others are installed on your local server or desktop machine. What you use will depend in large part on what you need and what you and your clients feel comfortable with. Don't feel pressured into using a project-management application that produces charts, figures, and graphs galore. The fact of the matter is, long project reports rarely ever get read. Keep things short, simple, and to the point to avoid misunderstandings.

Summary: the best advice

The best advice for project management is the best advice for the actual development of the project itself: keep it simple. If you have a schedule in hand, a budget, and a rough idea of what needs developing, you're ready to go. There is no reason why projects need to get blown out of proportion. Keeping things simple will free you up to concentrate on what's important: delivering the best possible product for your clients.

The greatest single skill in project management is experience. It's one of those things that really do get easier as you go along. You not only become more confident in what you're saying and doing, but you're also able to do more things "off the top of your head." It's really handy to be able to sit down with a client in that initial meeting and be able to give her some ballpark estimates on time and cost, without going through hours of estimation calculations. Early on, you'll want to put heavy disclaimers on these estimates and say that you're going to need more time to "crunch the numbers." After a while, though, your ballparks come pretty close to the actual numbers, and you can drop the disclaimers.

You won't always find clients who can agree with keeping things light and agile. At that point, you have a decision to make. If you're in a position where you can pick and choose your clients, I strongly urge you to do so. Honestly, the best projects are those that don't have to fall down over a waterfall. If you're not in a position to turn down any client work, then know what you're getting into. Plan for a good deal of contingency time (and money) to account for all of the planning, re-planning, and controlling of the scope. Also, plan to keep a tight handle on things as far as changes go once development has started, and try to complete the website as quickly as you can. The longer a project goes, the more likely it is that it will fail.

Additionally, if you're able to, hire a PMP to oversee things; or, at the very least, plan to devote as little as 50 percent of your time to just managing the project. It's pretty onerous keeping tight control on things and making sure that the project is proceeding in lockstep with the plan.

Profiling professions: Jason Fried

Jason Fried is one of the founders and is CEO of 37signals LLC, a Chicago-based former web development consultancy turned web application product provider. 37signals offers a number of excellent products, from its flagship Basecamp project-management software to its latest offering, a CRM-like tool called Highrise.

In addition to having a great deal of expertise working with large-scale applications, Jason and his team are also pioneers in the field of "getting real," a variation of the agile development practices we discussed earlier in this chapter. The people at 37signals believe that more software isn't necessarily better software and that keeping things small and simple is always the best way to go.

Lane: What's your role at 37signals, and what does that translate to in terms of day-to-day activities?

Fried: My role is pretty varied. I'm one of the founders, and technically the CEO, although we don't tend to use titles like that. I'm in charge of running the company, coming up with new products, and guiding the company in terms of strategy, as well as guiding the overall design and look and feel of the products.

So, I do a little design, although not as much as I used to; we have another person who does the lead design now, but I set up the overarching look and feel and the corporate identity of the products. I tend to do a lot of writing as well, but most of all these days it's marketing and strategy, coming up with new products, keeping an eye on everything, and guiding the products in the right direction.

Lane: Tell me a bit about your background working with computers—things like education and previous work experience—that led you to what you're doing today.

Fried: I'm not actually technical, so I don't do any programming. My expertise with computers revolves around design: HTML, CSS, graphic design, that sort of thing. My background is actually not related to that whatsoever. I've got a degree in finance, but I've always been interested in design, and I've always been designing stuff, ever since I got a computer in junior high—just kind of messing around and learning how to design things.

Around 1996 when the Web hit, I was just getting out of college, and I always wanted to start my own business, so it was a great opportunity to do that and design stuff, which is what I always wanted to do. I started learning how to design websites, and nobody else knew how to do it at the time, so I was on equal footing, and it just took off from there.

Lane: 37signals started out as a web design company, working on projects for clients, and you've now transitioned into creating products of your own that you now resell to customers. Could you talk a bit about how that transition happened?

Fried: It was kind of by accident. We were a web design firm, and we started getting really busy doing a lot of client work. We were managing our projects basically like most people do, sending e-mails back and forth, and it was really messy. It wasn't a good way to stay organized, and it showed. I think clients didn't feel particularly comfortable working with us in that way because they didn't know what was going on with their projects all the time.

We realized that we needed something to keep track of this sort of thing and have clients be able to give us feedback and to follow along in a project. We looked around for some tools and didn't like what we saw, so we decided to build our own. And as we started using it (it took about three months or so to build), our clients were saying "Hey, you know I could use something just like this, too. This is really handy, and I could use it for projects with my own company." Some of our colleagues that we showed it to said, "I need this for my own business," so we decided that there might be a product there.

We polished it up a bit and gave it a name, Basecamp, and put some prices on it and put it out on the market, and that's how it all got started. About a year later, Basecamp was generating more revenue than our consulting business was, so we stopped doing client work, and we focused exclusively on building our web-based applications.

Lane: One of the things you're most famous for, aside from your great products, is your philosophy of "getting real." Could you briefly talk about what that means and how someone would go about "getting real"?

Fried: The whole "getting real" philosophy is basically about just what it says: doing the real work and not talking about it or writing it down; just doing and figuring things out as you go. Our feeling is that you never really know what you're doing until you're doing it. You can write about it all day long, you can think about it all day long, and you can plan it out all day long, but until you're actually doing the work, you don't know how it's going to turn out and whether it's any good.

So, we get rid of all those abstractions—things like documentation and information architecture diagrams and functional specification documents—and we just dive right in. It's about iteration: putting our heads down, doing a bit of work, lifting our heads up looking around. Where do we need to go next? What do we need to do next? And we follow that reality instead of following a plan we wrote six months ago or a functional specifications document that we wrote before we even knew what we were actually building. That's the overarching philosophy of "getting real."

Lane: In terms of actually developing a project, what's the process? Where do your product ideas come from?

Fried: We always scratch our own itch. Every product we've built, we've built for ourselves first because we had a need; it just comes to a point where you realize that you have a need. There's no science behind it; it's just a moment where you think: "Gosh, I've been doing this wrong for so long that there must be a simpler way." And that's where the genesis of a new product idea comes from.

So, for example, Highrise, our most recent product, is a contact manager and simple CRM tool. It came about because we were talking to a lot of people in the press and doing a lot of interviews, and we weren't really keeping track of who we were talking to and what we said to them and articles they'd published and their contact information. So, if someone at 37signals needed to talk to one of these people again, we didn't know what had been said before or when the last time we talked to them was; and it was just a mess, so we needed something like that.

Again, we looked around for stuff because it's hard to build things. So, if we could find something that we thought worked well, we would use that; but we just really couldn't, so we decided to build our own. That's how all of the products have started. It just comes from a need. And then, what we do is, if we decide to go forward with it, we don't need to make a huge commitment to it. If we start on it and then three weeks later we don't like it, we stop—unlike a traditional process where you make a commitment, you write a functional specifications document, and you spend a lot of time doing a lot of things first, before you know if it's any good.

Then we start with the interface; we start designing what the thing is going to look like first. That dictates the rest of the project; the programming is then plugged into the interface, so it's not the other way around. It's not the programming first and the interface second. Once we've got the basic screens done, we hand them over to the programmers, and they hook it up; and then we start using it, and we go back and forth: Does this make sense? Is this too slow? How does this feel? And we just keep tweaking it until we find that we're really satisfied with what we have for an initial version, and then we put it out on the market. We'll then continue to tweak it over time based on people's feedback.

A lot of people talk about engineering when it comes to software, but we don't like that word. Engineers are people who build bridges. We're software programmers, and I think that when you start thinking about them as engineers, you start falling into that trap of, "what is an engineer?" An engineer is someone who makes these big, important decisions that are long-term, and I just think that that's the wrong mindset.

Lane: What advice do you have for people who are just starting out in working with the Web?

Fried: My suggestion for everything is to start with as simple a version as possible, not only with software, but with business. If you're going to start a business, start as simple a business as you can, which is probably just you or maybe another person if you need to. Whatever business structures are available to you in whatever country you're in, start with the simplest possible form. In the United States, the LLC is pretty much the simplest structure there is, so start there.

Don't make any huge decisions up front. Just start working on something, see if it works, and start using it as you're building it. You'll know pretty quickly if it's going to be any good or not; and if it is, hopefully other people will like it and just take it from there.

Definitely don't go out and get funding; don't go out and feel like you have to have a big business attitude or image. I think a lot of small companies try to act big for some reason, and you really don't need to. Just act your size and be who you are, and things will probably work out if you have a good product and you know how to pay attention to the right things. Running a business isn't all that hard; nothing is that hard unless you make it complicated. Most things are pretty simple and pretty easy as long as you take the easy route and build things as simply as you possibly can, to start at least.

Every mistake we've ever made as a business is because we've tried to do something too complex or too hard. It wasn't because we tried to do something too simple. Whatever you're going to do, take the easy way first and see if it's worth putting more time into it afterward. If so, then maybe you can make it more robust, but don't go there at first. Start as simple as you can.

Lane: 37signals has never used traditional advertising for any of its products (paid advertising). What can people who are just starting out do to get their names out there, get some customers, and spread the word about the work they're doing?

Fried: My suggestion is to be as public as you can. The best example of this is a guy named Gary Vaynerchuk of Wine Library TV. He is, to me, the perfect example of how to do it right. He's incredibly passionate. And let's say you're not good on video; let's say you write instead. But I'm going to use him as an example. He came out of nowhere, out of complete nowhere, and now he's an Internet celebrity, and a lot of people know about him. He's been on many TV shows, he's gotten tons of press, and he hasn't spent a single penny on PR.

What he does is, he shares. He shared his passion; he goes out there and tells people what he loves and helps them out. Whenever you share and teach, people pay attention, and they will begin promoting for you. It's really a great model, and Gary is spot on when it comes to that sort of thing.

I think that that's how we built it. We share a lot. We share a lot about our business, about what we do and why we do it, about what works, and about what doesn't work. We have strong opinions, and we're not afraid to share them, and I think that when you go out there and share your heart and whatever it is that you're doing, I think that people pay attention, and it's a great way of getting the word out.

Also, when you're a teacher, people pay more attention to your actual words, and I think that they appreciate what you're doing more. It's not just about trying to sell someone something; it's actually trying to help someone learn something, and that has a lot of weight to it as well.

My suggestion would be to find out what you really love to do and tell people about it every opportunity that you get. If it's a video blog, like Gary started out with, or if it's just writing a weblog or if it's writing articles in a magazine or writing a book, or whatever it might be—figure out what you can do to share what you know.

Lane: One of the things you talk about in your book, *Getting Real*, is choosing the right customers. How do you go about finding good customers? How do you avoid bad ones?

Fried: I think it's the same way you recognize a good friend compared to a bad friend or someone you wouldn't be friends with at all. Customers are people; and if you don't want to hang out with them or be around them, then they're probably not going to be good clients. You look for those sorts of matches on a personal level, I think.

You have to respect the other person and appreciate who they are and enjoy them as a human being. That's really the best way to find great customers or great clients. If you go to a meeting with somebody and they're rude or they're dismissive or they're impossible to deal with for whatever reason, they're not going to be a good client. If the initial meeting is bad, the client is going to be bad. If the request for proposals is bad, the client is going to be bad. You have to look for those signs just like you would with a friend. That's the best way we've found to do it.

I also think that the way you present yourself on your own website will hopefully attract the right kind of people. There are lots of people who wouldn't work with us when we were doing website design because we didn't have a traditional website with a portfolio section like a typical web design firm website would. Our initial site was simply text, black-and-white text, which no one was doing at the time. When we launched in 2000, everyone was doing really colorful stuff and animated stuff, and we were just doing plain text. We were telling a story; this is what we thought was important. The kind of clients who read that and could relate to that and thought "We like these people"—those were the kind of clients we found. The potential clients who said, "This is ridiculous, I don't get it"—were the people who wouldn't work with us. So I think your site has a lot to do with self-selection, and I would recommend that you stick to your point of view early on, because that's a great way to find the right kind of people who will work with you.

Chapter 3

Planning and High-Level Design

It's entirely by design that we spent the better part of the previous chapter discouraging too much up-front planning. But please don't call us hypocrites now that we're offering you an entire chapter that covers the planning and pre-project process. The reality of the situation is that it can be to your advantage to do a little work up front before digging into the development stage. Every project you embark on isn't going to be crystal clear; you will more than likely end up working outside your comfort zone on more than one occasion. Although it's easy to get a general feel for most projects, there will undoubtedly be specialized areas in which you will need to consult a subject-matter expert. Your clients may or may not have some idea of what they're looking for; and even then, after talking it over with them you may come to the realization that their vision of what they want makes absolutely no sense for their end users. The temptation might be there to simply do what the client wants, collect your paycheck, and walk away; however, it's far more fulfilling to work on projects where you can see the value that will be produced and where people will actually use the product you produce.

Disagreement with your client, particularly in the early stages of a project, can be really stressful. You want to get along and work collaboratively to produce something great; you especially don't want to have to fight over every point. The tools and exercises we'll present to you in this chapter will help you strike that collaborative note with your clients. We hope that, after working through some of these sections, you will draw similar conclusions and move forward as a united front with your clients. And remember: although you're an expert in your field and your instincts for what's good and what's bad are probably better than the average Joe's, your clients are the experts in their field. They know their customers, employees, partners,

...cesses better than you do; so if they're adamant about a particular point, don't automatically ... wrong. Arrogance is not a productive working methodology.

...n to find yourself working as part of a larger team, as opposed to freelancing, it's likely that ... of the activities described in this chapter will be done by the person responsible for client rela-... individual could hold any number of titles; on very large teams, he is the producer, the account ...r, or occasionally the project manager. In smaller groups, it may be a designer or developer (or a ...er/developer) who works closely with the client. Regardless, it never hurts to have an understanding of how things work, even if you aren't directly involved in them.

The toolbox

All the activities described in this chapter are optional. Just as with our discussion of project management in the previous chapter, you have to do what feels right for you and your client. We suggest that the only activity that isn't optional is the first one: you need to have a discussion with the stakeholders on a project to deter-mine your starting point. Most importantly, you need to know and agree upon what that finish line looks like.

If you need to get things straight in your head, you can do some of these activities without your client. Others are better to work through with your client, so that you're both on the same page. If you feel strongly about something, be prepared to defend your position. If your client insists on using the Comic Sans font throughout her entire website, you're going to need a better argument than "No, it's ugly and unprofes-sional" to dissuade her (even though we all agree with you). Just consider this a little advance warning.

Remember all of those times in school where your teachers would pester you to "cite your references" and "defend your position"? Unlike calculus, those skills they taught you are actually useful in real life. There really would be no arguing with you if you came in with a research paper discussing the poor readability characteristics of the Comic Sans font.

Goals and objectives discussion

The first order of business, once you've landed a project, is to sit down with everybody involved and have a quick discussion about some of the basics of the project. This is often called the *project kick-off meet-ing.* In addition to hashing out the details of a timeline and a budget, you will find it helpful to answer a few key questions. A lot of these questions overlap in some way; that's OK. Sometimes it helps if people think about them differently and phrase their answers accordingly. You can handle this step remotely if you need to by forwarding a questionnaire to your clients, but it's generally faster and easier to schedule a one-hour meeting with everyone involved to answer these questions:

- ■ *What is the goal of this project?* The answer to this question should be a little more specific than "to build a website." Why are you building a website and what is its purpose? Are you trying to sell something? Are you trying to provide better customer/technical support to your customers? Goals are often difficult to identify because they're sometimes really nebulous. Another good way to phrase this question is like this: "If I told you that, no matter your budget and no matter your timeline, I can build only one thing for you—what would that be? Would it be a set of pages where products can be purchased? Would it be a blog?" This generally gets people to focus on the biggest problem you're trying to solve by building this website. Most websites should have no more than one or two goals; anything more, and you're probably looking at something that's too complex for a single project, and you should consider breaking it up into stages.

■ *What are the objectives of this project?* Again, keep it general. (Note that there is a difference between general and vague; these objectives will help you define the project's scope, so lay them out in such a way as to be able to "check them off" a list. Try to identify specific user groups for each.) Things like "Give the media a place to get information about our company" and "Provide our agency with a professional online presence" are the level you want to stay at. If you're meeting with a group from your client's company, this is the stage where every department can have their say. Sales, PR, customer support, and even the CEO may have some input as to what objectives they want to accomplish. Again, to rephrase the question, try asking "What sorts of things can we do to accomplish the goal we've identified?" or "What is your vision of what the end product will look like?" These can be really fun questions to ask in a room full of people with different backgrounds (hint: if there are 10 people in the room, expect 10 different answers!).

■ *Can you provide a short description of this project?* This should be a couple of lines long, maximum. Ideally, this is the answer you would give if the company's CEO were to ambush you in the elevator and ask you what you're working on. You would get bonus points if you were to phrase the answer in language that's simple enough to get the point across to your family at reunions. Wouldn't it be nice, for once, to be able to explain to your Uncle Irv that you do something more than just "make websites"? This question really helps to answer the peripheral question of, "Why are we doing this?"

■ *What are the benefits of doing this project?* Will it save the organization money in the long run? Is it a good recruiting tool for prospective employees? Will it help the sales team move more products? This is the "dream big" section where everyone can pitch in his two cents about his biggest problems and how he hopes this project will solve them. If the room goes silent at this point, it can be interesting to approach this question from the opposite direction: what won't this project accomplish? In other words, ask for the "anti-scope"—things that will not be solved by what you're going to produce. Having limited knowledge of the organization, it will be easier to get the ball rolling by throwing out some completely absurd suggestions (this website will not solve illiteracy world-wide).

■ *What's the scope of this project?* This is usually one of the hardest questions to answer because it's not entirely clear at the outset. Regardless, everyone will have some idea of what the end product will look like, so it's good to get that out there. Again, you can hit this question from the opposite direction. This differs from the prior question in that we're looking for something a little more specific and concrete.

■ *What are the deliverables?* This can also be phrased as, "How will we measure success?" The answer to this question may be as simple as "a completed website with supporting documentation." Or, it might be something a little more abstract, such as "an increase in our Google search ranking." Make sure that what emerges from this question is something realistic, measurable, and attainable. If your client responds "to improve customer satisfaction," don't accept that at face value. How is customer satisfaction currently measured? Maybe it's the number of phone calls to customer support. If you decrease that number, have you improved customer satisfaction? How much does that number need to decrease? By at least 25 percent? If there's no existing measure of customer satisfaction, suggest coming up with some way to assess that before your project launches, and then after. A customer survey might be a good way to go; you also might be able to come up with some key statistic you can use.

We suggest sending these questions out a week in advance of your scheduled meeting. That gives all the participants a chance to think about and jot down their ideas, so that you can have a really productive discussion. It's OK to have debates and disagreements at the project-kickoff meeting, and they may turn ugly; however, it's better to get these out of the way at this point rather than on the day you go to launch. Your role at this meeting will be to mediate it. Draw on your background and try to propose solutions that will accommodate everybody.

We mentioned at the outset that this meeting should take an hour. In general, the more people involved, the longer it will take. Regardless, set a one hour limit on the meeting and make it a goal to get through as much of this material as possible. If you need to schedule a follow up, that's OK; however, don't let this meeting stretch into a two or three hour marathon. Nobody will be putting forth her best ideas after an hour.

You should also plan on bringing an audio recorder with you. Or, you might have a co-worker accompany you to take notes. You're not going to have time to both furiously write things down and participate in the discussion. You want to be available to take part in the answers to these questions, not just passively record other folks' opinions.

Brainstorming

The term **brainstorming** is often abused in the business community and has gotten a pretty bad reputation as a result. There is a right and a wrong way to brainstorm, though; and doing it properly is an extremely useful tool for getting a flood of ideas. To brainstorm properly, you'll need a few things: a bunch of sticky notes (or index cards), some pencils or pens, and a countdown timer (see Figure 3-1).

Figure 3-1. The high tech toolbox you'll be using in this chapter. Sometimes getting people off their computers helps with creativity!

It's important that you clearly outline what you're working on, so that everyone is on the same page. It may be a broad topic such as "the technical/functional features of our new website"; or, it might be something specific, such as "ways we can promote the launch of our new service." Tell everyone in the group that the next minute is just about getting ideas out there on the topic; it's not about discussion (that will follow).Participants should write their ideas on a sticky note (one idea per note) and call them out as they write them. No idea is stupid at this point, and it doesn't have to be completely clear what the idea is—just something memorable, so that the thought won't be lost.

Set the timer for one minute and tell everyone to start. As the leader of this activity, you shouldn't participate; rather, you should "police" the activity. Make sure people don't start talking about the merits of an idea while the timer is running. There should not be any judgments being made on ideas at this stage, so "that's dumb" or "forget about that" or even "hey, great idea" should be strongly discouraged.

Calling out ideas will reduce the amount of duplication you get from this activity; but inevitably, you'll still get some duplicate ideas. Calling out ideas also serves to spark ideas in others; so if one person calls out "professional product photos," then that may spark the idea of "multiple product angles" from someone else. Once the timer runs out, get everyone to sit back while you collect all of the index cards. Read each idea to the group while you have everyone's undivided attention; and if anything is a little ambiguous, ask the contributor of that idea to clarify her thinking (write it down). At this stage, weed out any duplication of ideas that may have occurred, as well.

Once the list has been pared down, start grouping ideas. So, if you look at our "ways to promote our new service" topic, you might group the ideas by "cost money" and "free." Next, you might further break them down into "online" and "offline" media. It's at this stage that ideas can be discussed and the advantages and disadvantages of each can be explored (see Figure 3-2).

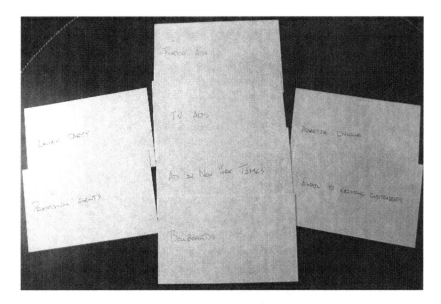

Figure 3-2. Group the ideas by similarity. This will help focus the discussion on what's feasible, and what's just a pipe dream.

User stories and user personas

User stories and user personas are similar in that they call for you to get inside the head of your end users and describe what they need or what they're thinking or doing at any given moment. A *user persona* involves creating a fictional character whom you envision is one of the target users of your website. You then create a profile and background information for this person, describing her age, occupation, technical background, and likes and dislikes. The biggest benefit to developing user personas is that they're great at serving as a reminder that you're not (necessarily) developing a particular website for yourself. Thus you should create your personas in such a way that they can serve as a constant reminder to the project team throughout the entire design and development phase. If you construct personas and then file them away, they aren't going to do anyone any good.

We think that there's a fundamental problem with personas, though, in that you're inventing a fictional character to deal with a real-world situation. If you're a 29-year-old male, you probably can't imagine what on Earth an 18-year-old female would think of a website you created. If you have a background in computers, you might have a tough time seeing what a website would look like to someone with little or no computer experience (such as your grandmother). Trying to determine facts based on fiction just seems counterintuitive. If the target user group of your product will be someone outside your realm of understanding, then we recommend involving someone from that target market in your project team. You don't have to bring this person in immediately; but once you have something that person can interact with, even in a limited capacity, you can have him take a spin around your website and give you some feedback.

User stories (sometimes called *use cases*) look at the individual needs of a user or features of the website you intend to produce. This is another great activity to complete as a group, and it's an even better activity if you can involve individuals from your target audience.

Start with a stack of index cards and ask the participants to start writing down features or functions of the website that they see as essential. The ideas need to be really concrete, such as "a five-star product rating system" or "people who purchased product X also bought product Y." Things such as "an easy-to-navigate website" are too broad. If the title alone isn't sufficient, ask people to write a short paragraph that spells out what they mean/envision; drawing diagrams is OK, too. The real purpose of this exercise is to clearly capture any and all ideas.

Give your group 20 minutes or so to produce its stack of cards and then come together as a group to discuss what everyone has come up with. Eliminate duplicates (if applicable), and then discuss the priority of each story (high, medium, or low). If there are disagreements over the priority of a particular story, the person who wrote the story gets to decide.

After you leave the meeting, assign an ID number to each story and estimate how long it would take to develop this feature (see Figure 3-3). It could be something like three days or one hour. You can now look through your stack of stories and quickly see what's really important, but also really easy to do; what's really important, but really hard to do; and what's not so important, but easy or hard to do.

We find that user stories help us answer the question of "What's next?" We talked about taking care of the core of the website first; that is the single thing that the website needs in order to function. What do you work on after that? Start tackling your high-priority stories, starting with the least time-consuming ones and proceeding through to the more time-consuming ones. Next, attack the medium-priority stuff and, finally, the low-priority stuff.

It's normal to add user stories throughout the life of an agile project or to make revisions to the priority or effort (perhaps implementing the user database for the forums has made single-click checkout

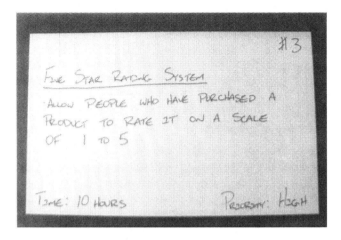

Figure 3-3. A completed card. Number these cards for easy reference, estimate a time, and then assign a priority based on group consensus.

really easy to implement). Feel free to keep revisiting your stack and making additions and updates as required.

Feature/unfeature list

Brainstorming and user stories provide great ways to get everyone's creative juices flowing; however, all of the ideas generated may not be what's best for your website. Also, although it's important to know what the competition is doing, you shouldn't let it dictate your work. Just because your biggest competitor has introduced live video chat on its website doesn't mean you should do the same. Heck, let your competition do the market research on it and spend the money figuring out whether it's a killer feature. What you're producing should stay focused on your end users and what they need. Keep it simple; you can always add things later.

The feature/unfeature list is exactly that: a list of what you must include in your project to make it useful and successful, as well as a list of what you aren't going to include. That might seem like a silly notion—why should you bother creating a list of what you're *not* going to do? However, doing so can really help to define what you're working toward. It can also really help with scope definition and in determining the budget and timeline for a website. If you can get everyone to agree up front that you're not looking to develop a music player, you'll have a ready answer when that pesky VP of marketing all of a sudden decides to get involved with your project and asks where the music playback controls are. Specifically, you'll be able to point to your unfeature list and say that it hasn't been overlooked, but was discounted earlier in the process.

For example, say you've been asked to create a social application that focuses on music. Your feature/unfeature list might look like what is shown in Table 3-1.

This list gives you some clear direction as to what the project team wants to avoid and what it expects the end product to look like.

Example Feature/Unfeature List

t is...	This project is not...
ne web application	A Facebook application
iere fans can come to discuss their favorite inds	A place where fans can come to trade audio files of their favorite bands
A news resource for upcoming CD releases and concert dates	A news site providing interviews and general information about bands
Meant for individuals who are at least 18 years of age	Meant to be a hangout for pre-teens to discuss the latest *American Idol*
About the music, the artists, and the fans	About the money (as long as we break even)
A place for discussion	A file-sharing outlet

Wireframes

You can think of wireframes as the thumbnail sketches of the web world. *Wireframes* are outlines of your pages using lines and boxes to represent where various elements will be placed (see Figure 3-4). Their primary purpose is to get the team focused on content, functionality, and navigation (or flow)—not on appearance. They are extremely quick to construct; in fact, a number of designers we know don't even

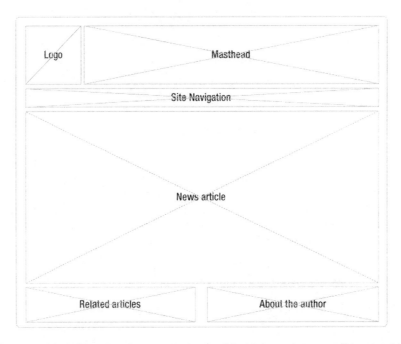

Figure 3-4. The goal of a wireframe is to focus on the layout of the elements in a page. Stay away from using colors and graphics, and just use boxes to represent various elements.

bother using a computer. They'll simply sketch them on a piece of paper, which they will then scan and send off to a client for feedback.

If you mock up a page in Adobe Photoshop using stock photos and placeholder graphics, we guarantee you that the majority of the comments you receive will focus on the images you selected or the shade of yellow you used for your highlights. We once did a mockup using "Lorum Ipsum" text, only to have it returned from the client with the comment that the website will need to be in English. Go ahead and roll your eyes—we did. It can be really frustrating when, despite your best efforts, your client still focuses on the wrong thing entirely. Do what you need to do to center their attention. If it means removing all text and replacing it with dashes (or replacing images with gray boxes), then do it.

In removing graphics, colors, and text, you force individuals to focus on the layout and content of a page. This activity is designed to get people thinking about what placement leads to the best interface for your pages and the nature of the content they will contain. At this stage, you'll hear questions such as, "Does it really make a lot of sense to split the navigation between a horizontal bar along the top and several vertical columns of links?" It's also common to hear remarks that the company's logo isn't prominent enough or that the content area doesn't have enough space (or, unfortunately, that there isn't enough room for advertising).

The biggest drawback to producing wireframes is that it's difficult to display interactive elements. If you have a box that will expand and collapse, it's tough to represent that in a simple sketch. You can use arrows to indicate motion of elements, but showing the expansion of a particular element can be challenging on a single page.

Wireframes are really only useful in larger groups where you're trying to get everyone to focus on one thing at a time. If you're working one-on-one with a client, don't even bother with wireframes; cut right to the prototype. Instead, let the client see and work with the website in a browser; he'll be able to gain a deeper understanding of the right way to do things.

Mock-ups

Several designers will still produce Photoshop mock-ups of a website for their clients ahead of time. Some will even produce two or three variations, so that their clients can pick the one they like best. As you may have gathered, we think this is largely a waste of time.

For starters, only one of the variations you've produced will be selected, so all the time and effort you put into the others will go into the great digital landfill. Why divide your time among several options? Instead, produce one design and make it the absolute best you can. Get everything pixel-perfect!

And then present it to your client in HTML/CSS. We understand that Photoshop is ingrained in the designer's thought process. If you're one of those folks who need to start with a blank canvas to get your creative juices flowing, so be it. But take it only as far as you need to before jumping to code. As soon as you have that vision in your head, start realizing it in a real-life web page.

Similar to wireframes, Photoshop is terrible at exhibiting dynamic content. You can flip layers on and off, we guess, but why spend the time? It's just as fast to code it, and then make small changes to the code as needed. Going to code gets you thinking about the best way to produce a page, instead of the best way to replicate your Photoshop mock-up. Another big benefit of the "straight-to-code" method is that it introduces the constraints of designing for the web immediately. We've had several designs handed to us that use commercial fonts that aren't widely available. Short of producing graphics of all of your text (do not do this), there's just no way to implement that design online.

The best-case scenario is that designers can write code, and coders can design like artists—but that's rarely ever the case. Chances are, if you're working in an organization that's big enough to have both designers and developers, then the existing workflow will incorporate mock-ups. In cases like that, just make sure, once you have the mockups "converted" to something interactive, that you work closely with your designer to review what you've done and whether it matches the direction he envisioned.

Information architecture

Your goal with this activity is to lay out the *site map* of the website and to come up with the nomenclature and taxonomy you'll be using for links (you haven't suddenly slipped into a biology textbook, don't worry). Will you be calling the page containing company information "Contact Information," "Contact Us," or simply "Contact"? Maybe you'll go with the more casual "Drop Us a Line" or perhaps "Feedback." There's no right answer here; it depends on a number of factors.

If you're developing a new website, your best bet may be to surf around a bit and see what other people are using for their naming schemes. Go to some of the biggest websites and try to draw parallels between their pages and yours. We're not suggesting here that "the big players" are always right; it's just that a great deal of people have been exposed to those websites before, so their naming schemes have caught on.

If you're redesigning an existing website, it might make sense to keep the existing labels for things. The existing users already know that when they click "Dude, hook me up," it means your site will take them to the online store. It's a judgment call that will be guided by the goals and objectives of the website (perhaps one of the objectives is to increase sales; making it easier to find the link to your online store might help that!). If your client is hoping to rope in new customers, it might be smart to rename your links to lower the bar for entry. Deciding how to implement your site's navigation is one of the key decisions that will impact the success of your website. Once you think you have it figured out, ask a neutral third party to see whether he "gets it," too. On the other hand, if the main goals are simply to update a site's look and increase sales to existing users, then don't go hog-wild. Existing users are existing users because they like the site as it is. Don't risk alienating them with sweeping changes for the sake of change.

A typical site map is just a series of boxes labeled with page names (see Figure 3-5). If you find that your website is oozing Web 2.0 machismo and you have more Ajax than you have images, then number each of the pages on your site map and provide a paragraph or two describing some of the functionality and interactions on that page.

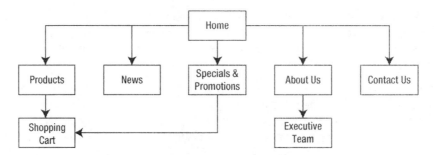

Figure 3-5. A site map can be a great way to identify content for the web site and to work out how site navigation should function.

Prototype

But that's not a tool, that's actual production work! It's crazy, we know, but getting to a working product is the single best design tool available. In a working product, there are no miscommunications or misconceptions. It's just the first step toward finishing a project. Sure, you may get absolutely everything wrong in the first version and have to change it all, but at least you know what not to do now. We want to pause for a second and just remind you that we're not presenting these tools to you in a particular order, but rather, as a collection from which you can pick and choose. The reason you should have this thought currently in your mind is because skipping every step except the prototype can produce a successful project. We've launched a lot of wildly successful projects that had no up-front planning except for preliminary discussions and a prototype that eventually evolved into the final deliverable. That said, there's nothing stopping you from calling a brainstorming session after a prototype has been built. If you've got that sinking feeling that not everybody's voice has been heard, then call on those people. It's better to do so late than never.

Start simple; don't even worry about the design for the first little while. White backgrounds and black text with simple text links are just fine for laying out a product and getting a feel for how things go together. Create some basic pages with titles (and content, if available), and then start building the hierarchy (see Figure 3-6).

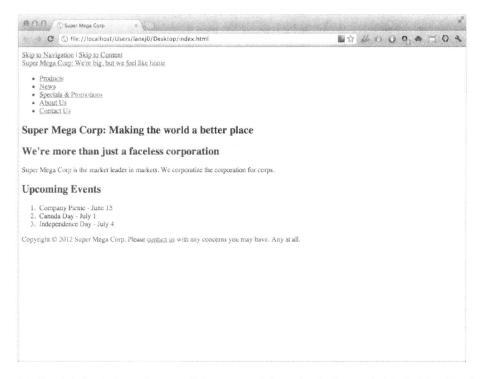

Figure 3-6. Simple is fine in the early stages. This prototype is just using the browser's default styles. If you're trying to work out site structure, that's fine! The links to other pages are all there, and there's no styling information to distract you.

Elaborate as you go along. Drop the company logo into the corner of the page, and let your client tell you whether it's too big, too small, or the wrong shade of purple. Also, keep a list of the changes requested, so that you don't let anything slip through the cracks. Better yet, let your client make the list for you. Tools such as Basecamp or Trac (which we discussed in the previous chapter) will let you add to-dos or tickets to keep track of what has been requested and what has been accomplished.

Let's go to an example

Hey, congratulations! We heard you just landed a contract with this hot new startup in Silicon Valley to produce a sales website for its cutting edge product that it's launching in a couple of months. That's awesome!

You're a little freaked out? This is your first major project besides that softball website you put together for your uncle in Cleveland last month? Don't worry about it; let's walk through the initial stages together.

OK, so you already know that the startup has scheduled the launch of its service to take place in two months (60 days). The startup is composed of entrepreneurs, so it is still on a bit of a tight budget. However, the company has managed to scrape together $2,000 for the project. You're just starting out in your career anyhow, so you're charging your standard rate of $20 an hour. You're reasonably confident that you're going to be the only one working on this project, and it doesn't sound like the company needs anything too complex (in fact, "simple" came up 35 times in your initial conversation with its people!).

So, where do you start? Well, this book you read once suggested that the best way to start a project is with a project kickoff meeting. It's lucky for you that you're taking a vacation to the Silicon Valley area next week, and you've already set up a time to swing by the company offices. (Man, this project is just one lucky coincidence after another!) What on Earth will you talk about, though?

First things, first. You've been talking exclusively with the CEO and VP of marketing. You fire off a quick message to these people, thanking them for the company's business and confirming the date and time of the meeting. In this message, ask these people whom you will be meeting with, and suggest that they include anyone who may have a stake in the project. At this stage, leave it wide open; it may be useful to have some of the folks who actually developed the product on hand. Along with this e-mail, you forward the six questions outlined in the "Goals and objectives discussion" section. Ask these people to take some time to think about the questions in advance and jot down a few ideas. Also, request that they forward these questions to anyone who will be in attendance.

Fast-forward one week, and you're on-site with your clients. After brief introductions, you jump right into the meeting. You start up the voice recorder on your phone. Luckily, everyone is well prepared, and you're able to zip through the six questions with little disagreement or conflict. Something interesting does emerge from the discussion, however. The management team is concerned about how it will receive feedback from its customers, including suggestions for improvement, so that it can continue to improve the company's product.

It's the perfect time to break out the second weapon from your arsenal and engage everyone in a brainstorming session. You set your timer for one minute, hand out a pad of sticky notes and a pen to everyone in the room, and remind those gathered to focus on their customers. Who are they? What is their level of expertise? And go!

Ideas start flying back and forth, and everything from "a toll-free hotline" to "a user discussion forum" to "a wiki" are tossed onto the table. Time runs out, and you collect all the notes and head over to the wall to start grouping them.

One by one, you read each idea aloud, asking for clarification when necessary. You group the ideas by the level of technical knowledge required, ranging from "little to none" (e.g., the toll-free phone number) to "advanced" (e.g., the wiki).

There is something intriguing about the wiki idea, however. People in the room start to talk about it and remark that it could enable the company to drastically reduce support costs, allowing "pro" users to help out new customers. The company's staff members would need to swing by only occasionally to answer the "dead-end" questions and add in their pro tips. Additionally, it's widely agreed that, because of the nature of the product, most users will likely be pretty technical, so a wiki isn't likely to scare them off.

You sit back for a minute and reflect that it's not completely unreasonable to include this in the original project. There's already a bunch of really great open source wikis out there; it would really just be a few hours of work to integrate one into your client's website. You know that they have a hard $2,000 budget limit, but you're pretty sure that you can shuffle some things around. You pipe up, telling those assembled that you'll take care of it for no additional cost.

You've set the right tone for the project. You've established that you care about your client and its success, and that you're willing to do what needs doing to produce the best possible finished product. You leave the meeting feeling great about the way things went and with a promise to get back to your client soon once you have something worth seeing. Now it's time to visit the wine country, and enjoy the rest of your vacation!

Two weeks later (remember, you were on vacation), you send your client a link to a prototype you've put up on your testing server. The client immediately starts clicking through it and sending you comments about what it likes and dislikes. Communication continues back and forth, with you posting messages to Basecamp about what you're currently focused on and where you'd like feedback. Something seems to click with this project, and there aren't a lot of revisions. You end up finishing ahead of schedule.

Summary: achieving balance

Your goal in the planning stage is to get a better idea of what the finished product will look like. Don't expect a photograph right out of the gates, but an abstract sketch is a good objective. The tools outlined earlier are really nothing more than a few standard ways of communicating with clients that may help you to get thoughts across. If you feel the need, you can repeat any of these exercises at any point during project development. It may prove interesting to see how things have progressed over the course of a project.

Don't feel obliged to run through everything outlined here as if it's a road map to project bliss. Before you begin any of these activities, ask yourself whether you (or anyone on the project team) will ever look at the output of these activities ever again. What is the point of developing an information architecture/site map if it's going to be completely ignored when you produce your prototype?

A really important point to note is that none of the output of these activities should be considered "locked-in" material. The agile project dictates iterations and changes once more information has been discovered. If someone creates a user story outlining the need for a discussion forum—and it later becomes evident that nobody is interested in using a discussion forum—then ax it. Constant improvement is the order of the day, and no decision is so big that it can't be changed after the fact.

Profiling professions: Daniel Burka

Daniel Burka is well known throughout the web community as a pioneer in Web 2.0 design. His exceptional implementation of a clean and simple design for the wildly popular community news website, Digg.com—and his ongoing efforts to incorporate community feedback to constantly improve and evolve Digg—has made him a sought-after designer and speaker.

After Digg, Daniel went on to work on Pownce, and then to Milk to focus on mobile application design. He has recently accepted a position at Google. This interview is from a few years ago, when Daniel was still at Digg/Pownce and his thoughts very much still apply today.

Lane: Give us a rundown of what you're working on these days.

Burka: By day, I'm the creative director at Digg, and by night (and in all my spare time) I design the user interface for Pownce. Being the creative director at Digg means that I manage a small team of designers who handle all of the user interface tasks on the site. I work closely with Kevin Rose, Digg's founder, to spec out concepts, determine how features will be incorporated into the interface, and generally defend all things related to the user experience. The role I play at Pownce is similar, though we have a tiny little team, and I spend a lot more time developing new things than refining existing features.

Lane: Tell us a bit about your background: things like education and work experience that led you to your work in web design.

Burka: I luckily stumbled into web design when I was in high school. My twin brother and some friends were experimenting with graphic design tools, and I joined in. We then discovered we could make some easy money in the summers doing government-sponsored web projects through a Canadian government program. Over a few years, that group of friends coalesced, and we formed a company called silverorange that eventually evolved into a very strong web development shop. I actually studied history at university and eventually (eight years in!) got a BA with a minor in art history. I think this academic education helped me in many ways, but I learned most practical design practices through trial and error with my friends at silverorange.

Lane: Step us through the process you went through when you were designing Digg.com. Where did your initial ideas come from?

Burka: Starting Digg was actually somewhat intimidating because it was a very large project already at the outset. Instead of tackling the whole thing at the beginning, I tried to identify the core component that made Digg unique, which were the story items on the home page. I isolated that one part and spent several days breaking it down, reorganizing the pieces, and developing a visual language. This groundwork established many ideas that percolated through the rest of the site as we increased our scope.

Lane: What are some of your favorite websites and why?

Burka: A List Apart: fantastic content that's well organized in a layout that happens to be very attractive. Those attributes are important in precisely that order. Apple: Apple's ability to keep the home page as a single focused element is impressive. CNN: I don't agree with every design decision on CNN's site, but the evolution of the CNN website has been impressive over time.

Lane: What advice do you have for people just getting started in working with the Web today?

Burka: I'd advise people to find a tight group of like-minded people to work with. Whether you're attending a design school or starting out with a small business, finding a group of people that you can bounce ideas off of, receive critiques on your work from, and generally have fun learning together with is an invaluable resource. It's certainly possible to learn web design on your own, but I doubt it's as productive or as much fun. Oh, and take Jeffrey Zeldman's advice—get half your money up front.

Lane: What tools do you use when designing a website?

Burka: Start with a whiteboard, move on to Photoshop, jump into the code in Coda. I can't draw with a pen and paper to save my life.

Lane: Web technology progresses pretty quickly. What are some of the ways you use to keep up on the latest trends in design and technology?

Burka: RSS feeds and talking to the right people. One of the great things about working on the Web is that almost all of the discussions happen online. I spent the first seven years of my web design career in eastern Canada, and we had no trouble keeping up with changes in the industry. Bloggers and sites like A List Apart really keep you in the loop.

Lane: If there were one thing you could completely change about the Web (or add/get rid of), what would it be?

Burka: Obviously, it'd be a fundamental shift, but getting rid of the statelessness of the Web would make a huge difference. Being able to haphazardly jump back and forth through a website using browser controls makes us do all kinds of weird design decisions that we don't even think about much of the time.

Lane: Where do you see things going with the Web in the next couple of years? What are you excited about?

Burka: I'm excited about the renewed potential of the mobile Web. People have been predicting the rise of mobile for years, and it's finally starting to show some promise. And, the best part is that, with devices like the iPhone, the gap between mobile and standard web experiences is narrowed.

Lane: What can new web designers/developers do to get their names out there and get noticed?

Burka: Seriously, the first thing is just to do really good work. A long time ago, I was speaking to one of the best graphic designers no one has ever heard of, and he told me that if you do good work, everything else will work itself out. It was very good advice.

Better short-term advice is that you shouldn't sit around waiting for good work to arrive. If you have any extra time, develop fictional projects and experiments. The 37signals early conceptual redesigns of banking, shipping, and payment sites are great examples. This will help you build out an impressive portfolio even if you don't have impressive clients yet.

Chapter 4

Giving Your Pages Structure: HTML5

Start paragraph. Take a minute to imagine what it would be like to have to describe the function of (strong emphasis) everything (end strong emphasis) you're saying. How (emphasis) irritating (end emphasis) would that be in a conversation? Give it a try: try reading this paragraph out loud. End paragraph.

That's enough of that. Writing the entire chapter in that style not only takes quite a bit longer, but is a pain to read, no? In dropping those annotations though, we lose some meaning to the text we've written. If only there were a way to describe the meaning of a particular piece of text for the purposes of publishing that text!

Wait! There is! When you're reading through a book like this, you may see certain pieces of *text written in italics* or in **bold**. You've probably seen that on the Web, as well. The trouble with bold and italic is that, while you and I can discern the differences, a computer can't. That's where we bring in HTML, or HyperText Markup Language.

What are web pages, really?

It may take you by surprise that, even though the web pages you look at are full of pictures and videos and things like that, underneath every page is just a single (albeit possibly very long) string of text. Not all of it is in English, of course, because computer programs such as your web browser don't actually speak or understand English. Nevertheless, your web browser does understand a kind of language: the Hypertext Markup Language (HTML).

When you go to a website in your web browser, you're actually telling your web browser to download a file. This file, called an HTML document, is nothing more complicated than a bunch of text that your web browser knows how to read. The HTML you download is then interpreted by your web browser and displayed to you as a web page.

If it's all just a single string of text, you might be wondering, then how does the web browser know that a picture should go in the top-left corner or that two pieces of text are in different paragraphs? The answer is that, in addition to all the content that's in the HTML document (such as the text of the two paragraphs), there's also information about the content. This information about the content isn't actually visible to you on the web page, but it's there behind the scenes.

All of that extra information, called *markup*, tells the web browser what kind of thing each content piece is. For example, it tells your browser where things begin and end in that long string of text, as well as what purpose they serve (remember our opening example—start paragraph, end paragraph).

The basics of markup

Everything that ends up on a web page has to be specifically prepared to go there. As much as you might wish it so, you can't just copy everything in a Microsoft Word document, paste it into an empty text file, and call that a web page. That file is missing all of the information that a web browser needs to interpret its contents. Preparing a document for the Web—or marking up a document—is actually a pretty simple process that involves working with a specific set of tools (tags). The rest of this chapter will give you an introduction to that set of tools and start you off with a sample project that we'll work with throughout the rest of this book.

Elements (or tags)

A *tag* is the basic building block of HTML. Most tags have both an opening tag and a closing tag (to show the start and end of an element), but there are some exceptions to that rule. There are also different types of tags, but we're getting ahead of ourselves:

```
<header>Your header content goes here</header>
```

In its simplest form, that's all there is to a set of tags. Of course, "simple" doesn't always translate to "most powerful" or "most useful," so tags can be extended through the use of attributes:

```
<a href="http://www.google.com/">Google: a handy search engine</a>
```

In this example, href is an attribute that tells the <a> tag where to link to. An element is nothing more than text wrapped between a pair of tags. Angle brackets, the < and > characters, delimit the beginning and end of a tag. But before we dive into the intricacies of HTML, let's look at a quick XML example. XML allows you to create your own tags on the fly, instead of using a pre-defined set, as is the case with HTML. Because of that, it's easier to read and follow along with. It will be useful to give you a taste of a markup language before diving into HTML. Take for instance, this piece of text:

```
Where the Streets Have No Name
```

You might easily identify this text as a song title written by the band U2. However, someone else might not be able to recognize this song title, so you need to indicate what it is in proper markup form (especially when it's dropped into the middle of a book about building websites). Let's label what it is and identify it as a title, like so:

```
<title>Where the Streets Have No Name
```

You've now identified where the title starts by annotating the beginning of the song title with the `<title>` tag; but in XML, that's not enough. You also have to identify where this title ends. To do that, you simply use the same tag again and include a forward slash directly after the left angle bracket:

```
<title>Where the Streets Have No Name</title>
```

Now you have successfully marked up the title of this song by annotating its beginning and end explicitly, using opening `<title>` and closing `</title>` tags. What you've created is a `<title>` element that, in this case, is nothing more than the title of the song.

Next, let's add the artist information so that readers of the XML document will know what band wrote the song. All you have to do is mark up the text U2 as a similarly obvious element. Let's call it `<artist>` and add that directly after the title:

```
<title>Where the Streets Have No Name</title>
<artist>U2</artist>
```

You can continue adding information about the song in this way and include all sorts of information. For instance, this song came out on the album titled, "The Joshua Tree" in 1987. You can add that to your list of information, marked up as follows:

```
<title>Where the Streets Have No Name</title>
<artist>U2</artist>
<album>The Joshua Tree</album>
<released>1987</released>
```

By now you have a good deal of information encoded in the XML document about this song. Let's take this one step further and encode information about many songs in the same document. To do this, you need a way of grouping all the elements related to a single song together, so you can clearly delineate where the information about one song ends and the next one begins.

In XML and most other markup languages, elements can be nested (placed inside one another) if the information can be grouped together in a meaningful way. So, you could take all the markup you have already defined for your single song and put it inside a `<song>` element, like this:

```
<song>
  <title>Where the Streets Have No Name</title>
  <artist>U2</artist>
  <album>The Joshua Tree</album>
  <released>1987</released>
</song>
```

Now, you have defined one `<song>` element in your document. Since that `<song>` element encloses four other elements, it is said to have four children. `<song>` itself is called the parent element of those child elements.

Any element that is nested inside another element is typically indented, and the enclosing element's start and end tags are on their own lines. This is done purely for ease of reading and editing by humans. Software programs written to interpret this markup will typically ignore all this whitespace between the tags (including the indentation, the line breaks, and so on), as well as any extra whitespace inside elements or an element's content. Technically, all these tags could be right next to each other and still be just as meaningful. The browser simply interprets any number of consecutive spaces or tabs as a single space. Nevertheless, it's good practice to keep to this style of indentation because it's much easier to edit the markup when its structure is visually obvious.

Now that your song's information is properly grouped, it's easy to expand this document to include other songs. For instance, you might want to have a document with information that encodes one of your favorite mixes. You can duplicate your single song markup and simply change the information held in the child elements for the different songs, as shown here:

```
<song>
  <title>Where the Streets Have No Name</title>
  <artist>U2</artist>
  <album>The Joshua Tree</album>
  <released>1987</released>
</song>
<song>
  <title>Hungry Like the Wolf</title>
  <artist>Duran Duran</artist>
  <album>Rio</album>
  <released>1982</released>
</song>
<song>
  <title>Dream On</title>
  <artist>Aerosmith</artist>
  <album>Aerosmith</album>
  <released>1973</released>
</song>
```

This isn't right quite, yet, because all you have now is a bunch of individual songs, not a playlist for your mix. You still need to group these songs together in some way. Let's use a <playlist> element for that purpose:

```
<playlist>
  <song>
    <title>Where the Streets Have No Name</title>
    <artist>U2</artist>
    <album>The Joshua Tree</album>
    <released>1987</released>
  </song>
  <song>
    <title>Hungry Like the Wolf</title>
    <artist>Duran Duran</artist>
    <album>Rio</album>
    <released>1982</released>
  </song>
  <song>
```

```
    <title>Dream On</title>
    <artist>Aerosmith</artist>
    <album>Aerosmith</album>
    <released>1973</released>
  </song>
</playlist>
```

Finally, you have a complete playlist of four songs that's been properly marked up in XML. Using just the very basic building block of XML elements, you can create arbitrarily complex documents that encode information about whatever topic you like in a hierarchical fashion. This hierarchical structure is known as a tree. However, if all you had to work with were elements, your tree would grow very big very quickly, and it would quickly become unwieldy. So, in addition to elements, there are two more very important parts of the XML markup language that allow you to add extra information about your data: attributes and values.

Attributes and their values

As mentioned previously, *attributes* are a means of adding extra information to elements in an HTML or XML document. Attributes always specify some value, so you'll always see attributes and values together in this form:

```
attribute-name="attribute-value"
```

Generally, in XML each element can have an unlimited number of attributes, though in practice each specific application of XML has a certain set of valid attributes and valid values for those attributes. Part of learning any dialect of XML is learning which elements can have which attributes and what values are allowed for those attributes.

Attributes and their values are specified by adding their name and value inside the opening tag for the element to which they apply. For instance, you can include the date this playlist was created as an attribute of the <playlist> tag. For example, let's specify that your playlist was created on May 28, 2012. You could add this data to the <playlist> tag, as follows:

```
<playlist created="May 28, 2012">
```

Alternatively, if you wanted to specify the author of the playlist, you might add that data like so:

```
<playlistauthor="johndoe">
```

To include both the author of the playlist and the date it was created, you simply include multiple attributes in the same element:

```
<playlist author="johndoe" created="May 28, 2012">
```

This brings up an interesting question: what data should be marked up as an element, and what data should be marked up as an attribute/value pair? You could have just as easily created an <author> element and defined johndoe as its content inside the playlist tag or a <created> element in the same way. Although there is no real right or wrong answer here, it's generally considered best practice to use attributes and values for metadata (or data about data) and to use elements for everything else.

In other words, if it's data that's meant to be seen by the end user, it's best to mark it up in an element. If it's data that describes some other data in the document, it's best to use an attribute/value pair. This is often a confusing topic, so don't think you have to get it perfect right away. Oftentimes, you just have to step back and take a look at how you're intending to use the data to determine the best solution for your markup based on its application.

Empty elements

There's one other way you might encode information inside an XML document, and that is through the use of an empty element. Empty elements are just like regular elements, except that they don't contain any content, neither text nor other elements, inside them. Such elements are well suited for things such as embedding pointers to other documents or objects (such as pictures) inside an XML document or for storing important yes/no (Boolean) values about the document.

For example, if you want to use your playlist document in an automated CD-burning application, you might embed an empty element inside the <playlist> element called <burn>, which could have an attribute called format, the value of which would indicate the kind of CD format to use when ripping the mix:

```
<burn format="music" />
```

Notice that empty elements, like their nonempty counterparts, are both opened and closed. In the case of empty elements, however, the closing tag is the opening tag and is denoted simply by including the closing forward slash right before the right angle bracket.

Document types

When marking up a document, you must conform to some kind of standard of what elements, attributes, and values are allowed to appear in the document, as well as where they are allowed to appear and what content they are allowed to contain. If web developers didn't conform to these standards, every website in the world might use a different set of elements, attributes, and values, and no web browser (much less any human!) would be guaranteed to be able to interpret the content on the web page correctly. For example, where you used a <playlist> element to enclose your favorite mix in the previous example, someone else might have used a <favorite-mix> element.

Luckily for us, the standards that web pages and most other kinds of XML documents use are published publicly and are known as document types. Every XML document declares itself as a specific type of document by including a special <!DOCTYPE> tag. The DOCTYPE tag used to be a long string of text referring to some obscure web page (that nobody could remember); so with HTML5, this tag has been simplified:

```
<!DOCTYPEhtml>
```

As a brief exercise, let's figure out what elements, attributes, and values are allowed in the earlier simple example. First, you need to allow for the existence of the following elements: <playlist>, <burn>, <song>, <title>, <artist>, <album>, and <released>. Next, you need to specify that the attributes called created and author are permitted to be attached only to the <playlist> element and that the format attribute can be attached to the <burn> element. You can say that any values are valid for these attributes, or you can say that only *date values* are permitted for the created attribute and only *text values* are permitted for the author and format attributes. If you do that, you'll also have to explicitly define what "date values" and "text values" are.

Document Type Definitions (DTDs) are useful, not only so you can understand how to formulate your markup properly, but also so that your markup can actually be checked by a computer. Software programs called validators can read a document of markup and its corresponding DTD, and they can alert you to any inconsistencies between the two. Using the preceding example, your DTD could alert you if you accidentally mistyped and created a <spong> element or tried to specify the author attribute on a <title> element instead of <playlist>.

Starting with HTML5

There have been several flavors of HTML over the years. HTML5 is the latest flavor to hit the scene, and it is being developed to address a lot of the shortcomings of its predecessors. Thankfully, instead of adding to HTML's complexity, the contributors to HTML5 took the following approach: "HTML is pretty complicated—what can we do to make things better/more intuitive?" Sure, there's still a learning curve, but trust us when we say that things have gotten much better with this release (and if you have had exposure to one of the earlier versions, or to XHTML, hopefully you'll nod your head in agreement).

Document shell

When creating a new HTML document, it's easiest to start with a basic template because there are several elements, attributes, and values you'll always need, and most of them are difficult to remember. First, create a new folder on your computer called HTML, and inside it create a new blank document using a text editor. On Windows, you can just use the built-in Notepad application that comes with Windows to get started. On a Mac, grab a copy of TextWrangler from the Mac App Store (it's free) and save your new file as index.html with the following code:

```
<!DOCTYPEhtml >
<htmllang="en ">
<head>
  <meta charset="utf-8">
  <title></title>
  <link rel="stylesheet" href="style.css">
  <script src="javascript.js"></script>
</head>
<body>

</body>
</html>
```

If you opt to open this file in a web browser like Internet Explorer, Firefox, Safari, or Chrome, you'll see a blank page. Just a word of caution: You may get an alert if you're using Internet Explorer. We've specified a JavaScript file that doesn't exist, and IE interprets this as a potential security issue. Before moving on, let's examine what this markup means, piece by piece.

This is the code to identify the doctype of this document:

```
<!DOCTYPEhtml>
```

This is hands-down one of the greatest improvements (from our perspective) when it comes to HTML5. In previous versions of HTML, we had to remember a long, convoluted string including a URL pointing to the actual document type definition (.dtd) file on the Web. No longer! HTML5 has done away with some of the legacies of its past, including a reliance on external document type definitions.

This is the opening tag of the <html> element:

```
<htmllang="en">
```

Doctype excluded, everything else in the document will be inside this *root* element. This has also been massively simplified and/or improved from previous versions. You used to have to specify an XML namespace (with XHTML), as well. Now, it's just simple: state that it's an HTML document and that it's written in English (or for whatever language you're using, change the lang attribute).

The head

This is the <head> of the document:

```
<head>
  <meta charset="utf-8">
  <title>New Document</title>
  <link rel="stylesheet" href="style.css">
  <script src="javascript.js"></script>
</head>
```

A large amount of information may go into the <head>, much more than we currently have in this example. The important distinction here is that none of the information in the <head> of the document actually displays in the web browser window (except for the information in the <title>). The browser will, however, read some of the information and use it in a wide variety of ways.

The first element you see inside the <head> element is the (empty) <meta> element. As mentioned earlier, metadata is data about data, and this element is used to provide information about the document itself. In this case, it says that the content inside is encoded using the UTF-8 (unicode) character set. This gives a web browser access to the widest range of character glyphs available, so that, if your document is written in Russian or in Arabic, there is a likelihood that the letter you're looking for is actually available.

The next element is quite possibly one of the most important in the document: the <title> element. It is simply a place to name the content of your document. The content inside the <title> element is normally shown in the title bar of the web browser's window or on the browser tab where the page is being viewed. The <title> of a document is also the default name associated with a page if somebody bookmarks that page (either in her browser or when using something like PinBoard). To change the value of the <title> element, simply change New Document to whatever is most accurate and descriptive of your page content.

The title is also commonly used as the headline in search results from search engines such as Google and Yahoo. When people are searching for content that is on your page, and search engines find and show your page as a result, the title of your page is often the only thing they have to decide whether your page is what they want. If you intend your page to be found by people using search engines, pay close attention to the <title> element.

Finally, our <head> section is rounded out with a link to our style sheet and our JavaScript. Style sheets provide the formatting information (e.g., colors, fonts, and backgrounds) for our document. We'll learn more about formatting starting in Chapter 5. JavaScript gives our page all kinds of interactivity and advanced functionality. We'll learn more about that in Chapter 8.

The body

The body is where the meat of your document goes. It's currently empty, but you'll be filling it with the content for your page soon enough:

```
<body>
</body>
```

Finally, you need to end the `<html>` element you opened near the top of the document:

```
</html>
```

Marking up content

Now that you have the shell of your document in place, it's time to start adding real content. There are many elements at your disposal in HTML5 (some old and some new), and all of them serve a different purpose. Let's walk through some of the most important, starting with headlines.

As you start adding marked-up content to your HTML5 document, pay close attention to the names of the elements you use. Since the purpose of markup is to explicitly label the content to define what kind of building block it is intended to be in the document, all the elements in HTML5 are designed to be semantically rich; in other words, they are designed to provide meaning to the content they define.

A lot of the new elements introduced in HTML5 are geared towards making documents more semantically relevant. There are new tags for grouping content together and for defining what part is a header, what part is a footer, what the main body is, and what sections are within that. Basically, the contributors to the HTML5 specification sat down and looked at most pages on the Web and asked themselves what most of them have in common. The following sections outline what they came up with.

Sections

Used for grouping together content of similar meaning, the `<section>` element should replace a lot of overuse of the`<div>` tag. The`<section>` element is a big improvement because it actually has semantic meaning—it means that "this content is related" (div could have been used to denote a sidebar, or a *pagewrapper* used to apply formatting to the entire document; it didn't necessarily mean that the content contained within had any connection):

```
<section>
  <h1>HTML5 Overview</h1>
  <p>HTML5 is used to structure documents on the web.
 It contains a lot of useful elements (or tags).</p>
</section>
```

Article and aside

Similar to a `<section>`, an `<article>` was introduced as a way to group together related information in a document. A lot of the elements in HTML5 translate well to thinking about a blog. For example, an `<article>`

would contain a single post in your blog, whereas a `<section>` may contain a month's worth of posts on a page and list all that content chronologically.

An `<aside>` is perfectly suited to a sidebar (not a bar that is physically located on the side of a page, but rather "additional information"). Think of a sidebar as it relates to a newspaper: news outlets will frequently include pullquotes and/or additional (related) articles in their sidebars. That's all perfect fodder for the `<aside>` element.

Headers and headlines

Another new addition to the HTML5 element family is `<header>`, which is to be used for grouping together introductory content (just as a header would). Traditionally, when you think of a header, you imagine that there would be one header per page. That's not necessarily the case in HTML5, though; you can have as many headers as needed throughout your document, and you group those headers with their associated content using a `<section>` element.

In almost any document you create, you're going to come across the need for headlines to introduce the sections of text or other content in the document. If you've dealt with any form of publishing in the past (even just MS Word), you'll understand that there are different levels of headlines: primary, secondary, tertiary, and so forth. In HTML5, you can use six levels of headlines, and the elements for these are called `<h1>` to `<h6>`. The `<h1>` tag is for the most important headline in a section (which is also new to HTML5; it used to be for the most important headline in a document), and `<h2>`, `<h3>`, and so on decrease in importance until you get to `<h6>`, the least important (or most esoteric) headline in the section. Let's take a look at an example:

```
<h1>How I Learned to Ride a Bike</h1>
```

Headlines, as you would expect, cannot be nested inside each other, but they can be right next to each other:

```
<h1>Overview of How I Learned to Ride a Bike</h1>
<h2>Step 1: Practice with Training Wheels</h2>
<h2>Step 2: Practice Balancing Without Support</h2>
```

In essence, headlines create an outline for your content. So when you mark up a section with headlines, be sure to think about what kind of outline makes the most sense.

Another element commonly found within the `<header>` element(s) of a page is the `<nav>` element. This element is used to denote navigation information, like a list of links. While it isn't required that the `<nav>` element appear within the `<header>`, it is a good place for it to go.

Footers

Also new to the HTML5 scene (you might get sick of us saying that by the end of this chapter), the `<footer>` element is used to contain information commonly found in the footer of a section. This content may be contact information, copyright information, or possibly some metadata about the author of an article. As with the `<header>` element, you may have multiple `<footer>` elements per page, each grouped into a different `<section>`:

```
<footer>
  <p>Contents of this page licensed under a Creative Commons Share Alike license.</p>
</footer>
```

Blocks of text

Most likely, a majority of your document will simply be blocks of text such as paragraphs, asides, block quotations, and other such things. HTML5 has elements specifically meant for each of these items. Most are just as easy to apply as headlines. Let's look at an example with a few paragraphs:

```
William Shakespeare was an English poet and playwright. He is widely regarded as the
greatest writer of the English language and the world's pre-eminent dramatist. His surviving
works include approximately 38 plays and 154 sonnets, as well as a variety of other poems.
Shakespeare was also respectively modest about his innovative works, never truly boasting
about his tremendous ability. He is often called England's national poet and the "Bard of
Avon" (or simply "The Bard").
Shakespeare was born and raised in Stratford-upon-Avon, and at age eighteen married Anne
Hathaway, with whom he had three children. Sometime between 1585 and 1592 Shakespeare moved
to London, where he was an actor, writer, and part-owner of the playing company the Lord
Chamberlain's Men (later known as the King's Men), with which he found financial success.
Shakespeare appears to have retired to Stratford in 1613, where he passed away three years
later at the age of 52.
```

You specify to the web browser that these blocks of text are paragraphs by marking them up with the element designed for such content. Since paragraphs of text are such a common occurrence on web pages, the element for them is given the shorthand name, <p>:

```
<p>William Shakespeare was an English poet and playwright. He is widely regarded as the
greatest writer of the English language and the world's pre-eminent dramatist. His surviving
works include approximately 38 plays and 154 sonnets, as well as a variety of other poems.
Shakespeare was also respectively modest about his innovative works, never truly boasting
about his tremendous ability. He is often called England's national poet and the "Bard of
Avon" (or simply "The Bard").</p>
<p>Shakespeare was born and raised in Stratford-upon-Avon, and at age eighteen married Anne
Hathaway, with whom he had three children. Sometime between 1585 and 1592 Shakespeare moved
to London, where he was an actor, writer, and part-owner of the playing company the Lord
Chamberlain's Men (later known as the King's Men), with which he found financial success.
Shakespeare appears to have retired to Stratford in 1613, where he passed away three years
later at the age of 52.</p>
```

Again, there's nothing complicated here. Simply start the paragraph with the open paragraph tag (<p>) and end it with the close paragraph tag (</p>).

In addition to paragraphs, you can indicate that a selection of text is quoted from another source by using the <blockquote> element (an abbreviation of block quotation). Since the only thing that the <blockquote> element indicates is that its content was sourced from somewhere else, inside each <blockquote> element you will still need to use elements such as headlines and paragraphs to mark up the quotation's content. It is by nesting elements in this way that you begin to provide rich meaning to your content. Here's an example of a block quotation that quotes a couple of paragraphs:

```
<blockquote>
  <p>Through the release of atomic energy, your generation has brought into the world the
most revolutionary force since prehistoric man's discovery of fire. This basic force of the
universe cannot be fitted into the outmoded concept of narrow nationalisms.</p>
```

```
<p>For there is no secret and there is no defense; there is no possibility of control
except through the aroused understanding and insistence of the peoples of the world. We
scientists recognize your inescapable responsibility to carry to your fellow citizens an
understanding of atomic energy and its implication for society. In this lies your only
security and your only hope - you believe that an informed citizenry will act for life and
not for death.</p>
</blockquote>
```

Most of the time when you're quoting an outside source, you want to cite that source along with the quote. As you might have guessed, there's another HTML5 element designed to do just that: the `<cite>` element. `<cite>` has been slightly redefined in HTML5, but frankly, the "redefinition" doesn't make a lot of sense. `<cite>` is only supposed to be used to cite the title of a quoted work, not the author. Unfortunately, there is no similar element for citing the author; so really, I think this is a case where you can break from the rules. Unlike the `<blockquote>` element that contains other blocks of text, however, the `<cite>` element is permitted to contain only other text (and not blocks of text). This is what it looks like when you cite the previous quote:

```
<blockquote>
<p>Through the release of atomic energy, your generation has brought into the world the
most revolutionary force since prehistoric man's discovery of fire. This basic force of the
universe cannot be fitted into the outmoded concept of narrow nationalisms.</p>
<p>For there is no secret and there is no defense; there is no possibility of control except
through the aroused understanding and insistence of the peoples of the world. We scientists
recognize your inescapable responsibility to carry to your fellow citizens an understanding
of atomic energy and its implication for society. In this lies your only security and your
only hope - you believe that an informed citizenry will act for life and not for death.</p>
<p><cite>AlbertEinstein</cite></p>
</blockquote>
```

One good reason why the `<cite>` element must be placed inside the paragraph here is so that you can more accurately indicate the cited reference. Say, for example, the content you wanted in that last paragraph is "Original Quote by Albert Einstein." Rather than citing that whole sentence, which wouldn't make much sense, you can mark up the reference as such:

```
<p>Original Quote by <cite>Albert Einstein</cite></p>
```

This is much more accurate because it specifically and explicitly isolates the cited reference, Albert Einstein in this example, and thus this example provides far more meaningful markup.

Similar to the way that the `<blockquote>` element is used, two additional common elements are used to mark up specific blocks of content. First, the code element indicates that the enclosed text is, as you would guess, computer code of some sort. (What sort of code isn't typically specified, although you can do so using certain attributes if you like.) The code element can be used to mark up large blocks of content or just a single piece of code or even a word in a sentence, much like the `<cite>` tag.

Then there is the `<pre>` tag, which indicates that the content inside it is preformatted with line breaks, whitespace, tabs, and so on; and it should be rendered the same way in the browser window as it appears in the actual physical markup. The `<pre>` tag is most often used in combination with the `<code>` tag to show computer language excerpts or to display certain kinds of formatted text such as poetry.

Identifying content

There are two core attributes defined in an HTML5 document that can be used to give elements names that you can refer to later (mostly in Cascading Style Sheets, described later in this book). These attributes are id and class, and they can both be used on any element. The id attribute is simply a way to give a unique identity to an element. The class attribute serves a similar purpose, but instead of being unique throughout the document, the same class can be specified any number of times.

A common example of this is to set the id attribute on particular elements to provide a little more meaning to the group. For example, say you have a headline and a paragraph about a featured product on your website:

```
<h1>SwinglineStapler</h1>
<p>This workhorse stapler brings you a solid and consistent performance that makes it an
industry standard. An all-metal die-cast base for years of durability. A performance driven
mechanism with an inner rail for long-term stapling integrity. Ease of use, refined design,
time-tested features: exactly what you'd expect from America's #1 stapler.</p>
```

Let's nest these two elements inside an <article> element to group them together:

```
<article>
<h1>SwinglineStapler</h1>
<p>This workhorse stapler brings you a solid and consistent performance that makes it an
industry standard. An all-metal die-cast base for years of durability. A performance driven
mechanism with an inner rail for long-term stapling integrity. Ease of use, refined design,
time-tested features: exactly what you'd expect from America's #1 stapler.</p>
</article>
```

Now you can identify that <article> element as a *feature* on your web page by using the id attribute:

```
<articleId="feature">
<h1>SwinglineStapler</h1>
<p>This workhorse stapler brings you a solid and consistent performance that makes it an
industry standard. An all-metal die-cast base for years of durability. A performance driven
mechanism with an inner rail for long-term stapling integrity. Ease of use, refined design,
time-tested features: exactly what you'd expect from America's #1 stapler.</p>
</article>
```

Since you've used the id attribute, you've also implied that you'll have only one feature on your web page at any given time. If this isn't true, and you'll in fact have multiple "features," then you need to use the class attribute instead. You can still use unique values in id attributes to identify individual features if you like:

```
<article class="feature" Id="feature-1">
<h1>Swingline Stapler</h1>
<p>This workhorse stapler brings you a solid and consistent performance that makes it an
industry standard. An all-metal die-cast base for years of durability. A performance driven
mechanism with an inner rail for long-term stapling integrity. Ease of use, refined design,
time-tested features: exactly what you'd expect from America's #1 stapler.</p>
</article>
<article class="feature" Id="feature-2">
<h1>Black Standard Stapler</h1>
<p>Not as exciting as the Swingline Stapler, but a classic stapler nonetheless! </p>
</article>
```

Most importantly, `id` and `class` attributes should add meaning to the markup and describe what the content is. You should avoid `id` values that are presentational in nature, such as left-column or blue-box. Presentation and styling will be completely handled using CSS, so your markup should remain as semantic as possible.

Links

Of course, the breakthrough that HTML introduced was the ability to allow page authors to create links from one document to another by marking up specific text with an element that created a reference (also called a *pointer* or a *hyperlink*) to another page. The element that was created for this purpose is simply called the `<a>` element, which stands for the anchor element. Authors would place anchors in their pages that each linked to some other page, and those pages in turn would provide their own anchors that pointed at other pages; this was the beginning of hypertextual navigation, or web surfing.

Like the `<cite>` element, anchors are typically parts of a sentence. To actually create a link, the anchor needs to do two things. First, it needs to designate something to be the link itself. This is what the user ends up being able to click. Second, it needs to specify the destination to which the link points. This is where the web browser will take the user when the user clicks the link.

The link itself is created just like any other element, by enclosing a word or phrase (or other item) within the `<a>` element. The resulting content of the link is referred to as the anchor text. Since the destination at which the link points is metadata, it is specified in an attribute of the `<a>` element. This attribute is called the hyperlink reference and is abbreviated to `href` for short. You can set the `href` attribute to any URL on the Internet or to any local page on the current site. Let's take the following sentence as an example:

```
For more information, visit Wikipedia, the free online encyclopedia.
```

It would make sense to link part of this sentence to Wikipedia, located online at `http://wikipedia.org/`. So, use the `<a>` element and set the `href` attribute to the Wikipedia website:

```
For more information, visit <a href="http://wikipedia.org/">Wikipedia </a>, the free online
encyclopedia.
```

From a technical perspective, this is absolutely correct. The element is in the right place, it's wrapped around the right word, and the attribute is valid. However, there's something else you should think about whenever you create links from one page to another. Forgetting to think about this is one of the most common mistakes that web developers make. What you need to remember to think about is how you can link up as much relevant text as possible.

There are several reasons why this is an important thing to do:

- It provides a larger clickable area for the visitor of the website. Rather than having to hover over a single word, multiple words together provide more room to click, and that makes it easier to use.

- It creates more descriptive anchor text, and that can help people decide whether that link is really what they want to visit. It also improves accessibility by screen reader applications (for folks who are visually impaired).

- It's better from an SEO (search engine optimization) perspective to provide descriptive links to pages. Descriptive text in a link to another page is one of the factors Google takes into account when determining how relevant a page is to a certain subject.

How do you know whether the anchor text you've provided is good enough? A good rule of thumb that you can use to test it is that you should always be able to extract all the anchor text of all the links on your page; and without any supporting context, the links should clearly imply their destination. Avoid linking words that have nothing to do with where you're linking to, such as "click here," or just "here." These types of links aren't helpful to anyone. So again, the more descriptive a link's anchor text is, the better.

To help this along, HTML5 has introduced the ability to create links out of multiple elements. So now, if you'd like to turn a large part of your header into a hyperlink, there's nothing stopping you:

```
<header>
  <a href="http://www.cnn.com/">
    <h1>CNN.com &mdash; Your source for news</h1>
    <p>CNN.com provides local and global perspectives on the news that matters to
      you.</p>
  </a>
</header>
```

The only exception to this rule is that one <a> element can't be nested inside another <a> element; but apart from that, there are no restrictions.

The href attribute, URLs, and web page addresses

Without links, the Web wouldn't be the Web, so it behooves you to pay a little more attention to the href attribute and the values it can take.

For obvious reasons, the href attribute is always going to contain a hyperlink reference, which is really just a fancy way of saying a web page address or, more formally, a URL. The acronym URL stands for *Uniform Resource Locator*. For the purposes of this chapter, a URL is just a way to generalize the kinds of resources that you can request through a web browser. A web page is one kind of resource, an image is another, and a video is yet another. Most of the time, hyperlink references refer only to web pages. All URLs, including those that specify web page addresses, can be written in three distinct ways. Each of these ways is a valid value for the href attribute.

The most verbose form of a web page address is called a fully qualified URL. Fully qualified URLs are so named because they are composed of all three pieces of a URL: the scheme (also called the protocol), the domain name (also called the host name), and the path. In the example link to Wikipedia in the previous section, the scheme was http:, the domain name was //wikipedia.org, and the path was the trailing / (which means "the home page").

Another way to specify a URL is called an absolute link. Absolute links require that only the path portion of the address is to be placed in the href value, but that the path begins with the website's root, or initial forward slash (/). These are called absolute links because they specify the web page's full path from the root of the website (typically the home page) to their current location.

The final method is called a relative link. Like absolute links, relative links also require that only the path portion of the address be present. Unlike an absolute link, however, a relative link must not begin with an initial forward slash. Relative links always use the context of the current location of your web page to infer the complete URL, so they are by definition restricted to always link to pages hosted at the same domain name. Relative links can be a little harder to grasp, so let's look at a few examples.

A website's structure is just like the files and folders on your computer. If you have a file called overview.html on your server and you want to link to messages.html, you could simply place messages.html as the href value, like this:

```
<a href="messages.html">Messages from fans</a>
```

If you want to link to john.html in the people folder, you will have to add the folder (also called the directory) before the file, with a forward slash between the folder name and file name:

```
<a href="people/john.html">John's Contact Information</a>
```

Both of these are relative links that link to different pages on the same website, relative to their own positions. Relative links are handy because they don't need to be updated if the structure of some part of your website changes. They need to be updated only if the file that they reference moves (or if they themselves move).

What if you're currently looking at john.html in the people folder and you want to link back to the overview HTML page above it? In this instance, you need to use a special symbol to indicate you want to move up one folder level before looking for a particular file. That symbol is two periods, which just means "the folder above me." Like all folders, you then follow this symbol with a forward slash:

```
<a href="../overview.html">Overview of our service</a>
```

The preceding snippet tells the browser to go up one level in the website tree, and then load the overview.html page. This ../ sequence can be used multiple times if you need to go up two or more levels.

It's almost always best to link to files on your own site with relative or absolute links, as opposed to fully qualified ones. This saves you from having to type your own domain name over and over again (which makes your HTML files that much shorter); it also makes your site more portable in case your domain name changes in the future.

Emphasis

When working with almost any kind of content, some parts of that content will need to be emphasized more than others. For instance, many times when marking up a document, you need to make words bold or italic. Back in the old days, before web developers realized the importance of having semantically rich and meaningful HTML documents, this was most commonly done using the <b> and <i> elements. If you were to wrap a word or phrase in the <b> element, it would render as bold in the browser window. That seems simple enough, right? But let's analyze this for a minute.

What does "bolding" some part of a sentence really mean? It doesn't mean "make it bigger"—that's just how it ends up looking. What it means is, "make it stand out." The key concept, of course, is that when you think of making something bold, all you really want to change is its presentation, or how it looks. Well, as we all know, thanks to being the enlightened semantic web developers that we are, markup should be about what the content means and not what it looks like.

In modern HTML, you typically replace all occurrences of the <b> element with the <strong> element, which simply means "strong emphasis." Similarly, you replace all occurrences of the <i> element with the <em> element, meaning simply "emphasis." When you enclose words or phrases inside the <em> element, the browser automatically defaults to italicizing the text. Similarly, the browser defaults to bolding words or phrases inside the <strong> element.

> **Note:** *We'll see how <b> and <i> are treated in HTML5 in the next section.*

Be sure to use the <em> and <strong> tags only when you mean to emphasize text. If you're looking to achieve italic or bold on text without meaning to emphasize it (e.g., on a book title), then you can stylize the text appropriately using CSS (this topic is discussed in future chapters). Don't put <em> or <strong> tags around text just because you want it to be italicized or bold; instead, use a <span> tag with a class specified. Be sure to keep your markup meaningful and accurate.

Other inline elements

<strong> and <em> are called inline elements because they can be included in the middle of a block of text, and they won't cause breaks or added spacing within that text. <cite>, which we discussed earlier, is also considered an inline element. Let's take a look at a few other inline elements that will allow you to give your content even more meaning.

The old: redefined

In previous versions of HTML, <small> and <big> were used to format text as either bigger or smaller than regular paragraph text. In HTML5, <big> is gone, but <small> has taken on a new meaning: it's now used to represent that small print that lawyers love to use so often. HTML5 makes no lawyer jokes here; it makes them feel included by giving them their very own element to splash about liberally.

Similarly, the <b> and <i> elements mentioned previously have been redefined. Instead of just making something bold, <b> now has the semantic meaning of "an element to be stylistically offset from the normal prose without conveying added importance." So basically, it still does the same thing, but now it actually does it with feeling! <i> is a little more interesting; instead of meaning "italicize," <i> now means "in an alternate voice or mood." *I don't know about you, but I've been dying for a semantic way to represent my sarcasm online.*

The previously mentioned <span> is really a semantically void inline element used for wrapping things up (very similar to <div> at the block level). Spans will often have a class or id assigned to them, and they're used primarily as formatting hooks for a piece of text. In other words, if you can avoid using a <span> by using something a little more semantically rich, do it!

Look, shiny new elements!

HTML5 isn't just a redefinition of the same old stuff. It also introduces a wide range of new elements for your semantic enjoyment. For example, how many times have you said to yourself: "Self, I wish there was a way I could highlight a passage of text that is relevant within its context." (If your answer is anything other than "never," maybe we should have a talk over a warm cup of tea).

Fear not! HTML5 rides to the rescue with the introduction of the <mark> element. The <mark> element (besides being a snappy dresser) is intended to highlight a piece of text, but to not give it any added importance. The best example I've read of a situation where you'd like to do this would be in a set of search results. If somebody searches for the word "HTML5" in your document, and you want to highlight all instances of that word in the search results, <mark>'s your man.

HTML5 introduces a pile of new elements for marking up your data (and by a pile, I mean two). `<time>` and `<meter>` are handy for your date and time needs, as well as for any measurements you need to include. They allow you to include some machine-readable attributes that keep things consistent, but that also make it so that you can use any format you're comfortable with for display:

```
<time datetime="2012-02-14">Valentine's Day in 2012</time>will fall on a Tuesday. Remember
to buy your sweetheart <meter max="36" min="12" optimum="24" value="24">two dozen roses</
meter>to show how much you love him.
```

I went a little crazy in the preceding example, but it helps to show you the great attributes available to you.

Well, we've made some great progress with this chapter so far. Wait, that reminds me—there's one more element worth mentioning: `<progress>`. Progress can be used to mark up a measure of progress (think: download or upload of a file). Just like `<meter>`, it's got some great attributes to enhance its meaning:

```
<progress min="0" max="100" value="30">You're now about 30% of the way through this
chapter!</progress>
```

Lists

Lists are another common item in publishing. Using HTML, you can have three different kinds of lists: ordered, unordered, and definition lists. *Ordered lists* are meant to itemize sequential items, so they are prefixed by numbers that are listed in order by default. In contrast, items in an *unordered list* are meant to itemize things that don't imply a sequence, so they're prefixed by bullets by default. *Definition lists* are meant to hold glossary terms or other title and description items in a list, so they're not prefixed by anything by default.

The elements you use to define these lists are `<ol>` for ordered lists, `<ul>` for unordered lists, and `<dl>` for definition lists. In each case, the only children these elements are allowed to have are the appropriate list items. So, let's start building a list.

Unordered and ordered lists

For this example, let's mark up a grocery list:

```
Milk
Eggs
Butter
Flour
Sugar
ChocolateChip s
```

Here, an unordered list makes perfect sense because the order you buy these items in really makes no difference. If this were not a shopping list but, say, a list of directions for making chocolate brownies, then perhaps the order you add these items to your mixing bowl would matter, and an ordered list would be more appropriate. But let's stick with your shopping example and add the `<ul>` element to your list:

```
<ul>
Milk
```

```
Eggs
Butter
Flour
Sugar
ChocolateChip s
</ul>
```

So, you have all the items in your list inside the appropriate element. Next, each item of an unordered (or ordered) list must be contained within a list item element, which is defined with <li>. Let's insert the <li> elements into your unordered list:

```
<ul>
  <li>Milk</li>
  <li>Eggs</li>
  <li>Butter</li>
  <li>Flour</li>
  <li>Sugar</li>
  <li>Chocolate Chips</li>
</ul>
```

Great! Aided by your shopping list, you go out and gather your ingredients for chocolate brownies. When you are ready to mark up your brownie recipe, however, you find out that these were actually put in this order for a reason (that's the order you need to add them to the mixing bowl). Marking that up is as simple as replacing your <ul> element with an <ol> element. The <li> elements work inside both ordered and unordered lists, and the browser will render the appropriate prefix to each list item.

So, let's see the markup for your newly ordered list:

```
<ol>
  <li>Milk</li>
  <li>Eggs</li>
  <li>Butter</li>
  <li>Flour</li>
  <li>Sugar</li>
  <li>Chocolate Chips</li>
</ol>
```

Notice that you didn't need to put the numbers in the list at all; the browser does that on its own. This turns out to be especially convenient when you need to add items to the top or middle of an ordered list. There is no need to redo the numbering yourself because it's handled automatically. This is one example of the power that can be harnessed by using semantic, meaningful markup.

It's interesting to see how you can start to use multiple elements in concert, if needed, to continue encoding semantic meaning to your list's content. For instance, if you wanted to emphasize the text inside a particular list item, you could nest the <em> element inside the <li> element, like this:

```
<li><em>ChocolateChips</em></li>
```

Similarly, you could link a particular list item to another page on the Internet:

```
<li><ahref="h ttp://www.aeb.org/">Eggs</a></li>
```

You could even, if you wanted, emphasize the text that's being linked:

```
<li><em><ahre f="http://www.aeb.org/">Eggs</a></em></li>
```

You can also nest lists inside each other to create a list of lists. For example, you could expand your shopping list into item categories and their actual ingredients:

```
<ul>
  <li>Baking Ingredients
  <ul>
    <li>Milk</li>
    <li>Eggs</li>
    <li>Butter</li>
    <li>Flour</li>
    <li>Sugar</li>
    <li>Chocolate Chips</li>
  </ul>
  </li>
  <li>Cereal
  <ul>
    <li>Fruity Pebbles</li>
    <li>Cheerios</li>
    <li>Cinnamon Toast Crunch</li>
  </ul>
  </li>
</ul>
```

What you have here is an unordered list nested inside the list item of another unordered list.

By default, most web browsers will automatically switch the bullet styles of the inner lists when you create nested lists to make it easier to tell them apart.

Many elements in HTML can be nested inside the same elements (like these lists). Some, however, cannot. These rules are all defined in HTML's DTD, although oftentimes the best rule of thumb is just to think about whether it makes sense for the element to be found inside another element of the same kind. Lists, as you can see, make perfect sense. Paragraphs, however, do not. What sense would it make to put a paragraph inside another paragraph? It wouldn't make very sense at all (but you can certainly put a paragraph inside a list item).

Definition lists

Let's quickly examine how to mark up definition lists because they are slightly different from ordered and unordered lists. Instead of the single <li> element for the list items, you have two elements to work with inside definition lists. These are <dt> for the definition's title and <dd> for the definition's description:

```
<dl>
  <dt>body</dt>
  <dd>Holds content of the document</dd>
  <dt>head</dt>
  <dd>Holds additional information about the document</dd>
  <dt>HTML</dt>
```

```
<dd>Root element of the document</dd>
</dl>
```

You can see the basic premise is what you're already used to: a <dt> element wrapping the definition's title, followed by a <dd> element wrapping the description. All of these are held together by being enclosed inside a definition list.

Images

So far, you've explored various kinds of elements that deal solely with text. However, web pages can be a lot more interesting than that. Let's find out how you can add images to your pages next.

When placing images in a document, you use the <img> element. Image elements are empty elements because they will be replaced with the image you're referencing. However, to work properly, you need to tell the web browser where to find the image you'd like to insert, as well as give it a brief textual description of what the image is.

These two pieces of metadata are specified inside the two required attributes that <img> elements hold. First, the src attribute points to the actual image file to be loaded into the document. The same rules apply to the src attribute as apply to the href attribute on the <a> element. Relative or absolute, the src attribute gives the browser the URL that tells it where to look for the image.

The second attribute is alt, short for the alternate text for the image. (You might also hear people calling this the image's *alternative text*, or *alt text*.) It's used to describe what the image is and what meaning it has in the document:

```
<img src="/images/moose.jpg" alt="The Majestic Moose">
```

Recall that this is an empty element, so it contains no other content, and thus it is opened and closed with a single tag. The attributes here indicate that you want to load in the moose.jpg file found in the images folder relative to the website's root and that you want to provide the alternate text of "The Majestic Moose."

The src attribute's purpose is obvious, but the alt attribute's purpose isn't. Usually, the alternate text doesn't even show up on the page when you look at it in your web browser. So, what's it there for?

The alternate text actually provides several very important features. First, in keeping with the semantic importance of markup, it's what lets the image provide some meaning to the document. In the previous example, if this were a page about wildlife, then the picture of the moose would likely be considered part of the content of the page. Without the alternate text in the <img> element, the image would be essentially "meaningless," and the document would lose some of its semantic value.

On the other hand, if the rest of the page were about grocery shopping, and the picture of the moose were just there for visual ambiance, then the image would be probably superfluous and might be considered "not content." In this case, you would leave the alternate text completely blank to indicate that the image is used only for visual reasons and shouldn't be considered an important part of the content of the page (so that it's not picked up by assistive technologies):

```
<img src="/images/moose.jpg" alt="" />
```

Note that you still need to include the alt attribute in the <img> element code, but that the value of the alt attribute is missing (or null). Determining what images on your page should be "real content" and which ones shouldn't is part of the art of web development. There often isn't a clear or right answer, so you simply need to use your best judgment.

Assuming the picture does add some value to the page, the alternate text also helps out in a few additional, concrete ways. For example, even though it does not show up on the page in the normal sense, many web browsers will show the alternate text for an image if you hover your cursor over the image for a few seconds or if you give the image keyboard focus. You can think of it like a transient caption; it's there if the visitor to your web page requests to see it, but it's otherwise hidden.

Of course, some visitors to your website won't be able to see at all. These visitors might be humans with visual impairments or they might be machines, such as Google's search engine spider (googlebot). For these visitors, the presence (or absence) of the alternate text is more important than the image itself.

Visually impaired people browsing the Web often do so with a special kind of web browser that reads the content of web pages aloud to them. These programs are called screen readers. When a screen reader happens upon an image in your document, it uses the alternate text to describe what the image shows. Providing good alternate text for your images is crucial to making your web pages accessible and understandable to these visitors.

Similarly, when Google or Yahoo is reading the markup of your page, good alternate text in your `<img>` elements can help a search engine make sense of the purpose and content of a given image, allowing it to be more effective in ranking your web pages appropriately in the search result listings. Generally, the better your alternate text describes the content in your images, the higher your search result rankings will be.

Finally, if for any reason the image you've told the web browser to include in the page can't be found (the image file itself) or loaded, most web browsers will replace the `<img>` element with the text of the `alt` attribute. This provides a sort of contingency plan to help ensure that visitors to your website get what they came for, even if they can't get it in the preferred form. Similar techniques are used all the time in web development, and collectively they're called *graceful degradation*.

When using images on your sites, be mindful of how many you have put on each page, how big they are, and what purpose they serve. Excessive use of images will make a page slow to load, and it might also be visually disruptive. Compared to HTML, images are extremely large. On most pages, the bulk of the time it takes to download a page is caused by its images.

What if you want to draw?

While your friend the `<img>` tag is great for displaying photos and other pre-generated images, what if you want to draw a picture or generate a chart of some data on the fly? HTML5's got you covered on that front with the `<canvas>` tag.

The `<canvas>` element is very simple (by itself). All you do is specify the dimensions (and give it an id so that you can target it with the JavaScript you're going to use to draw the picture):

```
<canvas Id="a_simple_box" width="640" height="480"></canvas>
```

If you put anything between the canvas tags, browsers that don't yet support `<canvas>` will render that instead:

```
<bodyonload="drawIt();">
  <canvas Id="a_simple_box" width="640" height="480">
```

```
   <p>Sorry, you can't see the beautiful box drawn here. Get with the times.</p>
  </canvas>
</body>
```

It's a bit of a tease, but this chapter is already long enough without discussing the JavaScript necessary to actually draw the box. We'll look at a listing of some sample code, but avoid discussing it in any detail (we will go into more about JavaScript in later chapters):

```
<scripttype=" text/javascript">
function drawIt() {
  var canvas=document.getElementById('a_simple_box');
  var context=canvas.getContext('2d');
  context.strokeStyle='#000000';
context.  fillStyle='red';
  context.fillRect(10, 20, 300, 300);
  context.strokeRect(10, 20, 300, 300);
}
</script>
```

I want moving pictures (and sound)!

You kids these days are never satisfied with just still pictures. You're always striving to engage more of your senses and incorporate video and audio. Luckily for you, the folks working on HTML5 are with you, and they've added a pair of new elements for just such outlandish purposes. Reader, meet <audio> and <video>.

Both <audio> and <video> have friends that play nicely together, but that come from very different backgrounds. There has been and continues to be some disagreement as to what file format should serve as "the video format" or "the audio format" for the Web. On the audio front, MP3 is hugely popular and it's supported by the majority of the players (Internet Explored, Safari, and Chrome). Unfortunately the MP3 format has a few patent issues surrounding it, whereas the OGG format is completely open and free. Currently, OGG is the only format supported in Firefox, so in order to support maximum compatibility, both must be included. It's pretty much an ideological battle at this point, and hopefully things will settle down eventually. But, for the time being, we've got to support both. Here's what that looks like:

```
<audio controls preload="auto">
  <source src="my_audio.ogg" type="audio/ogg" />
  <source src="my_audio.mp3" type="audio/mpeg" />
</audio>
```

The <audio> element has only a few attributes, but these attributes may look a little different than what we've seen previously. In HTML5, not all attributes have to have a value assigned. Certain attributes of the audio and video tags, as well as certain form attributes, can be used in a standalone manner and act as a true/false type of toggle. If it's present, the value is true; if it's absent, it's false. Here are a handful of standalone attributes for the <audio> element:

- The controls attribute will show a player with play, pause, and volume controls (this is a true/false attribute).

- The preload attribute will ensure that audio starts downloading "in the background" before somebody goes to play it.

■ There are also loop (one guess what that does!) and autoplay attributes. However, you should be careful with that last one because it can be really disorienting when you load up a web page and all of a sudden audio starts playing. Under most circumstances, it's better to let your users control playback.

The <video> element has file patent problems similar to those of audio. The big options here are MP4 video and Theora; but just as with <audio>, there's no harm in providing and specifying both. Here's what that looks like:

```
<video controls width="640" height="480" poster="img/slam_it.jpg">
  <source src="my_video.ogv" type="video/ogg" />
  <source src="my_video.mp4" type="video/mp4" />
</video>
```

The controls attribute should be familiar to you from audio. We're also specifying the height and width of the movie here, as well as providing a *poster*. Basically, that's a static image that will display when the page loads, but the user hasn't clicked the video's play button, yet.

Tables

When you have to mark up data that is best presented in rows and columns (tabular data), that calls for the <table> element. Some common examples of tabular data are calendars (where rows are weeks and columns are the different days of the week) or comparison charts. When you think of tabular data like this, you often think of spreadsheets and all the riveting data that goes along with them.

Fortunately, marking up tabular data is relatively easy, and HTML gives you plenty of semantic elements to organize your data appropriately. Let's start with some example data and walk through the process of marking it up with semantic HTML elements:

```
<table>
</table>
```

Next, let's add the first row. Table rows are defined with the <tr> element:

```
<table>
  <tr>
  </tr>
</table>
```

This row has three distinct cells. HTML table cells are marked up using the <td> element, which stands for table data:

```
<table>
  <tr>
  <td>First Name</td>
  <td>Last Name</td>
  <td>Birthday</td>
  </tr>
</table>
```

You now have a table with one row and three cells in that row. But you can do even better, since this row is obviously a header that introduces what data you'll find in the rows that follow. Using HTML5, you can use the <thead> element to mark up your header data and indicate that this row has this special purpose:

```
<table>
  <thead>
    <tr>
    <td>First Name</td>
    <td>Last Name</td>
    <td>Birthday</td>
    </tr>
  </thead>
</table>
```

This introductory row is special, but so too is each of the three cells, which are column headings, not ordinary table data. To indicate this in your markup, you'll replace the <td> elements with <th> elements, which indicate table headings. The <th> element is used for any table cell that is a heading for either a column or a row (a column, in your case) to differentiate it from regular table data:

```
<table>
  <thead>
    <tr>
    <th>First Name</th>
    <th>Last Name</th>
    <th>Birthday</th>
    </tr>
  </thead>
</table>
```

Now that your header is in place, you can start adding the bulk of the table's data. Just as your header data was enclosed in a <thead> element, your body data should be wrapped in a <tbody> element:

```
<table>
  <thead>
    <tr>
    <th>First Name</th>
    <th>Last Name</th>
    <th>Birthday</th>
    </tr>
  </thead>
  <tbody>
  </tbody>
</table>
```

To insert your individual data cells, you use the <td> element, with each row put inside a separate <tr> element, as before:

```
<table>
  <thead>
    <tr>
    <th>First Name</th>
    <th>Last Name</th>
```

```
    <th>Birthday</th>
    </tr>
  </thead>
  <tbody>
    <tr>
    <td>George</td>
    <td>Washington</td>
    <td>February 22, 1732</td>
    </tr>
    <tr>
    <td>Abraham</td>
    <td>Lincoln</td>
    <td>February 12, 1809</td>
    </tr>
  </tbody>
</table>
```

An important thing to note about HTML tables is that, when using this minimal markup, columns are created by implication based on the number of individual table data cells that exist in each row. With three table data cells per table row element, you create a three-column table. If you add a table data cell to the rows, you make a table with four columns. And so on. You can modify this behavior slightly using certain attributes that will be described in just a moment; but the important thing to remember is that (in most cases), only table rows are structurally grouped together in the markup, whereas the columns are usually implied.

Astute readers will point out that there is, in fact, a way to explicitly label columns using HTML markup. You can do this by defining a set of <col> elements that are optionally contained within one or more colgroup elements before the start of the table data. Although semantically rich and mostly harmless to old browsers, these elements aren't widely implemented in the real world, so they are considered to be outside the scope of this book. Implementing them in this example is left as an exercise to the reader.

Before you call your table complete, however, you'll add a few more things that will make it truly exemplary of semantic HTML markup. By design, a data table is a very visual element that relates data in columns and rows, so a viewer can grasp a complicated concept or more easily understand a large data set. For much the same reasons that you added the alt attribute to the <img> element, you'll provide some additional data about this table in text form.

First, you'll add a <caption> element, which is (obviously) meant to be a caption for the table. You can use this to provide a title for the table or perhaps an overview of its purpose. In this example, you could use "American Presidents" as the caption. Next, you'll add a summary attribute on the <table> element. A table's summary attribute is meant to hold more detail about what information is actually displayed in the table, and, just like the alt attribute on <img> elements, the summary is read aloud to visually impaired users who are browsing your web page with the aid of a screen reader. Let's see this in code:

```
<table summary="This table compares the first name,
 last name, and birth date of George Washington
and Abraham Lincoln.">
  <caption>American Presidents</caption>
  <thead>
    <tr>
```

```
    <th>First Name</th>
    <th>Last Name</th>
    <th>Birthday</th>
    </tr>
  </thead>
  <tbody>
    <tr>
    <td>George</td>
    <td>Washington</td>
    <td>February 22, 1732</td>
    </tr>
    <tr>
    <td>Abraham</td>
    <td>Lincoln</td>
    <td>February 12, 1809</td>
    </tr>
  </tbody>
</table>
```

Tables can have as many rows and columns as you'd like. As mentioned earlier, the number of <th> or <td> elements inside the <tr> element(s) dictates the number of columns in the table, and the number of <tr> elements dictates the number of rows.

Both <th> and <td> elements accept attributes called rowspan and colspan. These attributes indicate how many rows or columns this particular cell spans. The rowspan attribute, as you can infer, describes how many rows the particular cell spans, and colspan defines how many columns the cell spans. Let's take a look at an example using your American Presidents table.

Instead of having the individual header cells for the first name and the last name, let's merge those into one title cell called Name. Similarly, let's take both birthday cells and merge them into one with new content that merely states, "A long time ago":

```
<table summary="This table compares the first name,
 last name, and birth date of George Washington
and Abraham Lincoln.">
  <caption>American Presidents</caption>
  <thead>
    <tr>
    <th colspan="2">Name</th>
    <th>Birthday</th>
    </tr>
  </thead>
  <tbody>
    <tr>
    <td>George</td>
    <td>Washington</td>
    <td rowspan="2">A long time ago</td>
    </tr>
    <tr>
    <td>Abraham</td>
    <td>Lincoln</td>
```

```
      </tr>
    </tbody>
  </table>
```

You'll notice in the markup that you need only two `<th>` elements now because the first one is taking the place of two of them. Similarly, you don't need the third `<td>` for the birthday column in the last row because it's being filled by the `<td>` from the previous row by the rowspan value.

As you can see, tables provide a lot of flexibility and can be a great way to display certain kinds of data. Before the advent of Cascading Style Sheets in modern web development, however, tables were more often used to control the visual layout of a web page, which polluted the document's semantics and made web designers bend over backward to try to find clever ways of making their designs fit into the grid-like structure dictated by tables.

Even today, some websites that simply have to look right in old browsers use tables for this purpose. If you can avoid doing this, great! But if not, then remember this if you remember nothing else: include an empty summary attribute on the `<table>` element. Just as you would provide an empty alt attribute value on an image that serves no semantic purpose, so too must you declare a meaningless table if you use one!

Forms

Filling out forms online is a great way to glean information from your visitors or provide enhanced services to them. Although the scripts that actually receive and process such form data are beyond the scope of this book, in this section we'll discuss how some of the various form elements work in HTML markup.

A quick note of caution before we proceed: A lot of the new elements in HTML5 aren't well supported by most browsers. That said, a browser will just fall back to a regular text box in cases where it doesn't yet support a particular element.

The first thing you'll need in any form you create is the `<form>` element:

```
<form>
</form>
```

`<form>` elements accept many attributes, but only one, the action attribute, is required. The action attribute is similar to the href attribute in the `<a>` element. It specifies a particular URL where the script that processes the form data can be found. Let's set the example form to be processed at /path/to/script:

```
<formaction="/path/to/script">
</form>
```

When this form is submitted, it will send the browser to the /path/to/script page along with all the data from your form. Right now, however, there's no data to be sent because you haven't defined any fields to fill in. So, let's add some fields to this form.

A `<form>` element is a lot like a `<blockquote>` in the sense that it can have only certain child elements. For simple forms, you can use the `<p>` or `<div>` elements that you've already seen used before, and you can place all the form's controls into these elements. However, since you're about to build a relatively complex form, you'll use the HTML element specifically designed to group form controls into groups: the `<fieldset>` element.

The fieldset element

The <fieldset> element, which (as you might expect) defines a set of related form fields, is a lot like the <div> element. Both elements are used to group related elements together in a single chunk of code. Unlike <div> elements, however, <fieldset> elements can contain a special element called a legend that gives the <fieldset> element a name that is visible to your web page's visitors. You might do well to think of this element in the same way you might think of the <caption> element for tables.

With the <fieldset> element and its legend in your form, your markup now looks like this:

```
<formaction="/path/to/script">
<   fieldset>
     <legend>Personal Information</legend>
</   fieldset>
</form>
```

Adding an input element

The most common kind of form field is a simple text field where users can type something. These (and most other kinds of form fields) are added to forms by defining <input> elements. Form <input> elements can be of a number of different types, such as text fields, check boxes, or radio buttons. The kind of form control any particular <input> element becomes is specified by the value of its type attribute.

If a type attribute isn't specified, the default of type="text" is inferred. For example, this is how you might ask for the visitor's first and last name using a text input field inside your form:

```
<formaction="/path/to/script">
<fieldset>
  <legend>Personal Information</legend>
  <input type="text" name="fullname" />
</fieldset>
</form>
```

There are two things you should notice about the <input> element used here. First, it's an empty element, like an <img>. Second, you've also included an attribute called name, and you've given it a value of fullname. All form elements that need to provide some data to processing scripts need to have a name attribute with a value. This is the name that the processing script will use to refer to the data in this <form> element after the form has been submitted. If you don't provide a name, then the processing script won't be able to see any of the data in the form element.

You can see that the name attribute isn't displayed anywhere (nor should it be), so there's currently no easy way for visitors to know what they're expected to type into that text field. To give the text field a name that human visitors can use to refer to it, you have to use the <label> element.

Adding a label

You can place <label> elements anywhere in the form—they don't have to appear right next to the input field that they label. For this reason, each <label> element needs to be uniquely associated with an input field in some way other than proximity. You've already learned how to uniquely identify elements on a web page using the id attribute, so let's first uniquely identify this form field with an id of fullname_field:

```
<input type="text" name="fullname" Id="fullname_field" />
```

Now that you have a unique identifier to refer to this input field with, you can add the ‹label› element to your form. You'll add it directly in front of the ‹input› element for simplicity's sake; but again, you technically could have placed it anywhere inside the ‹form› element. When using a ‹label›element, the text inside the element should describe the field that the element labels (as the anchor text does for links), and the value of the for attribute should match the id of the field being labeled. In code, that might look something like this:

```
<label for="fullname_field">First and Last Names:</label>
<inputtype="text"name="fullname"Id="ful   lname_field"/>
```

New attributes

In the last section, we hinted at some new attributes available to form fields in HTML5. Let's take a look at those now and see what they do:

```
<input type="text" Id="fullname" name="fullname_field" autocomplete="on" required autofocus />
```

The first part, you've seen before. We're creating a text input with the name of fullname. We've also created an id for that element with the value of fullname_field. Here are the attributes you haven't seen before, and what they do:

- autocomplete tells the browser whether to use the built-in auto-completion functionality on that particular element. By default, it's on (i.e., we didn't have to specify it in the preceding example; we did so solely for illustrative purposes).

- required indicates whether a form field is optional (if so, it's omitted) or required. If it's required, the browser won't allow the form to be submitted until that field is filled in. A word to the wise, though: This new attribute isn't very widely supported yet, so if you have a form where you absolutely need to have a certain field filled out, this isn't the way to go (yet). Browsers that don't support this attribute will just ignore it and treat the field as optional. You can turn to JavaScript and server-side processing to double-check the required fields (we'll show you the JavaScript version in Chapters 9 and 10).

- autofocus is a handy new attribute that replaces something that's been done in JavaScript for some time. Have you ever loaded a web page and had your cursor immediately appear in the search box (think Google)? That behavior is called autofocusing.

Along with these new, timesaving attributes, HTML5 introduces quite a few new field types. Some look no different from current field types; they just behave differently under certain circumstances. Others are a huge sigh of relief for developers who have had to develop complex JavaScript analogs over the years. Let's check them out.

New datatype fields

HTML5 ushers in a raft of contact data-type fields. Currently, in a desktop web browser, you won't notice any difference in these fields from a standard text input (text box). The real magic happens when you access these fields with a mobile web browser (like the one on an iPhone). If you use ‹input type="tel"›, a user will receive a numeric keyboard in Mobile Safari—because really, no one needs to enter a letter for her phone number:

```
<input type="email" name="email" Id="email" />
<input type="tel" name="mobile" Id="mobile" />
<input type="url" name="web" Id="web">
```

`<input type="email">` and `<input type="url">` will also yield special keyboard configurations, including an @ sign for e-mail addresses and a menu of domain suffixes (e.g., .com, .net, or .org) for URLs. This is nothing earth shattering, but it is certainly helpful when people are trying to type things out with tiny on-screen keyboards:

```
<input type="search" name="search" Id="search">
```

The search input type is another subtle variation from the standard text input. The only difference is that some browsers will style it differently than a regular text input. Arguably, using a search type is also better semantically if you're planning on including a search field in your pages.

Adding a check box

Another possible type value for the `<input>` element is check box. A check box is a simple "yes or no" input, and it is nearly the same as the text field's `<input>` element in code. Let's use a check box to ask somebody whether he is currently enrolled in a college or university:

```
<input type="checkbox" name="enrolled" Id="enrolled_field" value="1" />
<label for="enrolled_field">I am currently enrolled in a college or university</label>
```

One of the attributes you've added to the check box is the value attribute (careful, this is an attribute named value). The value of the value attribute will be sent to the processing script only if the box is checked. Here you've used 1, a simple approach to indicate that "yes, this box was checked on the form."

Let's stop for a minute and think about how best to display a form. If you think about it, what you're beginning to create is a list of inputs for the user to fill out. In this case, these inputs are in a particular order. It sounds like an ordered list fits this scenario perfectly. Let's nest a few of the inputs and labels from previous examples in list items, and then nest the list items in an ordered list element:

```
<formaction="/path/to/script">
<fieldset>
  <legend>Personal Information</legend>
  <ol>
    <li>
    <label for="fullname_field">First and Last Names:</label>
    <input type="text" name="fullname" Id="fullname_field" />
    </li>
    <li>
    <input type="checkbox" name="enrolled" Id="enrolled_field" value="1" />
    <label for="enrolled_field">I am currently enrolled in a college or university</label>
    </li>
```

```
    </ol>
  </fieldset>
</form>
```

There's one other attribute that you can use for a check box, for cases where you want it to be checked when the visitor first loads the form. In this case, perhaps a majority of your visitors will be enrolled in some college or university. All you need to do to make this happen is specify a checked attribute. The visitor can still uncheck the box; but in some situations, it might prove easier to have the field checked in the first place. Let's see the markup for the check box when it's checked by default:

```
<input type="checkbox" name="enrolled" Id="enrolled_field" value="1" checked/>
<label for="enrolled_field">I am currently enrolled in a college or university</label>
```

Adding radio buttons

Another input type that HTML forms permit you to use is a radio button. A radio button is similar to a check box, except it includes multiple options from which a user can choose, and only one can ultimately be selected. Radio buttons are thus almost always found in sets that ask the user to select one of a small number of items.

Each radio button is represented as an <input> element with its type set to radio. You associate multiple radio buttons as belonging to the same set by giving each one the same value in its name attribute. Each radio button's value attribute, however, should be unique among the radio buttons in the set. Like a check box, each radio button needs a label, so each radio button's id attribute should also be unique (in the entire document, not just for the set of radio buttons or even just for the <form> element they're in).

For example, let's ask a visitor her favorite color. You'll give her four colors to select from: blue, red, yellow, or green. While marking up this question for your form, you'll immediately notice that you have yet another list. This time, though, the items are not in any particular order, so you'll use an unordered list.

You will also need to introduce the question because now your <label> elements are labeling the actual choices, instead of the question at hand. You'll do that simply by including some text before you start the unordered list:

```
<ol>
<li>What is your favorite color?
<ul>
  <li>
  <input type="radio" name="favorite_color" Id="favorite_color_blue" value="blue">
  <label for="favorite_color_blue">Blue</label>
  </li>
  <li>
  <input type="radio" name="favorite_color" Id="favorite_color_red" value="red" />
  <label for="favorite_color_red">Red</label>
  </li>
  <li>
  <input type="radio" name="favorite_color" Id="favorite_color_yellow" value="yellow" />
  <label for="favorite_color_yellow">Yellow</label>
  </li>
  <li>
  <input type="radio" name="favorite_color" Id="favorite_color_green" value="green"/>
```

```
      <label for="favorite_color_green">Green</label>
      </li>
  </ul>
  </li>
  </ol>
```

You may be thinking that there's a problem using four checkboxes here: what if the user's favorite color is something other than one of the listed options? HTML5 comes to the rescue again with the new `datalist` element:

```
<input type="text" name="favorite_color" Id="favorite_color" list="colors">
<datalistId=" colors">
  <option value="Red">
  <option value="Blue">
  <option value="Green">
  <option value="Orange">
  <option value="Yellow">
  <option value="Periwinkle">
</datalist>
```

The `datalist` is an enhancement to a regular text input field. It provides a list of options that the user can choose from; or, the user can type in her own option if she doesn't like any options in the list. This is ideal in a situation where you're filling out a survey and being asked to select one of the options in the list or to select "other." The `datalist` will save you the trouble of having two separate elements for this type of question.

Dropdown list

Let's ask for your visitor's time zone and provide a free-form area in which he can type whatever text he likes. Since these two items are somewhat unrelated to the previous three questions, let's group them separately from the previous form items by using a new <fieldset> element.

To let the visitor select his time zone, you could display a set of radio buttons in a list, just as you did for his favorite color. However, radio buttons take up a lot of space. Furthermore, there are dozens of time zones in the world. If you used radio buttons again, your form would be gigantic. You could use the new `datalist` element, but there really are a finite number of options. We don't want somebody typing in "-56 Wonkaland."

Instead, let's use a different form control that HTML makes available: a drop-down list. This control is defined by the <select> and <option> elements in tandem, much like a regular ordered or unordered list:

```
<labelfor="timezone_ field">Timezone</label>
<selectname="timezone"Id="timezone_ field">
  <option>-5</option>
  <option>-6</option>
  <option>-7</option>
  <option>-8</option>
</select>
```

This markup gives the user four options to select her time zone from: -5, -6, -7, or -8. These are actually the number of hours offset from UTC time of the eastern United States through to the Pacific coast. It's how computers most often tell time (by keeping track of everything in UTC time, and then calculating offsets per time zone); however, this is not how people think of their time zones. So, using the value attribute for each option element, let's give the computers what they expect, but also show human visitors values that are more comfortable for them to read:

```
<labelfor="ti mezone_field">Timezone</label>
<selectname=" timezone"Id="timezone_ field">
  <option value="-5">Eastern</option>
  <option value="-6">Central</option>
  <option value="-7">Mountain</option>
<optionvalu  e="-8">Pacific</option>
</select>
```

Now, when the user selects Eastern as her time zone, the processing script that sees this form will see the value –5.

You can place as many <option> elements inside <select> elements as you like. However, when there are a lot of options, or the options are representative of different categories, it makes sense to group these options. For that, you use the <optgroup> element, just as if you were using <div> or <fieldset>. Let's add more time zones to the list, but let's organize them inside <optgroup> elements, so that the categorization is obvious:

```
<labelfor="timezone_ field">Timezone</label>
<selectname="timezone"Id="timezone_ field">
  <optgroup label="Mainland America">
    <option value="-5">Eastern</option>
    <option value="-6">Central</option>
    <option value="-7">Mountain</option>
    <option value="-8">Pacific</option>
  </optgroup>
  <optgroup label="Outlying States">
    <option value="-9">Alaskan</option>
    <option value="-10">Hawaiian</option>
  </optgroup>
</select>
```

Notice that inside the <optgroup> element, you're using a label attribute to give a name to your group of <option> elements. Be careful not to confuse this with the <label> element used to label the entire <select> element.

Adding a textarea

As a final touch, let's add that free-form area of text where you encourage your visitors to send you their comments. This is accomplished with a <textarea> element, which is one of the simplest form controls to use. It has just two differences. First, unlike most of the other form controls you've seen, the <textarea> element does not need a value attribute because its content becomes its value. Second, it requires two new attributes, rows and cols, to indicate its default height and width, respectively. (This sizing can later be overridden with CSS.) A <textarea> element's markup might look like this:

```
<labelfor="comments_ field">Comments</label>
<textareaname="comments"Id="comments_  field"rows="6"cols="65"></textarea>
```

Adding a submit button

At long last you have your form controls all set up to collect input from the user. There's only one thing you're missing: a way for the visitor to actually submit the form to the processing script. For that, you need to use one more type of `<input>` element: the submit type. This type of `<input>` element will create a button that the user can click to submit the form.

Typically, when using elements that create form controls that operate on the form (such as a submit button), you can skip specifying a label for that element because the form control itself effectively serves that purpose. Since you're not using a `<label>` element for your submit button, you don't have to use an `id` attribute either, so your element is really quite simple.

```
<input type="submit" value="Submit this Form" />
```

Now your visitors will be able to click the Submit this Form button to send the form to the processing script.

All the rest

Of course, there's even more you can do with HTML5 forms. For instance, there are a few more options for the type attribute that you can specify on `<input>` elements. An important one to know about is the password type, which creates an element that is identical to the text type, except that it renders all the characters that the user types into it as asterisks (*) or bullets (•) instead of actual text. The text that's typed is, in fact, unchanged, but it doesn't show up on screen for security purposes. There's also the file type, which allows the visitor to select a file from his computer to upload through the form using his operating system's native file-selection dialog box.

There are also a few more kinds of buttons that are similar to the submit type of input. For example, there's a button type that displays a button that you can control through JavaScript, although it won't do anything at all by default. There's also a button element that can be used to turn certain other elements (such as an `<img>`) into a button. (These kinds of buttons will, by default, submit the form.) There's also the image type of `<input>` element, which provides another way to turn an image into a button. This element takes a src attribute, just like the `<img>` tag.

Finally, there's also a reset type of the `<input>` element that also creates a button; however, instead of submitting the form, this kind of button will restore the form to its original state, removing any input the user may have entered. There's rarely any real need for this kind of button (especially on longer forms), but it's there if you ever need it.

As you can see, designing forms can be quite an undertaking on the Web. They introduce a kind of interactivity that you can't get from other kinds of media like television or magazines. Forms—and the capabilities they provide to enable two-way communication between the website creator and the website visitor—are what make the Web a truly unique publishing platform.

Less well supported

In addition to the subtle additions discussed earlier, there have been some other great additions made to the form element library. Unfortunately, a lot of these elements are not yet supported at all by most browsers, so I would encourage you to use a great deal of caution if you choose to use them. Testing your form with a range of browsers and providing fallbacks or alternatives is a good idea here.

`<input type="date">` scratches an itch that a lot of developers have had for a long time. It provides a browser-native date picker that lets you control the input and formatting of the date in a form. The problem this solves is that there are a lot of ways to write a date. For example, you can write any of the following: 12-Oct-2012; October 12th, 2012; 2012-10-12; or even 12/10/2012. All are acceptable formats for you, but a computer (database) generally expects dates to be in a particular format (the mySQL date type is YYYY-MM-DD, for example). If somebody provides you with something other than what's expected, you either need to validate that and get her to fix it, or fix it yourself using Javascript and/or some type of server-side script. `<input type="date">` will give you better control over what can be input, and it will put it in a very user-friendly format!

Similarly, `<input type="color">` will help you control the input on your forms, so that they can prompt the user to enter a proper color value. Most on-screen color values are represented in hexadecimal format (#FFFFFF is white, for example). Eventually, when browsers support it, this input will yield a beautiful color picker (like the one you see in PhotoShop) that will translate colors into six character strings for you. Until that day, dream on!

The last two new input types focus on numerical values. `<input type="range" min="10" max="1000">` will display a slider control that allows the user to slide a knob back and forth and select a value within a range of values. Meanwhile, `<input type="number" min="0" max="1000">` will give you a text box with an up and down arrow that allows the user to pick a precise value within that range (the range input just gives you a graphical representation, allowing the user to "ballpark" it).

Special characters

When marking up content, you're bound to notice that there are certain characters that just don't display properly when you put them directly in your markup. Perhaps the most obvious of these would be the less-than and greater-than symbols, which are also called left and right angle brackets (< and >). Instead of treating these like angle brackets, the browser assumes these are the beginnings and endings of tags.

Because of the double duty these characters serve, if you actually want to use < or > in your content, you need to use special codes called entity references to refer to them. In computer speak, this is called *escaping* the characters. Escaping characters in HTML5 is achieved simply by replacing the character you intend to type with a combination of other characters that represent it. In every case, escape sequences such as these begin with an ampersand (&) and end with a semicolon (;).

The entity references for the less-than and greater-than symbols are < and >, respectively. This, however, poses a new problem. How do you mark up an ampersand symbol? The answer is the same: you escape it by using its entity reference. The entity reference for an ampersand is &.

There are hundreds of different entity references, and an exhaustive glossary would be superfluous in this book. However, keep these in mind when marking up your content because they will probably prove very useful. For example, assume you want to make the following sentence appear on your page:

```
I'm sure that using the <div>tag is more professional than "faking a layout"
using tables.
```

First, you can see that we'll need to replace the angle brackets with their entity references. Don't forget to mark up the HTML tag as computer code, either:

```
I'm sure that using the <code>&lt;div&gt;</code>element is more professional than "faking a
layout" using tables.
```

There is also the issue of the curly quotes around the words "faking a layout." Let's replace those:

```
I'm sure that using the <code>&lt;div&gt;</code>tag is more professional than &ldquo;faking
a layout&rdquo; using tables.
```

And finally, you'll need to escape the curly apostrophe in the word "I'm":

```
I&rsquo;m sure that using the <code>&lt;div&gt;</code>tag is more professional than
&ldquo;faking a layout&rdquo; using tables.
```

When you view this in a browser, it will look like your original sentence.

Using entity references is quite simple because you're simply replacing one character with a short sequence of others. They're helpful in keeping your markup portable across browsers, and they keep your content looking and acting properly. You can get a complete list of entity references at www.webstandards.org/learn/reference/charts/entities/.

Let's go to an example!

We're going to run with an extended example throughout the next few chapters. This chapter on HTML has shown you how to structure your pages and how to outline your content. Unfortunately, by themselves, these pages would look pretty plain. In the next couple of chapters, we're going to show you how to add some style to your pages using CSS, and then show you how to add some function and interactivity using JavaScript.

We thought that a good example to work with would be a registration form for an event. That will let us use a number of the new HTML5 elements and really kick the tires on things. So without further ado, let's start with our basic page shell:

```
<!DOCTYPEhtml >
<htmllang="en ">
  <head>
  <meta charset="utf-8">
  <title>Summer Smash 2012 Registration</title>
  <link rel="stylesheet" href="css/style.css">
  <script src="js/javascript.js"></script>
</head>
<body>
  </body>
</html>
```

The preceding code provides a good starting point. Next, let's outline some of the basic elements of our page between the <body> tags:

```
<body>
  <div Id="pagewrap">
    <header>
    </header>
    <section Id="main">
      <section Id="registration_form">
      </section>
      <aside>

      </aside>
    </section>
    <footer>

    </footer>
  </div>
</body>
```

So far, we've laid out the "block" structure for this page. It's a registration form, so we want to do away with a lot of the interface clutter we'd find on a regular web page, so that we don't distract our user from his goal here. (Have you ever noticed how the checkout process on Amazon lacks page navigation? It's intentional!) That said, let's provide a way to get back to the rest of our web site, in case the user isn't quite ready to register, yet:

```
<header>
  <a href="/">
    <h1>Summer Smash 2012</h1>
    <p>This summer's most smashing event!</p>
  </a>
</header>
```

Let's also put in a little contact information, just in case our user has some pre-registration questions. The <aside> is the perfect spot for this:

```
<aside>
  <h2>Questions about whether Summer Smash is right for you?</h2>
  <p>We're here to help! Our team of smashtastic smashers will
shatter any doubt in your mind. Why not give us a call, or send
us an email?</p>
  <ul>
    <li>Call: 1-800-555-5555</li>
    <li>Email: <a href="mailto: smash@example.com">smash@example.com</a></li>
  </ul>
</aside>
```

Finally, it wouldn't hurt to say who's behind this whole Summer Smash thing—you know, give it some credibility by associating our names with it. The footer seems like a good place to do this:

```
<footer>
  <p>Summer Smash 2012. A Barker and Lane Production.</p>
</footer>
```

We've got a lot of the peripheral elements assembled now, so let's put them together and see what that looks like:

```
<!DOCTYPEhtml >
<htmllang="en ">
<head>
  <meta charset="utf-8">
  <title>Summer Smash 2010 Registration</title>
  <link rel="stylesheet" href="css/style.css">
  <script src="js/javascript.js"></script>
</head>
<body>
  <div Id="pagewrap">
    <header>
      <a href="/">
        <h1>Summer Smash 2012</h1>
        <p>This summer's most smashing event!</p>
      </a>
    </header>
    <section Id="main">
      <section Id="registration_form">
      </section>
      <aside>
        <h2>Questions about whether Summer Smash is right for you?</h2>
        <p>We're here to help! Our team of smashtastic
smashers will shatter any doubt in your mind. Why not give us a
call, or send us an email?</p>
        <ul>
          <li>Call: 1-800-555-5555</li>
          <li>Email: <a href="mailto: smash@example.com ">smash@example.com</a></li>
          </ul>
        </aside>
      </section>
    <footer>
      <p>Summer Smash 2012. A Barker and Lane Production.</p>
    </footer>
  </div>
</body>
</html>
```

Things are looking pretty good. Now we just need to drop our form into the registration form section. What do we need for a registration form? Let's start with some basics:

```
<sectionId="r egistration_form">
<formaction=" /registration/">
<  fieldset>
  <legend>Registrant Information</legend>
  <ol>
    <li>
      <label for="name">Registrant name:</label>
      <input type="text" name="name" Id="name" required autofocus />
    </li>
    <li>
      <label for="email">Email address:</label>
      <input type="email" name="email" Id="email" required />
    </li>
    <li>
      <label for="phone">Phone number:</label>
      <input type="tel" name="phone" Id="phone" />
    </li>
    <li>
      <label for="party">How many people do you
have in your party (including yourself)?</label>
      <input type="number" name="party" Id="party" min="1" max="10" />
    </li>
    <li>
      <label for="dob">Your date of birth:</label>
      <input type="date" name="dob" Id="dob" />
    </li>
  </ol>
</  fieldset>
<  fieldset>
  <legend>A few quick questions</legend>
  <ol>
    <li>
    Is this your first Summer Smash event?
    <ul>
      <li>
      <input type="radio" name="yes_first" Id="yes_first" value="1" />
      <label for="yes_first">Yes, this is my first</label>
      </li>
      <li>
      <input type="radio" name="no_first" Id="no_first" value="0" />
      <label for="no_first">No, I've been to one before</label>
      </li>
    </ul>
    </li>
    <li>
    <label for="how_hear">How did you hear about Summer Smash 2012?</label>
    <input type="text" name="how_hear" Id="how_hear" list="media">
```

```
    <datalist Id="media">
      <option value="Google search">
      <option value="Magazine ad">
      <option value="A friend told me">
      <option value="An enemy told me">
      <option value="My dog told me">
      <option value="My dead uncle Henry told me">
    </datalist>
    </li>
  </ol>
</ fieldset>
  <input type="submit" value="Register now!" />
</form>
</section>
```

We've definitely taken some chances here, using those brand-spanking-new HTML5 form elements; however, the Summer Slam crowd is generally pretty tech savvy, and it's likely to be using the latest and greatest browsers available. Heck, even if it isn't, we'll give it some fallbacks—but not until we touch JavaScript, so that aspect of the site is just going to have to wait!

Our page is complete! It's ugly, but it's complete! We'll address that ugliness factor in the next couple of chapters when we dive into using CSS (Cascading Style Sheets) to fancify our markup. Just note at this point that, while we've laid out the basics for our page in this chapter, we the authors do hereby reserve the right to make changes to this markup in later chapters. That's life. Sometimes, the day before launch your client comes to you and demands that you ask for the user's shoe size on the registration form. No big deal.

Chapter 5

Exploring Fundamental Concepts of CSS

By now, you should have a solid understanding of how to create web pages using HTML markup. You should understand how to encode semantic meaning into your page content, and you should be familiar with the concept of page elements and how these elements can be nested inside one another to give a page an orderly structure. Finally, you should also understand the basics of how a web browser interprets your HTML source code and determines its rendering. All of these topics were covered in the previous chapter, and all the concepts in this chapter will build on them.

In this chapter, we'll take a much closer look at how the web browser actually displays elements inside its window, and we'll discuss the specifics of how you can control this behavior. We're going to dive into the world of Cascading Style Sheets (CSS). Before we get carried away writing code, however, we'll first explain where CSS came from and why it's such a powerful tool for web designers.

The origins and evolution of Cascading Style Sheets

Many web designers are surprised to learn that style sheets have existed in some form or another since the inception of HTML's ancestor, the standard generalized markup language (SGML), back in the 1970s. This is because, even before the Web was born, documents marked up in SGML needed some way to encode formatting information in addition to their semantic meaning. In the early days of HTML, both this visual formatting information (called presentational style) and the semantic meaning were encoded directly inside the markup of each element. Over time, as discussed in earlier chapters of this book, this proved problematic for many reasons.

CSS1 is born

It was clear that the Web needed a better way to encode formatting information both to ease the development and maintenance of content already published on the Web, as well as to increase the capabilities of web browsers. What you know today as Cascading Style Sheets (CSS) was first formalized in 1994 by the joint efforts of Bert Bos and Håkon Wium Lie, two developers involved in the World Wide Web Consortium's (W3C's) presentational style debates. Together, with the support of the W3C's HTML editorial review board, the CSS level 1 (more simply called CSS1) specification was officially published at the end of 1996.

Even then, CSS boasted some special features that made it especially well suited as a generalized presentation language. For example, CSS was not limited to applying stylistic information to web pages marked up in HTML; it could be just as easily applied to any other markup language. Today, CSS can be applied to such XML dialects as SVG (a markup language for describing vector-based artwork) and XUL (a cross-platform user interface language). Indeed, it's this ability to separate the information about specific content from the information about how that content is displayed that gives CSS its power.

Another advantage that CSS held over other display languages was its ability to apply multiple style sheets to a single document. This allowed one document to *inherit* the declarations of all the styles in each style sheet it referenced, with each successive style sheet *cascading* on top of the others. This cascading effect—the fact that later declarations about certain styles can overrule earlier declarations about the same styles—is part of what gave CSS its name. Later in this chapter, you'll see how this capability directly benefits web developers like you.

Best of all, CSS had an incredibly simple syntax that made extensive use of English keywords. This makes it easy to read and understand. For the same reason, as you'll see here, it's also easy to learn.

Followed quickly by CSS2

Even though the benefits of CSS were very quickly realized by the W3C and it took only another two years for CSS level 2 (CSS2) to become an official recommendation in 1998, it is only recently that reliable, widespread support for CSS in web browsers has given it a prominent place in the tool sets of web designers and developers. We know what you're thinking: if CSS was this good this fast, why did it take so long to make it into mainstream web browsers?

For many years after the original release of CSS, it was difficult for web developers to make full use of this technology. Thanks to competition between the major browser vendors to one-up each other on features; differing opinions regarding what the standards should actually be; and in the worst cases, the complete failure to even approach support for said standards; it became nearly impossible for a professional web developers to be able to rely on the use of CSS for web design. At the time, web developers used a patchwork of techniques that relied upon nested table layouts, presentational HTML markup, and the implementation of proprietary browser features that required developers to write browser-specific code or else completely abandon support for certain browsers.

Eventually, with the numbers of different browsers on the Web rising and the seemingly endless browser wars causing developers even more grief, it was the release of Internet Explorer 5.0 for Mac OS 9 on March 27, 2000, that finally gave everyone a way to move toward standards compliance. Specifically, the new version of the web browser from Microsoft, written partly under the direction of Tantek Çelic, implemented a rendering engine (called Tasman) that provided a means for web developers to explicitly choose one of a number of possible "rendering modes." Developers writing new code that conformed to the W3C's published standards could then switch the web browser into a *standards rendering mode*. Older pages that would likely be incompatible with standards mode, however, would use a different rendering mode that became widely known as quirks mode.

Enter CSS3

Work on CSS level 3, which began immediately after the release of CSS level 2 in 1998, now started to hit the scene. CSS3 picks up where CSS2 left off with a series of modules where each is designed to do different things (e.g., in addition to formatting, CSS can now facilitate some basic animations, as well). Taking a module-based approach has made it easier for web browser manufacturers to implement different sets of features of the CSS3 specification at different rates (which is a good thing for us!).

A word to the wise, though: CSS3 is still a work in progress, so support for some of the things we'll be talking about in this chapter and the next vary from one browser to the next. Sometimes, there's a workaround, and other times not. More often than not, we'll be using the more advanced CSS3 techniques to enhance the user experience, not to perform some essential function. So, if a link doesn't scale up and rotate around, at least that link will still be clickable!

How CSS works

To a lot of people, CSS often looks like magic. Admittedly, it's not easy to wrap your head around the idea that with two simple text files, one with HTML markup (that gives a page's content meaning and structure) and a completely separate one with CSS rules (that define the layout and presentation of this content), you can end up with a visual display that looks nothing like the original. How can a humble text file full of CSS rules change so much about a web page so dramatically? Let's find out.

Default browser styles

A style sheet is actually a pretty simple construct. Like HTML markup, a style sheet is just a plain-text file; but unlike markup, it contains no content of its own. A CSS style sheet is always applied to the content of some other document: it's this other content that the CSS declarations affect. By itself, a CSS file can't do anything.

Recall that in the previous chapter we developed a registration form for Summer Smash 2012 using HTML markup. Let's use the content of that page and apply some styles to it. Right now, that form looks rather plain—but it's not entirely devoid of formatting.

As you can see, you have a link at the top of the page ("Summer Smash 2012"), and the text of this link is blue and underlined. Beneath that, you have some smaller text (still linked) with the tagline of the event. We have some nice borders around our different sets of fields, and all form elements are displayed as they should be and are contained within lists.

So, if this is the page supposedly without any styling information, why is the page showing off some smarts about how you might envision these elements should look? The answer, my friends, is that each web browser has a built-in, default style sheet that it uses to display elements in the absence of all other styling information. Unfortunately, not all web browsers come with the same style sheet baked into them, which means that different browsers will display the same elements in different ways unless you define your own rules and override all the default ones.

Even though CSS brings with it incredible flexibility of presentation, the style sheets themselves must be constructed in a certain way, just as the HTML page you created in the previous chapter had to be written a certain way. But to start, we'll use the default browser styles you just discovered to explain the syntax CSS uses and to show how style sheets are constructed.

Anatomy of a style sheet

A single style sheet can contain an endless amount of presentational information. This information is organized into a sequence of statements and organized by selectors, each of which specifies one rule (sometimes also called a *ruleset*) that is applied to all the elements selected by the selector. Rules do all of the heavy lifting in CSS; they determine what stylistic information to apply and where. When you create a style sheet, you spend most of your time writing these rules.

Each of these rules can be expressed in plain English; and in fact, you've already done so in the example of the default styles. For example, "a link's text should be blue and underlined" is something a CSS rule might specify. Another rule might specify that "paragraphs should have a decent amount of whitespace between whatever is above and whatever is below it." In CSS, you would write these rules like this:

```
a:link{
  color: blue;
  text-decoration: underline;
}
p{
  margin-top: 25px;
  margin-bottom: 25px;
}
```

This snippet of CSS is a valid style sheet. If you apply these styles to a web page, all links (we specified a:link specifically; we'll talk more about that later with pseudo-classes) will turn blue and will have under-lined text, and all paragraphs will have exactly 25 pixels of spacing above and beneath them. We used a couple of keywords in our style declarations here to make things easier to read (i.e., blue and underline). There are a number of keywords you can use in CSS, and a listing of color keywords can be found at www.w3schools.com/cssref/css_colornames.asp.

Of course, our approach here is similar to how most browsers display links and paragraphs by default, so what we've done thus far isn't very exciting. However, what is exciting is that it's not very hard to make a simple change and make all your links green or to change the number of pixels above or below your para-graphs. For instance, check out the changes in the following snippet, which are highlighted in bold:

```
a:link{
  color: green;
  text-decoration: underline;
}
p{
  margin-top: 50px;
  margin-bottom: 50px;
}
```

```
  font-style: italic;
  font-weight: bold;
}
del{
  text-decoration: line-through;
}
abbr[title], dfn[title] {
  border-bottom: 1px dotted;
  cursor: help;
}
table{
  border-collapse: collapse;
  border-spacing: 0;
}
/* change border colour to suit your needs */
hr{
  display: block;
  height: 1px;
  border: 0;
  border-top: 1px solid #cccccc;
  margin: 1em 0;
  padding: 0;
}
input, select {
  vertical-align: middle;
}
```

There's a lot happening here, but let's take a quick look at some of the highlights! The first rule block lists the majority of elements we might use on our page. It sets them to a consistent size (100%) and makes sure that there are no borders, margins, or padding on any of them. We'll definitely want to override that later on for certain elements—more than likely, we'll want to make our headings larger than the rest of our text, and we'll want to put some space around things. Remember that we're just establishing a baseline with this CSS reset.

A little further down, there's a rule that starts with article, aside. This rule lists a lot of the new HTML5 block-level elements, and it's intended for browsers that don't support these elements yet. By putting this rule in, we can at least tell browsers to display these as blocks, rather than inline elements:

```
article,aside,details,figcaption,figure,
footer,header,hgroup,menu,nav,section{
  display:block;
}
```

Now let's clear out the styling on lists (i.e., remove bullets and numbers) and standardize the display of tables and table borders:

```
nav ul {
  list-style:none;
}
```

```
...
table{
  border-collapse:collapse;
  border-spacing:0;
}
```

Basically, if you thought that our page looked drab and boring before, this adjustment ramps things up a notch and really takes all of the fun out of it! That's okay though, because we're going to start putting the fun back into it now! Well, we will—after we touch on just a little more theory.

Applying styles to web page elements

So you now understand what CSS is, what it looks like, what it can do, and how it does it. It's almost time to write some new CSS rules to make the Summer Smash page sparkle. But first you need to figure out how to attach a style sheet to an HTML web page, so that the styles you write will actually be shown.

You can apply CSS rules to page elements in three ways.

- You can embed a CSS rule directly into an element.

- You can embed a whole style sheet inside the HTML page itself.

- You can link a style sheet from an entirely separate file to your HTML page.

Let's examine all three possibilities in detail.

Inline styles

Perhaps the simplest way of applying CSS styles to web page elements would be through the use of *inline styles*, or styles written directly into the element. By definition, an inline style applies only to the element in which it is placed, so there is no need to use a CSS selector in the rule. And since the style is already enclosed inside the element, a declaration block's curly braces aren't needed, either. All you need to specify for an inline style to work is the property and value you want to set on the element.

Inline styles are written into the value of the style attribute of an element, like so:

```
<p style="color: purple;">Look ma, i&rsquo;m purple!</p>
```

Naturally, inline styles don't give you much flexibility because they can't use the power of CSS selectors to target multiple elements of the same type on a page (in contrast to what our previous examples have done). Worse, inline styles embed presentational information directly into your document, which is exactly what CSS was developed to avoid. In general practice, inline styles really aren't a good solution for applying styles to elements.

There are some other cases where inline styles are useful, however. For instance, they make it easy to experiment with particular elements and to test what different values of different properties will do to an element. While you're learning about what CSS properties exist and what they can do, feel free to use inline styles to try them out. In an actual project deliverable, however, you shouldn't leave any presentational data inside your markup. So, once you've got things figured out, you should pull these inline styles out and place them in either embedded style sheets or external style sheets.

Embedded style sheets

Embedding a CSS style sheet inside an HTML file enables you to use every feature of CSS without limitation, but only within the single document that contains the embedded style sheet. By placing CSS rules in a <style> element, you're effectively creating a small area inside your markup where you can safely put CSS rules. When the browser encounters this special area, it stops interpreting your source code as HTML markup and begins to interpret the code as CSS rules. Let's check out some code:

```
<!DOCTYPEhtml >
<htmllang="en ">
<head>
    <meta charset="utf-8">
    <title>Summer Smash 2012 Registration</title>
    <style>
        h1 {color: red;}
    p {line-height: 2em;}
  </style>
</head>
```

Placing CSS rules inside embedded style sheets in this manner clearly gives you more flexibility regarding what you'd like your CSS rules to accomplish, but you're still limited to applying the rules to a single page (which can be a good thing, depending on the circumstances). Sometimes, you want to override the presentation of an element on more than one page alone, though. One of the greatest benefits of CSS can be seen when you use a single style sheet to define the presentation, not for a single web page, but for an entire website that may have 10, 20, 100, or 1,000 or more individual pages.

To accomplish this feat, you must completely separate the CSS styling from the HTML markup by placing it into a separate file.

External style sheets

The most common and efficient way to apply CSS to a web page—and indeed, to an entire website—is via the use of entirely separate files that are linked to a web page with a special reference element. This works similarly to the way the <img> element references an external image file. These separate files with CSS rules in them are called external style sheets because they are placed outside any containing markup. Even though these CSS rules are separated from the actual web page document, they still behave as if they were written in an embedded style sheet.

To reference an external style sheet from an HTML page, you use the <link> element to—you guessed it—link your CSS file to your markup. Since you can link many different kinds of things into a web page, the link needs to be of a certain relationship; specifically, it must have a style sheet relationship. This is specified in the rel attribute. As when using an <img> element, you need to tell the browser where to find this external style sheet. You can do this with the href attribute; and as you have probably already guessed, its value is any valid URL. Putting it all together, the <link> element might look like this:

```
<link rel="stylesheet" href="css/style.css" />
```

This (empty) element specifies that an external CSS style sheet can be found inside the css folder and that its file name is style.css. Inside the style.css file, you simply write CSS rules as you normally would. Since this entire file is going to be interpreted by the browser as CSS, there's no need to enclose the CSS rules within a <style> element.

Web pages can be linked to any number of external style sheets. There's really no technical limit, although in practice the more CSS files you link to, the longer it will take for your browser to go and fetch all of them. Of course, the benefit of an external style sheet is that more than one web page can be linked to it, which means you can reuse the style rules you write for one web page across an unlimited number of other web pages. This is what makes CSS so outrageously scalable. It doesn't matter whether your site has one page or one million pages; as long as these pages have the basic elements that need to be styled in the same way, a single CSS file can be used to style them all.

In our Summer Smash example, we'll take the just described route, linking to an external style sheet. While we're currently only working on one page, the registration form, chances are that this page will be part of a bigger website and that we may want to reuse some of the styling we're going to apply elsewhere. Let's go ahead and get started:

```
body{
  background-color: #cccccc;
}
header a {
  text-decoration: none;
  color: #ffffff;
}
```

There's nothing too fancy here. First, we change the background color of the page to a medium grey. The funny number shown is the hexadecimal representation of this color. Using hexadecimal values gives us a much broader range of color selections, and they're really easy to select if you just use a color picker to figure out the value. For example, the color picker at www.colorpicker.com/ displays the value you're looking for at the top.

Second, we create our header <a> element. Wait a minute—what's a "header <a>" element? This is one of the great features of CSS; it lets you target elements with greater precision by using their context.

More CSS selectors: targeting page elements with surgical precision

So far, you've seen how to apply CSS rules to specific types of page elements. Of course, specifying style rules based on element types is handy, but ultimately its usefulness goes only so far. For example, what if you wanted some links to look one way, and some other links to look some other way. Basing all your styles solely on the element type (<a>, or *anchor*, in our example) isn't going to cut it. You need a more precise way to select elements. That's where the different kinds of CSS selectors step in to help you.

As you already know, CSS selectors allow you to target elements in your markup to which you want to apply certain styles. You already know how to use one kind of CSS selector, the *type selector*, which (as its name implies) selects elements based on their type (or name). For example, a selector that reads as h1 will apply to all <h1> elements. Similarly, a selector that reads as h1, h2, h3 will target all <h1>, <h2>, and <h3> elements in the page.

To be more precise, the type selectors that you have used so far are called simple selectors because they are, well, pretty simple. In order to construct more complex CSS selectors, you combine, or chain, multiple simple selectors together in specific ways. These more intricate patterns enable you to target elements on your page with surgical precision. Let's take a brief look at what other kinds of selectors you can avail yourself of when using CSS.

Id selectors

Another kind of simple selector is the id selector. As you might expect, this selector targets an element whose id attribute has been given the specified value. For instance, on our Summer Smash page, we've created a <div> element with an id of pagewrap:

```
<divid="pagewrap">
    <header>
    <a href="/">
      <h1>Summer Smash 2012</h1>
      <p>This summer's most smashing event!</p>
    </a>
```

By using this selector, we can set the width of all of the contents on the page and make the page centered in our CSS:

```
#pagewrap{
    width: 75%;
    margin: 20px auto;
}
```

Id selectors always begin with an octothorpe (#) and are immediately followed by the id value of the element you want to target. In the previous example, the <div> element's id attribute value was pagewrap, so that's what goes after the octothorpe. This will have the same target as an id selector that explicitly specifies the <div> element, as in this example:

```
div#pagewrap{
  width: 75%;
  margin: 20px auto;
}
```

The first selector is more generic; it doesn't care what type of element the header is, as long as that element has pagewrap as its id attribute value. The second selector does care, and it will target the pagewrap id only if that element is a <div>. Since id attribute values must be unique across a web page, most of the time you can be assured that these two selectors are entirely interchangeable. In some cases, however, you need the more specific selector to override another style. We'll cover selector specificity a little later in this chapter.

Class selectors

Class selectors are yet another kind of simple selector. These selectors function in the same way as id selectors, except that, instead of targeting elements with an id value, they target elements that have been given a particular class value. We haven't given any elements in our registration form a class value, so let's head in and change the markup a bit:

```
<legend>RegistrantInformation</legend>
  <ol>
  <li class="formitem">
```

```
<label for="name">Registrant name:</label>
<input type="text" name="name" id="name" required autofocus />
</li>
<li class="formitem">
<label for="email">Email address:</label>
<input type="email" name="email" id="email" required />
</li>
```

Here, we've added a class name of formitem to each top level list item on our form (even those not shown in this code snippet). We can now target these list items specifically, leaving other list items (like those that appear in the footer) alone.

```
li.formitem{
  list-style: none;
  margin: 5px 0;
  padding: 0;
}
```

We've also taken out the numbers next to each item in our form and put in a little space between our form elements.

The real magic here happens if we have another form on the website, and we want to use consistent styling (e.g., a Contact Us form). Our class names are reusable, and all of our style information is contained within an external, linked style sheet. As long as we link in the style sheet on the contact page and give the form's list items class names of formitem, the formatting that we've just established will carry us through. This example highlights the importance of semantic markup. It's the sound semantic markup that underpins our web pages that enables us to leverage the benefits of CSS in this way.

pseudo-class selectors

We introduced a pseudo-class silently way back when we began talking about the syntax of CSS rules. That rule looked like this:

```
a:link{
  color: blue;
  text-decoration: underline;
}
```

The selector in this instance is a:link. Here, the type selector is simply a, and the pseudo-class is :link. Pseudo-classes will be discussed in more detail in the next chapter; so for now it's simply important to be aware of their existence and to recognize them as another kind of simple CSS selector.

Yet more simple selectors

If you thought type, id, class, and pseudo-class selectors weren't enough, there remain other kinds of simple selectors that we haven't touched upon yet. These include attribute selectors and the universal type selector. In fact, both the id and class selectors are a shorthand form for an attribute selector (because they select elements based on a particular attribute value, such as id or class). Since attribute selectors and the universal type selector are rarely used, they won't be discussed here.

Once again, the important point is that all of these kinds of simple selectors are merely building blocks for creating more complex patterns with which to target specific elements in a web page.

Descendant selectors

The other CSS selector we introduced earlier is known as a descendant selector. This selector consists of two type selectors separated by whitespace. And as its name implies, it targets elements of the specified type that are descendants of another element of the specified type. CSS rules with descendant selectors look like this:

```
header a {
  text-decoration: none;
  color: #ffffff;
}
```

This CSS rule says: "target all <a> elements that are nested within <header> elements, color them white, and remove any underlines they may have." In this example, the whitespace in the CSS selector is called a *combinator* because it combines two simple selectors. You can use the whitespace combinator to chain any number of simple selectors together to create more complex descendant selectors. For example, if you want to select all links in a document that are inside paragraphs, that in turn are grouped with other elements inside <div> elements, then you can use the following CSS selector:

```
div p a {
  color: teal;
  text-decoration: none;
}
```

Once again, this says: "target all <a> elements that are nested within <p> elements, if those <p> elements are nested within <div> elements." So, the previous CSS rule would affect the links in a markup structure like this:

```
<div>
  <p><strong>We appreciate your
  <a href="buy.html">patronage</a></strong>, and encourage your
  <a href="contact.html">feedback</a>.</p>
</div>
```

However, such a CSS selector would not affect links in a markup structure like this:

```
<div>
  <h3><a href="index.html">Oh won't you please take me home?</a></h3>
</div>
```

Note that, in the first example, the selector matches both of the links even though one link is inside a <strong> element and one isn't. The descendant selector matches elements regardless of how deeply nested they are, as long as they are nested in the order specified. In other words, the selector's only requirement is that the markup's tree structure must match the chain of simple selectors, regardless other of intervening elements.

Child selectors

If you did want to target elements that are nested only one level down from another element (e.g., the child elements of that element), then you could use the child selector to accomplish that. Like descendant selectors, child selectors are composed of at least two simple selectors and the greater-than (>) symbol, which is the combinator. For example, to target all links placed directly inside list items (and which are not nested inside any other element between the list item and themselves), you could use the following child selector:

```
li > a { ... }
```

Note that any whitespace between the simple selectors and the combinators is ignored, unless the only combinator between simple selectors is, itself, whitespace (that is, a descendant combinator). In other words, this CSS selector—which reads "li type selector, space, child combinator, space, a type selector"—is not a CSS selector with descendant combinators, even though it includes spaces.

Adjacent sibling selectors

The final kind of combinator that CSS provides is the adjacent sibling selector. This selector is again composed of at least two simple selectors and a combinator, which in this case is the plus sign (+). This selector gives you the ability to select a specific element only if that element is a sibling of another specific element that comes immediately before it in the markup.

Recall that a nested element in your markup is called a child, and the element that it is nested within it is called a parent. A sibling is thus an element that is also a child of this parent element.

For example, in this sample navigation menu, all the list items are siblings because they are all children of the unordered list:

```
<ul>
  <li><a href="index.html">Home</a></li>
  <li><a href="menu.html">Our menu</a></li>
  <li><a href="contact.html">Contact Us</a></li>
  <li><a href="about.html">About Us</a></li>
</ul>
```

The unordered list is the parent of the list items. It is also the ancestor (grandparent) of the links. The links are themselves children of the list items, but none of the links is a sibling of any other links because each link has different parents (that just happen to all be list items).

In the previous list, each list item child follows another list item sibling except the first (which can't follow anything, because it is, of course, first). Using the adjacent sibling selector, you could write a rule to select all but the first list items in lists and make them just a bit smaller, like this:

```
li + li { font-size: x-small; }
```

This can be a powerful tool for things like navigation lists, where you may want to style the items in that list slightly differently from one another.

Combining multiple CSS selectors in a single rule

So far you understand the building blocks of CSS selectors, what kinds of simple selectors are available to you, and how to chain them using specific combinators. You're now ready to take a quick look at a few complex examples. First, it's helpful to note that there is no law that says you can use only one kind of combinator in a CSS selector. This means you can use any combination of simple selectors and combinators to create arbitrarily complex selection patterns.

Let's amend the rule you used in the previous section, so that it will apply only to this question: "Is this your first Summer Smash Event?" Currently, your rule looks like this:

```
li + li { font-size: x-small; }
```

This rule affects list items in every list on the entire page, and that's too broad for your tastes. Let's narrow its subjects down to only the list items that are descended from the <ul> list. To do this, you simply add an element type selector targeting the <ul> and use a descendant combinator to chain it to your existing selector. The new CSS rule looks like this:

```
ul { font-size: x-small; }
```

While that currently works, it's still a bit broad. But what if you added another <ul> to the page, such as secondary site navigation? This rule would also apply to that list. Let's narrow this example down a bit more:

```
ol li.formitem ul { font-size: x-small; }
```

As you can now see, CSS selectors give you enormous power to target the elements you want—and only the elements you want.

CSS inheritance: making the general case work in your favor

As we discussed earlier, using properly structured markup and identifying the groups of those elements with ids and class names gives you the ability to apply certain styles to a big chunk of the elements in your web page using a single CSS rule. You've already seen one example of this in practice, where you styled all the text in the Summer Smash header in one fell swoop. Recall that the HTML markup you developed for the website header looks like this:

```
<header>
  <a href="/">
    <h1>Summer Smash 2012</h1>
    <p>This summer's most smashing event!</p>
  </a>
</header>
```

And here is the CSS rule you used to style all the text in the header with a particular font:

```
header a {
  text-decoration: none;
  color: #ffffff;
}
```

As you can see, we only targeted text contained in an <a> tag (which is currently all of the text). We didn't specifically target the <h1> and <p> tags themselves. Nevertheless, the text of each of these elements has been given the style you declared in the CSS rule. How did this happen? It's not magic; it's simply another feature of the CSS specification that the designers of CSS were clever enough to create.

This behavior is called *inheritance*, and it is so named because of the way child elements acquire certain CSS properties that their parents also have just by virtue of being that parent element's child. Another way to say this is that children inherit CSS properties from their parents and ancestors. This automatic inheritance saves web developers like you from the tedious task of explicitly defining CSS properties for every single element on a web page. Can you imagine what a nightmare that would be? There are four individual elements in just the previous HTML snippet! You'd be no better off with CSS than you were without it!

Another way to think about inheritance and how it works is to think of your HTML elements as steps, where each nested element is another step down from its parent element. When you apply a CSS property to one of the steps, it "cascades down all the steps" beneath it and gets applied to those elements, too.

As we remarked earlier, some CSS properties display this inherited behavior, and others do not. As a general rule, most of the properties that replace HTML elements for styling (e.g., text properties like font and color), including those that you've already seen in this chapter, are inherited properties and behave in this way. However, a number of properties are not inherited because it would make little sense for them to be (e.g., width and height). These and other properties that affect the layout of the web page (we'll discuss examples of these later in this chapter) are specific to the elements on which they are applied.

CSS inheritance is ultimately a way to allow you to get the biggest effect with the least amount of work. At any point, you can specify another, more specific CSS rule to override an earlier rule. For instance, using the previous example, you could give our tag line a slightly darker color to deemphasize it a bit (visually):

```
header a p { color: #eeeeee; }
```

Doing this is like pouring a new CSS property on your steps at the point of the paragraph, so that this new property cascades down on top of the one that was applied to the step above it, the <a>.

The CSS cascade and the rules of specificity

What happens when the declarations of two or more CSS rules conflict with one another? Far from being a one-off occurrence, these situations are actually at the core of how CSS works and are referred to as the cascade. Learning how the cascade works is fundamental to learning CSS.

The CSS cascade is just a fancy name given to a set of rules that define how conflicts among different CSS declarations should be resolved. These rules are based on the concept that more specific rules should override more general rules. Each CSS rule that applies to an element is examined and sorted based on its specificity. The most general rule is applied first, followed by the next most general rule, and so on, until the browser reaches the most specific rule. Each successive rule overrides the previous rule's declarations for the element's properties.

So, what makes one CSS rule "more specific" than another? It depends on a number of factors, such as where it was written in the source code (its source order) and the specificity of the CSS selector used. (There are other things that determine the specificity of a rule, such as its origin and its weight, but these are advanced topics that you will not likely encounter in the day-to-day web development process.)

These days, a number of tools are available that can help you visualize the cascade. Adobe Dreamweaver is one such tool, and it includes a good visualization feature for specificity in its CSS panel. The TopStyle and CSSEdit applications are also good tools to consider for getting on top of the cascade. Additionally, both the Firebug add-on for Firefox and the Element inspector in Safari and Google Chrome can also show you inheritance results and the cascade order. These two tools are especially convenient since they are embedded directly into their respective host browsers.

CSS selector specificity

The selector you use as part of your CSS rule determines a great deal about how specific your rule is. In most cases, it's really easy to determine which selectors are more specific than others because CSS selectors translate to English quite easily. For example, it's easy to see that a selector with multiple combinators will be more specific than a selector without any combinators:

```
header a { ... }
```

The preceding example is more specific than this one:

```
a { ... }
```

The first reads as "all links descended from the header," whereas the second simply says "all links." Clearly, links that are specifically inside the header are a more specific target than links that can be anywhere on a page.

As a general rule of thumb, the more simple selectors and combinators a CSS selector has, the more specific it is. Some simple selectors are more specific than others, however, and so are some combinators. For example, a type selector is more general than a class selector, which is more general than an id selector.

If you think about it, this is all simply common sense at work. You can have <div> elements all over your page, but a much smaller number of them might be classed as *features*, and only one of them might be given the feature-1 unique identifier. What this means is that given an element—for instance, <div class="feature" id="feature-1">—the following three CSS rules will all match. However, the rule that uses the id selector will actually be the one that the visitor sees applied.

```
.feature { color: green; } #feature-1 { color: red; } div { color: black; }
```

The result here is that this feature's text will be colored red. It doesn't matter in what order these three CSS rules are written down in the CSS file or even if they're not in the same style sheet at all. Since selector specificity is the primary sorting method the browser will use to determine the cascading order of an element's CSS properties, the most specific selector will always win.

Source order cascading

If two or more CSS rules conflict with one another, but their selectors have an equal specificity, then their source order is used to determine which rule actually gets applied. This can often happen in complex style sheets that have many levels of cascading rules.

For instance, you may choose to make all the text in your feature boxes green by default, so you place the following CSS rule in an external style sheet:

```
.feature { color: green; }
```

Next, you link this style sheet to your web page, so the <head> portion of your document might look something like this:

```
<head>
  <title>Fantastic staplers: Home page</title>
  <link rel="stylesheet" href="css/global.css" />
</head>
```

Now every page on your website that has been linked to this external style sheet will show feature boxes with green text. However, say that you want feature box text to be red, not green, in the special sales section of your website. How might you go about overriding the rule you wrote previously?

One possibility is to use a more specific CSS selector. For instance, perhaps each web page that is in the sales section of your site has a <body> element with the id of sale-section. In that case, you can just add the following rule anywhere in your style sheet:

```
#sale-section .feature { color: red; }
```

However, implementing this requires changing the HTML markup (i.e., adding an id="sale-section" attribute to your body tag), even if only a little bit. There are some situations when this isn't possible or, more to the point, isn't advisable. Recall that CSS was invented to separate style from content; therefore, it should be possible to make this change without affecting the HTML content at all. And of course, it is possible to do just that. By adding a new style sheet to your page, redeclaring the feature box text as red, and inserting this new style sheet closer to the <body> element than the other style sheet, you can use the CSS cascade's source order sorting to effect the change. Using this method, the <head> section of your document would now look something like this:

```
<head>
  <title>Fantastic staplers: sale page</title>
  <link rel="stylesheet" href="css/global.css" />
  <style>
    .feature { color: red; }
  </style>
</head>
```

Notice that this example is using an embedded style sheet to define the style sheet with the overriding rule. However, it doesn't have to be an embedded style sheet. In fact, if the sales section of your website is more than a single page, it behooves you to create a new external style sheet and link that in after the initial style sheet, as in this example:

```
<head>
<title>Fantastic staplers: sale page</title>
<link rel="stylesheet" href="css/global.css" />
<link rel="stylesheet" href="css/sale-section.css" />
</head>
```

In both examples, however, the concept is the same: style sheets defined further down the page (closer to the <body> element) will override ("cascade on top of") the styles defined further up the page (closer to the start of the <head> element) when the CSS rules that conflict have the same specificity.

It's also interesting to note that this is the same behavior you observed much earlier, when you overruled the browser's default styling with a style sheet of your own. Since the browser's default styles are defined "first" (they are at the earliest point of the cascade), any conflicting styles you define later overrule the browser's styling.

One final way to override

Finally, we'd be remiss if we didn't tell you about the one final way to override all rules: !important.

Before we show you this in action, we're going to caution you that using !important should not be done lightly because it completely breaks the cascade on the element you override. Specifying !important after a rule will ensure that that is the rule used in displaying the element—no matter what. Keeping this in mind might help you to troubleshoot a spot where the cascade doesn't appear to be working properly. Let's look at a new example:

```
a { color: red; }
.featured_item a { color: blue; }
```

The preceding snippet is somewhat similar to our previous example. It implements two rules:

1. Take all of the links on a page and color them red.

2. Next, look for any links contained in an element with the class featured_itema nd
    colort hosel inksb lue.

Given what we just learned about the cascade, we know that this will work in theory. However, in practice the site we're working on shows us a different result: all of the links are showing up green.

If we keep digging, we'll see another rule further down the CSS file:

```
a { color: green !important; }
```

According to the rules of the cascade that we've learned, this rule should override our color: red rule, but it shouldn't touch the .featured_item a rule. Why is it, then? That !important bit of the rule is giving it precedence over all other rules. It appears that somebody just got the order to "change all links to green" on the website; and instead of updating the current rules to make that happen, she took a shortcut and just overrode them all.

Visual rendering: document flow and the CSS box model

There are two final concepts to understand about CSS before you can honestly say that you know enough CSS to be dangerous. These are the CSS box model and how it relates to document flow. It's these two fundamental concepts that make designing for web pages radically different than designing for printed media. If you really want to become proficient with CSS-based designs, and especially if you're coming from a print design background, then these are the concepts you absolutely need to nail.

Computer screens are not magazine pages; and at least for the foreseeable future, they won't ever be exactly like them. When you design for the printed page, you make certain assumptions about what kinds of designs might work based on facts that you understand about how printed media works. For example, you know that a standard printed page is a rectangle about 8.5 inches wide by 11 inches high, so you don't put a picture that is 10 inches wide or 13 inches high on the page because it just won't fit. On the other hand, you know that you can put high-resolution images on the page because such images look really good when printed on paper (though they may not look so great on a computer monitor).

The web page, like the printed page, also has certain constraints, weaknesses, and advantages. For example, a web page can have a link or can change some of its content dynamically in response to a user's actions, such as hovering his cursor over a certain area. For obvious reasons, this is something a printed page couldn't dream of doing.

But let's take a quick step back. We'll begin by taking a quick look at what document flow is, and then we'll briefly introduce the CSS box model. After that, we'll discuss how the two concepts are intricately related. And finally, we'll show you some of the ways that you can use CSS declarations to alter these two things at will.

What is document flow?

Document flow is a fundamental concept to CSS designers. In fact, the concept of document flow (or just flow for short) predates CSS considerably. So, what is it?

Document flow is a system by which a renderer (such as a web browser) lays out pieces of visible content on a screen, so that they flow one after the other in predictable ways. Every element on a web page, every headline, every list item, every paragraph, and even every line of text and each individual character within every paragraph follow the rules of flow to determine where they end up on the screen.

For the most part, document flow just mimics what you would expect to see on a printed page. For example, while reading this book, you're looking at large chunks of text (paragraphs), each of which has a number of lines. These lines have printed characters on them that start from the left side and end at the right side. When you read the full paragraph, you're reading from the top-left corner of the paragraph, horizontally across each line, and ending at the bottom-right corner of the same paragraph.

This is the normal direction in which content flows in the English language. However, this is not true for all languages. Hebrew is an example of a language that reverses the direction of flow, so that it begins from the top-right corner and ends at the bottom-left corner. Arabic does this, too. As described in the previous chapter, web pages are really just long strings of sequential characters that a web browser sees one after the other, so it needs some way to know how to order these characters and elements on the screen. It uses the rules of flow to do this.

It's easy enough to see how flow affects characters in a paragraph. Based on the language specified in the web page's <html> element, the web browser simply places the first character at either the top-left or top-right corner of the paragraph, and then places each successive character it sees to the right or left of the one before it. Recall that your <html> element for Summer Smash 2012 began like this:

```
<htmllang="en ">
```

Since you've defined that this web page is written in English by specifying the lang="en" attribute, the web browser will assume a normal flow for what is expected in English. Specifically, it will flow text in a direction of left to right. If you're feeling experimental, go ahead and add the dir attribute with a value of rtl (short for right-to-left) to the <html> element—you'll see that now every headline and paragraph is right-aligned (previously it was left-aligned) and the punctuation marks are all on the "wrong side" of the words.

So, some of the rules of flow control things like the direction of text and where the beginning of an element's content should be placed. But, as you'll see next, there's much more to flow than that.

What is the CSS box model?

You'll hear the term box used a lot when talking about CSS. Obviously, the first question you need to ask yourself is, "What is a box?"

In CSS, a *box* is simply a rectangular region that represents the physical space that a certain thing takes up. Typically, for web pages, this space is a group of pixels on a computer screen. For example, for every <p> element you define in your web page, you create a rectangle inside of which the content of that paragraph is displayed, or flows into. You can use tools such as Firebug or the Web developer toolbar add-on for Firefox to see these boxes.

Notice how the CSS boxes of the paragraphs always extend to the paragraph's edges, even though the last line of text inside the paragraph may not. This is because it's not only HTML elements like the <p> element that create CSS boxes. Indeed, everything on a web page that is visible creates a box of a certain type, including strings of text content.

However, not all CSS boxes are created equally. These characters inside paragraphs do not create the same kinds of boxes that the <p> element does. This is very deliberate; and as you're about to see, it's a very important distinction (recall that we talked briefly about box-level versus inline elements in the previous chapter).

Inline-level vs. block-level boxes

The <p> elements create what are known as block-level boxes, whereas the strings of text within them create inline-level boxes. These two different kinds of CSS boxes flow onto the screen in very different ways.

Block-level boxes always flow onto the page one on top of another, like boxes (or bricks) in a vertical stack. Since paragraphs are declared by all web browsers' default style sheets to be block-level boxes, each time you define a new <p> element (and thereby generate a new block-level CSS box), the browser places that paragraph underneath any block-level boxes that came before it. This is why two paragraphs next to one another always create two distinct chunks of text, one atop the other, by default. Other elements that create block-level boxes are headlines, <div> elements, and lists (not list items, but the list items' containing elements such as <ul>, <ol>, and <dl>). There are also a host of new HTML5 block-level elements, including <header>, <section>, <article>, and <aside>.

Inline boxes are almost always inside some containing block-level box; but instead of flowing one after the other in a vertical stack as block-level boxes do, they flow one after the other horizontally. Each character of text (or glyph) that the browser sees is thus placed in the same horizontal line with any inline-level elements that came before it. It's only if there's not enough horizontal space for things to fit on the same line that inline-level boxes get bumped down to the next line. Some examples of web page elements that create inline-level boxes by default are images, links, and emphasized text (e.g., the <em> and <strong> elements).

Runs of text that aren't nested within any of these inline-level elements also create inline boxes implicitly. These implicit inline-level boxes are called anonymous inline boxes because they don't have an element that is specifically associated with them.

For instance, the following HTML markup you used for the paragraph of text on the Summer Smash website footer creates two CSS boxes (not one), one of which is a block-level box and one of which is an inline-level box:

```
<p>Summer Smash 2012. A Barker and Lane Production.</p>
```

The <p> element is the one that creates the block-level box. All the text inside the <p> element creates the anonymous inline-level box. If you then added another inline-level element into this paragraph, such as a <strong> element for some additional emphasis on the year, then you'd suddenly have four CSS boxes:

```
<p>Summer Smash <strong>2012</strong>. A Barker and Lane Production.</p>
```

In this paragraph, the <p> element still creates the block-level box, but the text "Summer Smash" creates the first anonymous inline box. Next, the <strong> element creates a second inline-level box (with the contents, "2012"). Finally, the text ". A Barker and Lane Production" creates the second anonymous inline-level box. Thus, we have one block-level box, plus two anonymous inline boxes, plus another (non-anonymous) inline-level box. That equals a total of four CSS boxes.

The kind of CSS box that an element generates (e.g., inline-level or block-level box) can be controlled with CSS. Specifically, the value of an element's display property determines what kind of box it will generate. The following example shows what the default CSS rules that web browsers use to make <p> elements block-level and <strong> elements inline-level might look like:

```
p { display: block; } strong { display: inline; }
```

Of course, you can override these default styles and make any element generate any kind of box you want—something that was flat-out impossible to do before the advent of CSS. For example, you could add a CSS rule that makes <strong> elements generate block-level boxes instead of inline-level boxes:

```
strong { display: block; }
```

If you add that CSS rule to the style sheets for Summer Smash's web pages, you'll see that you now have three lines of text inside one paragraph and that the number "2012" will be on its own line. This is because, as you now know, the rules of flow dictate that block-level boxes be stacked vertically. Since the <strong> element is now generating a block-level CSS box, it must be placed on its own line, so you end up splitting the footer sentence across three lines.

In this state, you still have four CSS boxes. But instead of having three inline boxes, all within a block-level box, you now have two inline boxes and two block-level boxes. One of the block-level boxes (the one generated by the <strong>element) is overlapping the one generated by the <p> element. You can make this more obvious by adding background colors to your <p> and <strong> elements:

```
p{
        background-color: blue;
}
strong{
        display: block;
        background-color: red;
}
```

There's another thing worth pointing out about this picture. Notice that each stripe goes all the way to the edge of the browser window. At first, you might be tempted to assume that all CSS boxes will always be as wide as they can be; however, this is not true, and this fact highlights another important difference between inline-level and block-level boxes.

Block-level boxes that have no specific width declared (such as the ones generated by both your <p> and <strong> elements) do, indeed, grow as wide as they can, while still fitting inside their containing element's CSS box. In this case, all the block-level CSS boxes are as wide as the browser window, or viewport, because none of them has an explicit width. This means they all grow to be as wide as they can be inside the web browser.

Inline-level boxes, however, grow only as wide as they need to be to make their content fit within them. Inline boxes are like shrink-wrap that surrounds whatever content they have. You can make this more obvious by giving a background color to your two remaining inline boxes.

Since both of your remaining inline boxes are anonymous, you need to use an element you haven't seen before—the <span> element—so that you can target them with CSS. The <span> element is just like the <div> element, except that, instead of generating a block-level box, by default it generates an inline-level box. The HTML paragraph looks like this with the <span> elements added:

```
<p><span>Summer Smash </span><strong>2012</strong><span>. A Barker and Lane Production.
</span></p>
```

And the CSS looks like this with the background colors applied to the <span> elements:

```
p{
  background-color: blue;
}
span{
  background-color: green;
}
strong{
  display: block;
  background-color: red;
}
```

The two inline-level boxes (colored green) shrink to the width of their content, but the block-level boxes (colored blue and red) extend to be as wide as they can.

Changing CSS box properties: the CSS box model explained

Every CSS box, whether inline-level or block-level, has four distinct areas within it. These are, from the inside out, the content area, the padding area, the border area, and the margin area:

- *The content area*: You're already familiar with this area. It is the rectangular area inside which an element's content, whether plain text or other nested elements, is placed.

- *The padding area*: This is a transparent space around the content where only the background properties of an element (if any) will show.

- *The border area*: This area frames the padding and the content, much like a picture frame.

- *The margin area*: This area defines the amount of whitespace the CSS box should have around it.

All of these areas always exist for all CSS boxes. However, much of the time, none of them is shown, except the content area. This is because the other three areas have zero width and zero height. That is, they take up no space in the layout of a page whatsoever. However, with CSS, you can make each of these areas larger, so that they will show up and thus affect the layout of the elements on your web page.

Firebug has a great layout tab that lets you see exactly what the dimensions of each of these areas are for any given element. Let's start by examining the content area more closely, and then do the same for each of the other three areas that the CSS box model defines.

Content area: defining the dimensions of content boxes

As you saw in the previous section, the content area of a CSS box behaves differently depending on the type of box being generated. For block-level boxes, the content area grows as wide as it can within the confines of its containing block or the browser viewport in the absence of such a container. For inline-level boxes, the content area shrinks so that it is only as wide as the widest part of its content. Both block-level and inline-level boxes grow as high as their tallest content—and no higher. This can be summed up in CSS with the following declarations:

```
width: auto; height: auto;
```

As you've probably guessed by now, changing the values of the width and height properties affects the content area's width and height, respectively. Say, for instance, that you want the footer for the Summer Smash website to be exactly 300 pixels wide. This is no problem:

```
footer { width: 300px; }
```

The width property (and any property that accepts a length value, such as the height property) can take as its value a number followed by an abbreviation (px, in this example) that indicates the unit of measurement. The abbreviation *px* is short for *pixels*.

In this example, you're setting the width of the element with the id of footer to exactly 300 pixels. Obviously, pixels make sense only for designs that are going to be displayed on a device that measures distances in pixels (e.g., a computer monitor, but not a printed page). There are other length units that CSS will allow you to use, and we'll talk about those later on.

So, with the earlier CSS rule applied to Summer Smash's footer, your footer text is now exactly 300 pixels wide all the time. Resizing the window will not change the width of your footer, nor will adding more text content to it. The footer will remain at a fixed width because you've told it to do exactly that.

Note that even though this example appears to be using CSS inheritance, it's not. The <p> element inside the footer <footer> still has a width value set to auto, since the width property is not inherited. However, since the <p> element is nested inside the footer <footer> (the footer <footer>'s CSS box is the paragraph element's containing block)—and since the footer <div> is constrained to be only 300 pixels wide—the paragraph inside the footer can also be a maximum of only 300 pixels wide.

Since an inline-level box's width is defined by its content, the width property does not apply to these types of CSS boxes, so the width we've set is ignored. In other words, if this inline element had no content, it wouldn't even display.

Padding area: giving backgrounds the floor

The padding area of a CSS box is the area immediately surrounding the content area. Padding is used to space the content of a box away from its edges. This helps a design look less cramped.

By default, most elements will not have any padding. The noteworthy exceptions are typically lists of some kind (e.g., unordered, ordered, or definition lists) where the child list item elements receive their indentation in some browsers through the application of a default padding value. (In other browsers, this same indentation effect is achieved with a default margin value. Margins are described later in the chapter.) In CSS, a box with no padding at all might be declared by using the following declaration:

```
padding:0;
```

Notice that there is no unit abbreviation, such as px, after the 0 in the value of the padding property. Since 0 is the same value whether it is specified in pixels or in inches (or any other length unit), no unit abbreviation is needed. It can be specified (so 0px will work), but it's not necessary to do so—and why would we want to type more than we have to?

Of course, all we need to do to give an element's box some visible padding area is to increase the amount from zero to some noticeable value. For example, let's give Summer Smash's footer 10 pixels of padding:

```
footer{
    width: 300px;
    padding: 10px;
}
```

This change is subtle, but using Firebug you can clearly see that you now have 10 pixels of padding surrounding the content of the footer. Any background properties you specify on a box, such as a background color or background image, will "shine through" the invisible padding area because a box's backgrounds, unlike its contents, start at the edge between a box's padding and its border, rather than inside the box's content area.

You can see from this example that, in fact, you've applied 10 pixels of padding to all four sides of the content area. You have 10 pixels on the top, the right, the bottom, and the left sides of the footer <div>'s content. Also notice that the width of your content area is still 300 pixels, just as you left it.

The important thing to infer from this is that any space you give the padding, border, or margin areas of a CSS box get added to any size you might specify for the box's width (or height) property. In effect, our 300-pixel-wide CSS block-level box is now a 320-pixel-wide CSS box because we've just added 10 pixels of padding to both the left and right sides of the box.

With CSS, we have the flexibility to define different sizes for each of the four individual sides of a box. The padding property used in the earlier CSS rule is shorthand that can be expanded to the following four declarations:

```
padding-top:10px;
padding-right:10px;
padding-bottom:10px;
padding-left:10px;
```

Every time you simply declare a value for a box's padding area with the padding property, you're really declaring each of those four specific padding properties with the same value applied to each property. CSS is full of shorthand properties like this, and it's important to be aware of them and what they expand to. When declaring rules generally, shorthand properties can save you quite a bit of typing (and quite a bit of bandwidth when downloading the finished CSS style sheet, too); however, when you're declaring rules to override other rules, it pays to be as explicit as possible.

A CSS box's padding area behaves slightly differently based on whether the box is an inline-level box or a block-level box. The padding area of a block-level box behaves as you would expect, causing the content area to move both vertically and horizontally to accommodate the additional padding. However, while the horizontal padding of an inline box (i.e., the right and left sides) behaves that way, too, the vertical padding (i.e., the top and bottom sides) does not. Specifically, an inline box's vertical padding will increase the area available for the box's backgrounds, but no other boxes will be affected by the inline box's occupation of the additional space.

Border area: drawing borders and outlines

The border area is, as its name implies, a space to define a border (or outline) for a CSS box. The edge between a box's padding and its border is where any background stops being visible. A CSS box's four borders (i.e., top, right, bottom, and left sides, as usual) have a number of different possible looks. Let's use a border to outline the footer on Summer Smash's website.

```
footer{
        width: 300px;
        padding: 10px;
        border: 1px solid black;
}
```

Borders behave in the same way that padding does. On a block-level box, all four sides affect their neighbors, but on an inline box, only the horizontal borders affect the layout of neighboring boxes.

The border property is another shorthand property. It sets a border width, style, and color for all four sides of a box. The example border declaration shown earlier expands to the following 12 declarations listed here, each of which can be set with a different value:

```
border-top-width:1px;
border-right-width:1px;
border-bottom-width:1px;
border-left-width:1px;
border-top-style:solid;
border-right-style:solid;
border-bottom-style:solid;
border-left-style:solid;
border-top-color:black;
border-right-color:black;
border-bottom-color:black;
border-left-color:black;
```

Borders have a lot of options—too many to go into at length in this chapter—so we encourage you to explore some of the other possible values for these properties on your own.

Margin area: defining whitespace and centering

The margin area of a CSS box defines the whitespace that surrounds the box's other areas. Most of the spacing of elements on web pages is accomplished with clever combinations of margins and padding. As with the padding and border areas, CSS allows you to specify different amounts of whitespace (i.e., margin sizes) on each of the four sides of a CSS box. Or, you can use the margin shorthand property to set the margins of all four sides in one declaration.

Margins can be thought of as a way for an element's CSS box to invisibly "push against" any other boxes next to it in exactly the same way as you've seen happen with padding. Like padding and borders, all four sides of block-level box's margins affect the layout of its neighboring CSS boxes, but only the horizontal margins of an inline box do.

Typically, headlines, paragraphs, lists, and many other elements have a certain amount of vertical margins defined by the browser's default style sheet. This CSS rules could look like this:

```
h1, h2, h3, h4, h5, h6, p, ul, ol, dl { margin: 1em 0; }
```

The selector for this rule is simply a group of individual type selectors that matches all possible headline levels, paragraphs, unordered lists, ordered lists, and definition lists. The declaration uses the margin shorthand property. With two values, the margin shorthand property expands to the following four CSS declarations:

```
margin-top:1e m;
margin-right: 0;
margin-bottom:1em;
margin-left:0 ;
```

That is, the first value sets the values for the vertical (i.e., top and bottom) sides, and the second value sets the values for the horizontal (i.e., right and left) sides.

The length unit being used here is an em. One em is the same length as the width of the letter m for the currently selected font for an element. Since the lowercase letter m is a different size in different fonts (and different font sizes), this unit is referred to as a relative-length unit because the actual computed value is relative to another value that may change. Contrast this with an absolute length unit, such as pixels, which are always the same size, no matter what. When working with text on a web page, it often pays to set sizes using a unit that is measured relative to a font size.

Why might the CSS rule for a margin use a relative unit that is defined by font sizes? If you think about it, the font size of an <h1> element is drastically different from the font size of an <h6> element, which is similarly different from the size of regular body text, such as the contents of <p> elements. It makes sense, then, that the amount of whitespace (margins) on top of and below the CSS box for each of these elements is different.

It would look a little weird if you had a huge level-one headline, but you had only a few pixels of distance between it and the introductory paragraph that came next. Using relative units allows you to be consistent in your declarations and yet apply different actual values to CSS properties based on the values of other CSS properties. This is the basis for creating what is known as a *responsive* (formerly known as *elastic*) layout, an advanced implementation of designs that results in the ability to "zoom in" on a page by increasing the text size in the browser.

The margins of a box are often used to center a block-level element horizontally within its containing block. Centering blocks is accomplished by setting both the right and left margins of the CSS box to the special value auto. You'll recall that this value simply means something like "automatically adjust this value based on the available space." For example, let's center the footer of Summer Smash's website:

```
footer{
  width: 300px;
  padding: 10px;
  border: 1px solid black;
  margin: 0 auto;
}
```

Again, the margin shorthand property is used to set the margins for all sides of the footer. The vertical sides are both given margin values of 0 (i.e., no extra whitespace at all), and the horizontal sides are both set to auto.

The footer is centered within the browser viewport because both its right and left margins automatically adjust their size to an equal share of the available horizontal space. To create available space in the first place, a width value other than the default of auto and less than the width of the footer's containing block (the browser window, in this case) must be specified, so that the element appears centered.

Margins have one other interesting property that can at first be confusing, but quickly becomes indispensable. When the bottom margin of one element is directly next to the top margin of another with no intervening areas (i.e., there are no padding or border areas separating them), then the two margins combine to form a single margin equal to the size of the larger margin. This peculiar behavior, called *collapsing margins*, occurs only for vertical margins and never for horizontal ones.

This behavior is handy because it means you don't have to specify a multitude of additional CSS rules in the common case where two block-level boxes follow one another in the document flow, such as a sequence of multiple consecutive paragraphs. In that case, setting a top and bottom margin of, say, 1em, on each paragraph will result in exactly 1em of whitespace between each paragraph (not 2em). If vertical margins didn't collapse, you'd instead have to specify something like 1em of bottom margin and zero top margin on every paragraph except the first in the series.

It can take a bit of time to get comfortable with the notion of declaring the sizes of what are essentially invisible areas of a page to define the layout of elements. This method of designing runs counter to the more natural feel achieved by directly manipulating the object itself. Nevertheless, you'll find that if you "go with the flow" of a web page, you'll end up creating designs that are far more flexible and far more maintainable.

Summary

This chapter covered an immense amount of technical material and a lot of theoretical ground. Don't feel discouraged if you think you may need to return to this chapter to get a handle on everything we've discussed. Thanks to its flexibility, power, and the unfortunately spotty browser implementations, actually creating complex designs with CSS can be tricky. However, knowing the foundations will prove invaluable just a short way down the line.

In this chapter, we introduced the majority of foundational concepts that explain how CSS actually works inside the web browser, such as the cascade, inheritance, document flow, and the box model. We also introduced a great deal of practical information regarding how to use CSS, such as how to apply CSS styles to a web page by using external or embedded style sheets and individual inline styles. We also covered the syntax and terminology of CSS rules and distinguishing between properties, values, declarations, declaration blocks, selectors, and rules. Next, we explored many possible CSS selectors and observed how you can have incredible flexibility over how you apply styles to elements by chaining simple selectors together with combinators. Finally, we introduced a plethora of CSS properties, including shorthand properties, each of which changes the way an element is displayed visually.

Armed with this knowledge, you'll next take a look at a real design and dissect it to discover how it was implemented. You'll then use this experience to help you implement a simple design for Summer Smash's website. Along the way, we'll introduce you to some additional CSS concepts and properties that will give you yet another level of appreciation for the power and flexibility of web standards.

Chapter 6

Developing CSS3 in Practice: From Design to Deployment

In the previous two chapters, we talked a lot about the theory and concepts behind standards-based front-end web development. You learned why and how to create structured, semantically meaningful HTML5 markup. You also learned how Cascading Style Sheets work, how web browsers display HTML content by default, and how to apply your own CSS rules to web pages. It's finally time to bring all your new-found knowledge to bear on a real project and turn your bland, unstyled web page into a beautiful, professionally implemented CSS design.

Since the easiest way to learn CSS-based design techniques is arguably to simply dive right into them, we invite you to think about this chapter as though you were looking over our shoulders while we show how to implement this design in code. We'll be carrying through the execution of an earlier example in this book: the Summer Smash 2012 registration form. Throughout this chapter, we'll be making references to topics covered in the previous two chapters, so we strongly urge you to read those chapters before beginning this one.

The visual source: understanding design documents

In any website design process, there always comes a point at which the developer (that's you!) needs to turn a visually presented layout into a real web page. The designs for websites are typically created in programs such as Adobe Photoshop. These files contain all the specific information about what a design looks like, including what fonts are used for each text element, the physical dimensions of all the items in the design, and the raw assets for each graphic.

As a front-end web developer, you are tasked with translating this design file into HTML and CSS to make your web page's look and feel match the look and feel of the design document as closely as possible. This is easier said than done because design files aren't constrained by the same limitations that web browsers are. Many times, design elements may need to be modified in some way, so that they are suitable for the web pages for which they're destined. For this reason, it really pays off to be familiar with one of these image-editing applications. Such software is beyond the scope of this book, however, so you'll be focusing solely on implementing a design in CSS in this chapter.

Diving into code: advanced CSS concepts applied

When developing any website design with CSS, you can follow some well-established best practices. Following these guidelines will make your life a lot easier, and they will ensure you end up with well-tested, standards-based code. One of the most important guidelines is to develop your style sheet in whatever browser most strictly adheres to the W3C's published standards. Since we're covering how to develop CSS3 now, we'll be testing our markup in Google Chrome. Whenever we refer to "our web browser" for the time being, that's the browser we mean. Although it's a good idea to occasionally check your progress in other browsers, for the sake of clarity in this text, we'll refrain from mentioning other browsers unless it adds to the discussion.

First things, first: Let's set up the source code file. In Chapter 4, we developed a basic HTML5 template for the registration page of the Summer Smash website. We saved this template as a plain-text file named `registration.html`. The content of this file is as follows:

```
<!DOCTYPEhtml >
<htmllang="en ">
<head>
    <meta charset="utf-8">
    <title>Summer Smash 2010 Registration</title>
    <link rel="stylesheet" href="css/style.css">
    <script src="js/javascript.js"></script>
</head>
<body>
<divid="pagew rap">
  <header>
    <a href="/">
      <h1>Summer Smash 2012</h1>
      <p>This summer's most smashing event!</p>
    </a>
  </header>
  <section id="main">
    <section id="registration_form">
      <form action="/registration/">
      <fieldset>
        <legend>Registrant Information</legend>
        <ol>
          <li class="formitem">
```

```
        <label for="name">Registrant name:</label>
        <input type="text" name="name" id="name" required autofocus />
        </li>
        <li class="formitem">
        <label for="email">Email address:</label>
        <input type="email" name="email" id="email" required />
        </li>
        <li class="formitem">
        <label for="phone">Phone number:</label>
        <input type="tel" name="phone" id="phone" />
        </li>
        <li class="formitem">
        <label for="party">How many people do you have in your party (including yourself)?</
        label>
        <input type="number" name="party" id="party" min="1" max="10" />
        </li>
        <li class="formitem">
        <label for="dob">Your date of birth:</label>
        <input type="date" name="dob" id="dob" />
        </li>
    </ol>
  </fieldset>
  <fieldset>
    <legend>A few quick questions</legend>
    <ol>
        <li class="formitem">
        Is this your first Summer Smash event?
        <ul>
          <li>
          <input type="radio" name="yes_first" id="yes_first" value="1" />
          <label for="yes_first">Yes, this is my first</label>
          </li>
          <li>
          <input type="radio" name="no_first" id="no_first" value="0" />
          <label for="no_first">No, I've been to one before</label>
          </li>
        </ul>
        </li>
        <li class="formitem">
        <label for="how_hear">How did you hear about Summer Smash 2012?</label>
        <input type="text" name="how_hear" id="how_hear" list="media">
          <datalist id="media">
            <option value="Google search">
            <option value="Magazine ad">
            <option value="A friend told me">
            <option value="An enemy told me">
            <option value="My dog told me">
            <option value="My dead uncle Henry told me">
          </datalist>
        </li>
```

```
        </ol>
      </fieldset>
      <input type="submit" value="Register now!" />
      </form>
    </section>

    <aside>
    <h2>Questions about whether Summer Smash is right for you?</h2>
    <p>We're here to help! Our team of smashtastic smashers will shatter any doubt in your
    mind. Why not give us a call, or send us an email?</p>
    <ul>
      <li>Call: 1-800-555-5555</li>
      <li>Email: <a href="mailto:smash@example.com">smash@example.com</a></li>
    </ul>
    </aside>
  </section>
  <footer>
    <p>Summer Smash 2012. A Barker and Lane Production.</p>
  </footer>
</div>
</body>
</html>
```

Recall that we've already set up a few rules for this page from the last chapter. For example, we decided to apply a reset style sheet to our page to bring the baseline formatting of all elements across all web browsers to roughly the same point. This reset stylesheet will also provide some older browsers with the ability to handle some of the newer, HTML5 elements we've used in our page, even though those browsers don't support HTML5. We also put in a few other rules while we were playing around in the last chapter, but they were just for the purpose of demonstration, so let's remove those for now. Our starting CSS file will look like this:

```
/* RESET STYLES */
html, body, div, span, object, iframe,
h1, h2, h3, h4, h5, h6, p, blockquote, pre,
abbr, address, cite, code,
del, dfn, em, img, ins, kbd, q, samp,
small, strong, sub, sup, var,
b,i,
dl, dt, dd, ol, ul, li,
fieldset,form, label,legend,
table, caption, tbody, tfoot, thead, tr, th, td,
article,aside ,canvas,details,   figcaption, figure,
footer, header, hgroup, menu, nav, section, summary,
time, mark, audio, video {
  margin:0;
  padding:0;
  border:0;
  outline:0;
  font-size:100%;
```

```css
  vertical-align:baseline;
  background:transparent;
}
body{
  line-height:1;
}
article,aside,details,figcaption,figure,
footer,header,hgroup,menu,nav,section{
  display:block;
}
nav ul {
  list-style:none;
}
blockquote, q {
  quotes:none;
}
blockquote:before,blockquote:after,
q:before, q:after {
  content:";
  content:none;
}
a{
  margin:0;
  padding:0;
  font-size:100%;
  vertical-align:baseline;
  background:transparent;
}
/* change colours to suit your needs */
ins{
  background-color:#ff9;
  color:#000;
  text-decoration:none;
}
/* change colours to suit your needs */
mark{
  background-color:#ff9;
  color:#000;
  font-style:italic;
  font-weight:bold;
}
del{
  text-decoration: line-through;
}
```

```
abbr[title], dfn[title] {
  border-bottom:1px dotted;
  cursor:help;
}

table{
  border-collapse:collapse;
  border-spacing:0;
}

/* change border colour to suit your needs */
hr{
  display:block;
  height:1px;
  border:0;
  border-top:1px solid #cccccc;
  margin:1em 0;
  padding:0;
}

input, select {
  vertical-align:middle;
}

/* END RESET */
```

Now that we've made a change to the CSS rules in our style sheet (by removing the extra styles), we can view the change by reloading the `registration.html` page in our web browser. Each time we save a new change, we typically check to see whether it got applied properly by reloading the web page in the browser. We continue by saving another change, and we repeat the process all over again. We simply lather, rinse, and repeat until the entire design is complete.

This is a good start so far. Let's begin defining the CSS rules specific to this design.

Page structure: laying out the page

Let's start by getting things to show up where we want. For the most part, we're going to be laying out our block-level elements here. Right now, everything is stacked on top of each other, and crammed up into the top-right corner of our page. Most pages these days center their content within the viewport—that seems like a good place to start. We put in a special `<div>` just so that we can target all of the content on our page:

```
div#pagewrap{
  width: 80%;
  margin: 4em auto;
}
```

We did a couple of things in the preceding code. We set the width of the page contents to occupy 80% of the browser window. Using "80%" rather than "800px" is an important step in coding our page so that it will scale for a range of different devices. We plan on making the Summer Slam registration form work on everything from an iPhone or Android device, through the range of tablet devices, and into desktop computers with (potentially) extremely large and extremely detailed screens.

We'll talk more about the specifics of this approach in the next chapter on responsive design; but for the time being, we'll try to use relative or proportional units as much as possible. Moving along, though, let's take care of our other block-level elements:

```
header{
  padding: 1em 0 2em;
}
section#main{
  float:left;
}
section#registration_form{
  width: 74%;
  float:left;
  padding: 0 1% 0 0;
}
aside{
  width: 25%;
  float:right;
}
footer{
  clear: both;
  padding: 2em 3%;
}
```

Let's take a look at what we've done here: for our header, we've simply applied a little padding to the top and the bottom of the element to give us some space between its contents and the element below. Once we start applying some background colors and graphics to things, padding becomes a lot more important.

On the #main section, we've applied a float. This is actually there so that this element will contain the two child-floated elements, #registration_form and <aside>. If we didn't float this section, then our footer would creep up and find its way into the #main section.

We want our registration form and our contact information to appear beside each other, so we've set our registration form to be 74% wide (with 1% right-side padding) and our aside to be 25% wide. At first glance, this might look confusing: didn't we set div#pagewrap to be 80% wide? Yes, we did. However, when you're defining a percentage width, you define it as a percentage of the parent element, and the parent is always 100% wide when you're inside it.

We've floated both the #registration_form and the <aside> to opposite sides, so that they won't interfere with one another. Finally, we've cleared the floats with the footer and applied a bit of padding to it.

OK, our design still isn't at the point where anyone would accuse it of being beautiful, as shown in Figure 6-1, but at least we're making some progress. Let's keep moving and adding style information in. We might come back and revisit some of these rules, but for now we've got the basic layout we want.

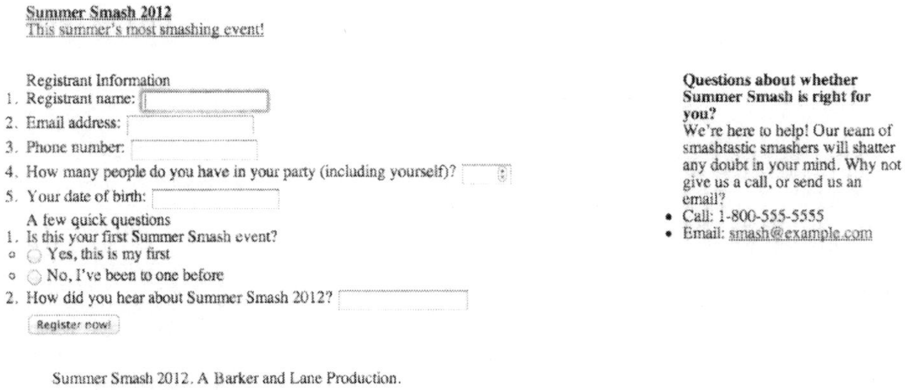

Figure 6-1. We have the basics of our page laid out, but we can go much further in the style department.

The header: start at the top

We'll start at the top of the page and work our way down. Our header right now is pretty plain and not very interesting to look at. It's really just a couple of links, both with the same font, size, and color. We can do better than that! First up, let's get those titles looking like titles instead of like text links:

```
header{
  background-color: #333;
}
header a {
  text-decoration: none;
  color: white;
  text-align: center;
}
header h1 {
  font-size: 3em;
  font-family: Helvetica, Arial, sans-serif;
}
header p {
  font-size: 1.2em;
  font-family: Helvetica, Arial, sans-serif;
}
```

OK, again we're making progress. We gave the header a dark gray background color, removed the underlines from the links, turned them white, and centered them.

We also increased the font size of both our header and our tag line, and changed the font to Helvetica. Figure 6-2 shows the progress we've made.

Helvetica just doesn't scream "Summer Smash" to us, though; we need a slightly more creative font for this role. Unfortunately, we can't really rely on folks to have a copy of our favorite font installed on their machine locally, so we can't just specify any font we choose. In the old days, this presented a real problem, and designers would frequently turn to displaying type using an image. But that isn't a very semantic way to do things, is it? There's got to be a better way!

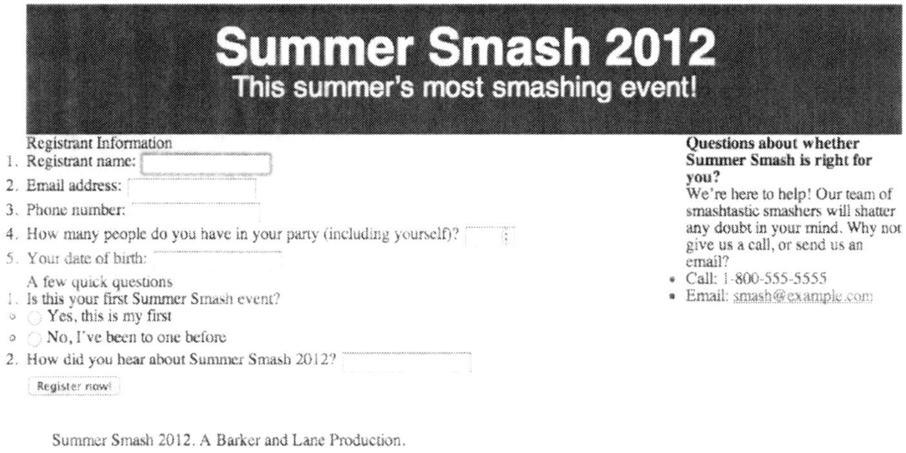

Figure 6-2. Our stylized header without our smashing font selection

Exploring the world of fonts

Thankfully, there is a better way to handle fonts. With modern web browsers, you can specify alternate font faces and provide the fonts to your end user (keeping in mind copyright restrictions on some fonts!). A few sites have popped up online to help with this process, including one from a well-known search giant, Google. At the time of writing, Google has more than 400 fonts on its "Google Web Fonts" website, which allows you to select a font, link to a special style sheet Google hosts for you, and then use that font on your site.

It's a bit hard to describe what this looks like, so let's just get right to the code. First, let's head over to www.google.com/webfonts and select something that will fit the bill for our Summer Smash needs. "Frijole" looks like a contender, so let's grab that one. Google makes it easy for us from this point; all we do is copy and paste some code it provides for us.

In registration.html, we replace the <head> </head> section with this:

```
<head>
  <meta charset="utf-8">
  <title>Summer Smash 2010 Registration</title>
  <link href="http://fonts.googleapis.com/css?family=Frijole" rel="stylesheet">
  <link rel="stylesheet" href="css/style.css">
  <script src="/js/javascript.js"></script>
</head>
```

Next, we make a couple of tweaks to our CSS styles for the header:

```
header h1 {
  font-size: 3.5em;
  font-family: "Frijole", Arial, sans-serif;
  color: #eee;
}
```

```
header p {
  font-size: 1.2em;
  font-family: "Frijole", Arial, sans-serif;
  color: #ccc;
}
```

Every font is a little bit different, so we tweaked the size of the <h1> element after settling on a font face. For example, using pure white was a little bit blinding with such a bold font, so we made both the <h1> and the <p> a light gray.

The font-family rule is where the magic happens. We linked in a style sheet directly from Google in the <head> of our document that describes what the Frijole font is; this style sheet provides the necessary files to users who don't have that font installed on their computer. We can then use font-family to build a stack of fonts that are acceptable here. Check out Figure 6-3 for a far more smashing experience.

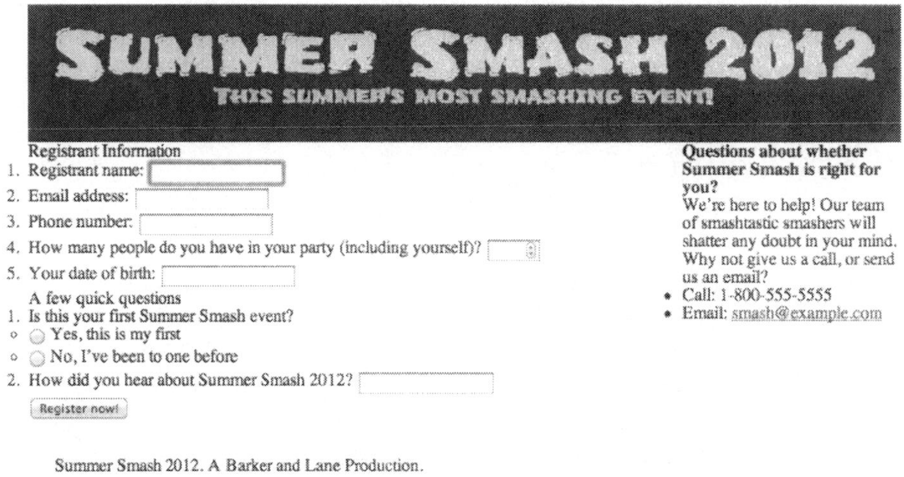

Summer Smash 2012. A Barker and Lane Production.

Figure 6-3. The Frijole font just screams "Smashing"!

While we're at it, let's change the default font for the page over to Verdana (instead of the default Times/ Times New Roman that most browsers use):

```
div#pagewrap{
  width: 80%;
  margin: 4em auto;
  font-family: Verdana, Arial, sans-serif;
}
```

Room to breathe: space it out

We've got everything roughly laid out now, but let's put a little space between the elements and make things look a bit nicer. Starting with the header, the page title (<h1>) and the tag line (<p>) look a little claustrophobic. Let's put a little space between them and also space out the individual characters in the tag line—they look a little mashed together.

```
header p {
  font-size: 1.2em;
  font-family: "Frijole", Arial, sans-serif;
  color: #ccc;
  margin: 0.7em 0 0 0;
  letter-spacing: 1px;
}
```

That's good enough for now. Now let's space out the blocks of content a bit:

```
section#main{
  float:left;
  margin: 2em 2%;
}
```

In the preceding code snippet, we're putting a 2em top and bottom margin on the #main section to give it a little room from the header and footer. We're also bringing the sides in by 2% on each side. Next, let's clean up the form a bit:

```
fieldset{
  padding: 0.5em 1% 1em;
}
legend{
  text-transform: uppercase;
  font-size: 1.2em;
  font-weight: bold;
  padding-bottom: 3px;
  border-bottom: 1px solid #333;
  width: 100%;
}
form ol, form ul {
  list-style-type: none;
  margin: 0 2%;
}
form li {
  margin: 0.5em 0;
}
label{
  font-size: 0.8em;
}
form ol li label {
  display: block;
}
form ul li label {
  display: inline;
}
```

There are a lot of margins and padding declared here. There are also a few other things to note. Both ordered lists <ol> and unordered lists <ul> in our form are being given a list-style-type of none. Even though the form elements are contained within a list, we don't want that list to have numbers and bullets the way a normal list would.

We've changed the display type for labels contained within the ordered list to block, so that the input fields will appear on the line below. We've also over-ridden this for labels contained within the unordered list (our radio buttons), so that the form elements appear inline with their labels.

Finally, we've styled the <legend> elements to give them a little more prominence and to help them stand out like the section headings that they are. Their text is slightly larger, and they will appear in uppercase and bold. We've also put a little 1px border on the bottom of those to give the page a little visual division. Now things are really starting to come together, as seen in Figure 6-4!

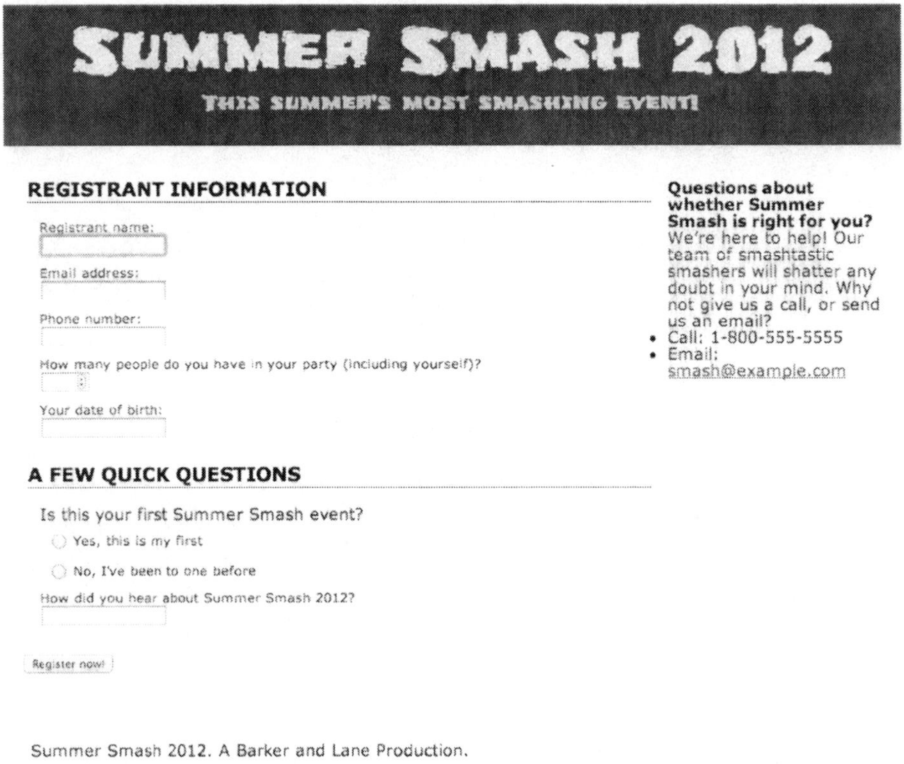

Figure 6-4. The page's formatting nears completion

Give those form elements some style

Our input fields are looking a little drab and boring. Let's give them a bit of a boost by applying some styles to them:

```
input[type="text"], input[type="number"], input[type="tel"], input[type="email"],
input[type="date"] {
  width: 50%;
  padding: 0.5em 0.7%;
```

```
    margin-top: 0.4em;
    font-size: 1em;
    color: #eee;
    border: none;
    background-color: rgba(0,0,0,0.6);
    -webkit-border-radius: 4px;
    -moz-border-radius: 4px;
    -o-border-radius: 4px;
    border-radius: 4px;
}
```

Here we're using an attribute selector (type=) to target everything except the radio buttons (we don't want them to be 50% wide; we'll handle those separately). We've set the width, font-size, padding, top margin, color, and border on all of these elements—those declarations are pretty straightforward. The background color and last four lines need a little explanation, though.

For our background-color, we didn't declare a color name (like red or green) or use a hexadecimal value (like #666666). Instead, we used an RGBA value, which is a new color model supported in CSS3. RGBA allows us to say how much red, green, and blue to use (the first three values respectively; in this case, three zeros produce black), as well as to specify the opacity for the color (the final value is set to 60% opacity).

Our number field and our date of birth field look a little funny. though; they're awfully wide considering the data they're going to hold. Let's override those widths:

```
input[type="number"], input[type="date"] {
    width: 20%;
}
```

Finally, it's a minor thing, but our submit button looks a little weird because it's a light gray color compared to the dark gray elements on the rest of the page. Let's correct that:

```
input[type="submit"]{
    background-color: rgba(0,0,0,0.6);
    color: #eee;
    padding: 0.5em 0.7%;
    font-size: 1em;
    border: none;
    -webkit-border-radius: 4px;
    -moz-border-radius: 4px;
    -o-border-radius: 4px;
    border-radius: 4px;
    margin-left: 2%;
}
```

There is nothing too strange, here: the code pretty much mimics what we did on our other form elements. We put a left margin on our button as well as brought the submit button into alignment with our other elements. Let's check on our progress in our browser (see Figure 6-5).

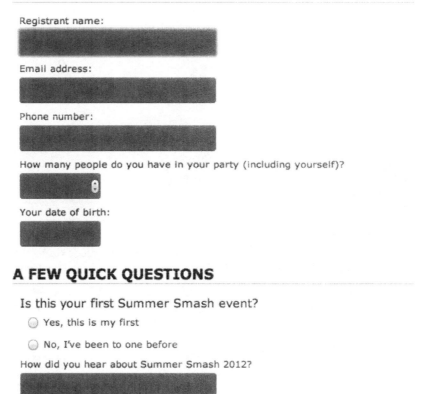

Figure 6-5. Our stylized form

Sidebar styling

The sidebar for our registration form contains some helpful customer service information. We've provided a way for folks to get in contact with us if they have any questions or concerns, but that information needs to stand out a bit:

```
aside{
  background-color: #ccc;
  padding: 1em 2%;
  -webkit-border-radius: 4px;
  -moz-border-radius: 4px;
  -o-border-radius: 4px;
  border-radius: 4px;
}
```

When we do this, we run into a little hiccup, and our sidebar ends up being pushed down the page. Remember back to our discussion of the box model? Here, by adding horizontal padding to the aside, we've widened that element enough that it won't fit floated beside our registration form. It's a simple fix—let's just subtract some width from our earlier declaration:

```
aside{
  width: 21%;
  float:right;
}
```

Instead of declaring the width to be 25%, we've set it to 23% with two 1% paddings (so the aside stays the same width as before). But there's still more work to do; our text looks terrible all cramped together in our aside. Let's clean up the various elements:

```
aside h2 {
  font-size: 1em;
  line-height: 1.3em;
  text-transform: uppercase;
  margin-bottom: 1em;
}
aside p {
  font-size: 0.8em;
  line-height: 1.2em;
  margin-bottom: 1.5em;
}
aside ul {
  list-style-type: none;
  font-size: 0.8em;
  line-height: 1.5em;
}
```

That's not too bad. We're not crazy about that e-mail link being the default underlined blue text. Let's do something special there: we'll not only change the style of that link, but we'll add a touch of interactivity, so that when a user mouses-over the link, some animation happens.

CSS3 transitions

Something new in CSS3 is the introduction of transitions. Transitions allow you to animate between two states of an element. What we mean by that is that, instead of having something change immediately from blue to red, you can have it fade through a series of shades of purple until it eventually reaches the red endpoint. Transitions usually come in three parts: the transition-property (what you're going to change), the transition-duration (how long the change is going to take) and the transition-timing-function (how fast the transition happens over time). Here's what that looks like:

```
aside a {
      color: #333;
      background-color: transparent;
      text-decoration: none;
      -webkit-transition: all 3s ease;
      -moz-transition: all 3s ease;
```

```
    -o-transition: all 3s ease;
    transition: all 3s ease;
}
aside a:hover {
      color: #c00;
      background-color: black;
      font-weight: bold;

}
```

In our first declaration, we've turned off the underlines, set our transitions, and set our link color to dark gray. We've also explicitly declared that our background color is transparent (this is required so that this works properly in Firefox) In the second declaration, we've used an a:hover pseudo-class to indicate what should happen when a mouse hovers over the link. In this case, we've changed the color of the link to red and changed, changed the weight of the typeface to bold, and the background color to black. Colors can have transitions, but font weights can't—all that means is that, when somebody hovers her mouse over our link, it will instantly become bold, but will fade to red over a half-second duration.

Let's pause for a second and take a look at these declarations in more detail. First, we've made a number of vendor- (i.e., browser-) specific declarations here that all do the same thing. You might be asking yourself why that is, but it's entirely because CSS3 is still in its infancy. Certain browsers support CSS3 transitions, and others don't. Here, we're specifically targeting a number of browsers that do have support, and then ending with the general transition: declaration. As time progresses and browser support improves, we'll be able to drop the vendor-specific rules; however, for the time being, they're required.

We should also dissect one of these declarations and explain what's going on. The first property, all, simply tells the browser to transition between all supported properties. We could also alter the size, rotation, or position of the link; and specifying all would ensure that a smooth transition happens for all of those.

3s indicates the length of time over which the transition should take place. Three seconds is slow enough that we'll actually be able to see the change. Also, ease indicates the timing function. There are six possible timing functions that can be used here, and the best way to get a feel for what they do is to experiment with them. For example, try swapping out ease for ease-in, ease-out, ease-in-out, linear, or cubic-bezier to see what all of these do. Don't worry; we won't go anywhere.

There are other properties you can transition between. Some handy ones include size (you can make things grow and shrink), rotation (make things spin), background colors and opacity (make things appear or disappear).

Footer beautification

We've finally reached the bottom of our page. The footer of a page is often overlooked because it's pushed all the way to the bottom. Footers often contain very valuable information, though. In our case, we're letting everyone know who's behind Summer Smash 2012—the infamous promoters, Barker and Lane! This calls for some style:

```
footer{
  border-top: 1px solid #666;
  color: #c00;
  font-family: Zapfino, Verdana, sans-serif;
  font-size: 0.8em;
}
```

We gave our footer a bit of flair by changing the text color to a nice crimson (red). We also decreased the font size a bit—there's no need to have it jump off the page!—and put in a font stack of Zapfino and Verdana. We didn't bother to include the Zapfino font as a separate style sheet (as we did with Frijole); this means that, if a person visiting our site has Zapfino installed on their computer, he'll see our footer in a nice cursive font face. If he doesn't, it's no big deal; we'll just show it to him in Verdana.

Some designers might cringe at this idea. If the font face really is essential to your design, then go the extra mile and include it. In this case, our footer just contains a bit of meta-information, so there's no real reason to obsess over it. Let's take one final look at our page now (see Figure 6-6).

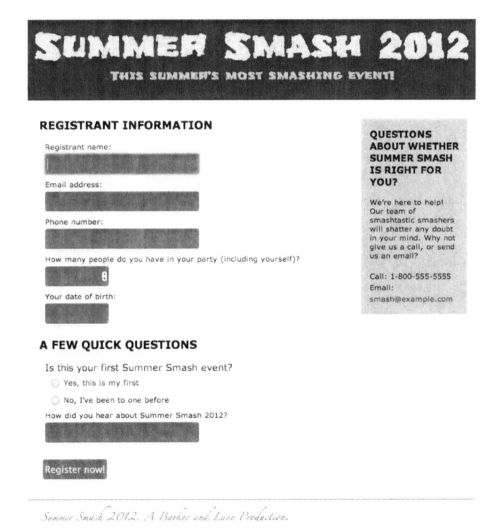

Figure 6-6. The completed page

All together

We jumped around a bit in this chapter, tweaking values here and there, so we thought that we'd give you a complete listing of the style sheet before moving on. Our completed `style.css` style sheet looks like this:

```css
/* RESET STYLES */
html, body, div, span, object, iframe,
h1, h2, h3, h4, h5, h6, p, blockquote, pre,
abbr, address, cite, code,
del, dfn, em, img, ins, kbd, q, samp,
small, strong, sub, sup, var,
b,i,
dl, dt, dd, ol, ul, li,
fieldset,form,label,legend,
table, caption, tbody, tfoot, thead, tr, th, td,
article,aside,canvas,details,    figcaption, figure,
footer, header, hgroup, menu, nav, section, summary,
time, mark, audio, video {
  margin:0;
  padding:0;
  border:0;
  outline:0;
  font-size:100%;
  vertical-align:baseline;
  background:transparent;
}

body{
  line-height:1;
}

article,aside,details,figcaption,figure,
footer,header,hgroup,menu,nav,section{
  display:block;
}

nav ul {
  list-style:none;
}

blockquote, q {
  quotes:none;
}

blockquote:before,blockquote:after,
q:before, q:after {
  content:'';
  content:none;
}

a{
  margin:0;
  padding:0;
  font-size:100%;
```

```css
    vertical-align:baseline;
    background:transparent;
}

/* change colours to suit your needs */
ins{
    background-color:#ff9;
    color:#000;
    text-decoration:none;
}

/* change colours to suit your needs */
mark{
    background-color:#ff9;
    color:#000;
    font-style:italic;
    font-weight:bold;
}

del{
    text-decoration: line-through;
}

abbr[title], dfn[title] {
    border-bottom:1px dotted;
    cursor:help;
}

table{
    border-collapse:collapse;
    border-spacing:0;
}

/* change border colour to suit your needs */
hr{
    display:block;
    height:1px;
    border:0;
    border-top:1px solid #cccccc;
    margin:1em 0;
    padding:0;
}

input, select {
    vertical-align:middle;
}

/* END RESET */
/* Layout Block level elements */
div#pagewrap{
    width: 80%;
    margin: 4em auto;
    font-family: Verdana, Arial, sans-serif;
}
```

```
header{
  padding: 1em 0 2em;
}

section#main{
  float:left;
  margin: 2em 2%;
}

section#registration_form{
  width: 74%;
  float:left;
  padding: 0 1% 0 0;
}

aside{
  width: 21%;
  float:right;
}

footer{
  clear: both;
  padding: 2em 3%;
}

/* Header */
header{
  background-color: #333;
}

header a {
  text-decoration: none;
  color: white;
  text-align: center;
}

header h1 {
  font-size: 3.5em;
  font-family: "Frijole", Arial, sans-serif;
  color: #eee;
}

header p {
  font-size: 1.2em;
  font-family: "Frijole", Arial, sans-serif;
  color: #ccc;
  margin: 0.7em 0 0 0;
  letter-spacing: 1px;
}

/* Form */
fieldset{
  padding: 0.5em 1% 1em;
}
```

```css
legend{
  text-transform: uppercase;
  font-size: 1.2em;
  font-weight: bold;
  padding-bottom: 3px;
  border-bottom: 1px solid #333;
  width: 100%;
}
form ol, form ul {
  list-style-type: none;
  margin: 0 2%;
}

form li {
  margin: 0.5em 0;
}

label{
  font-size: 0.8em;
}

form ol li label {
  display: block;
}

form ul li label {
  display: inline;
}
input[type="text"], input[type="number"], input[type="tel"], input[type="email"],
input[type="date"] {
  width: 50%;
  padding: 0.5em 0.7%;
  margin-top: 0.4em;
  font-size: 1em;
  color: #eee;
  border: none;
  background-color: rgba(0,0,0,0.6);
  -webkit-border-radius: 4px;
  -moz-border-radius: 4px;
  -o-border-radius: 4px;
  border-radius: 4px;
}

input[type="number"], input[type="date"] {
  width: 20%;
}

input[type="submit"]{
  background-color: rgba(0,0,0,0.6);
  color: #eee;
  padding: 0.5em 0.7%;
  font-size: 1em;
```

```
  border: none;
  -webkit-border-radius: 4px;
  -moz-border-radius: 4px;
  -o-border-radius: 4px;
  border-radius: 4px;
  margin-left: 2%;
}

/* Aside */
aside{
  background-color: #ccc;
  padding: 1em 2%;
  -webkit-border-radius: 4px;
  -moz-border-radius: 4px;
  -o-border-radius: 4px;
  border-radius: 4px;
}

aside h2 {
  font-size: 1em;
  line-height: 1.3em;
  text-transform: uppercase;
  margin-bottom: 1em;
}

aside p {
  font-size: 0.8em;
  line-height: 1.2em;
  margin-bottom: 1.5em;
}

aside ul {
  list-style-type: none;
  font-size: 0.8em;
  line-height: 1.5em;
}

aside a {
    color: #333;
    background-color: transparent;
    text-decoration: none;
    -webkit-transition: all 3s ease;
    -moz-transition: all 3s ease;
    -o-transition: all 3s ease;
    transition: all 3s ease;
}

aside a:hover {
    color: #c00;
    background-color: black;
    font-weight: bold;
}
```

```
/* Footer */
footer{
  border-top: 1px solid #666;
  color: #c00;
  font-family: Zapfino, Verdana, sans-serif;
  font-size: 0.8em;
}
```

A quick note about browser compatibility

We put in a disclaimer early on asking you to forget about other web browsers as you work through this chapter and to focus your testing on Google Chrome. The reason we made this request is that, at the time of this writing, Chrome has some of the best support for the new CSS3 properties we've discussed. We should really stress here that CSS3 is still a working draft and that CSS3 is not a fully approved standard at this point. We really are working with cutting-edge stuff here. Because of that, browser support will vary quite a bit.

CSS3 is fairly well supported in Safari, Opera, Chrome, and Firefox. Internet Explorer 10 and onwards has decent support as well. You may be asking yourself why on earth we'd consider using this technology that has such spotty support, and the answer is simple: when CSS3 is supported, the results are fantastic. And when it's not supported, nothing breaks (no harm, no foul). CSS3 provides an enhancement to the user experience when it's supported. Think of it this way: you, as a developer, are rewarding your end users for using the most up-to-date technology!

CSS media types and creating print style sheets

So far, you've seen how you can use CSS to create vivid designs on a computer screen. This is very handy, but CSS can do even more. Since its flexibility comes from its ability to use the same source document and display it in different ways, you can use everything you've just learned to create an entirely new look for the page when it's printed. You do this in two steps:

1. Create a new style sheet (or an additional portion on your existing style sheet) and declare it as a print style sheet.

2. Simply write new CSS rules that restyle your page in an appropriate way for paper.

To define styles specifically for printed media, you need to use CSS's predefined media types. Recall that the original style sheet is embedded in your HTML document like this:

```
<link rel="stylesheet" href="css/style.css">
```

This style sheet is effectively a style sheet for all possible media types. One of these media types is screen; and another, as you may have guessed already, is print. In other words, the style sheet element actually looks like this to the browser:

```
<link rel="stylesheet" href="css/style.css" media="all">
```

If we want to restrict all the CSS rules so they apply only to computer monitors, we could instead define the CSS style sheet like this:

```
<link rel="stylesheet" href="css/style.css" media="screen">
```

In fact, this is probably the simplest way to create a printed version of most pages because it will cause the browser to ignore all our CSS rules when the user prints the page, and our design will revert to the unstyled look we had before we started.

Let's create a new, very short print style sheet for the Summer Smash registration form (some folks don't like submitting their information online, so we'll let them print it out and mail it in). This style sheet builds on all the work we've already accomplished. We're not going to go crazy here, just clean up things a bit and remove certain unnecessary elements from the printed view.

With this new style sheet added to the mix, the HTML header of the page now looks like this:

```
<!DOCTYPEhtml >
<htmllang="en ">
<head>
  <meta charset="utf-8">
  <title>Summer Smash 2010 Registration</title>
  <link href="http://fonts.googleapis.com/css?family=Frijole" rel="stylesheet">
  <link rel="stylesheet" href="css/style.css">
  <link rel="stylesheet" href="css/print.css" media="print">
  <script src="/js/javascript.js"></script>
</head>
```

We don't want to burn through an entire forest worth of paper, nor do we want to drive ourselves nuts with constant trips to the printer. Thus, while we're developing our print style sheet, we'll leave the media="print" attribute out of our code. This will render our print styles on screen, so we can get things looking as we'd like (we can add these styles back when we're done). Doing this will signal the following to the browser: "This is just another style sheet that isn't specifically targeted to any medium, so apply it everywhere."

Let's create a new file called print.css in our /css directory and start writing new CSS rules to override the rules we already have. Just as we've done before, we'll simply go over the design (and its style sheet) from top to bottom, changing what we need to and leaving the rest the same. At the top, you have the global rules for the background of the page and the colors of the text and links.

Even though most browsers don't print backgrounds by default, let's turn off all the background colors and images explicitly. This will save some of your visitors some ink, and it's better for the environment, too. Also, since the notion of links is somewhat useless on printed pages, let's make all links look like normal text by turning them black and removing their underlines. After doing this, we can see yet another reason why descriptive anchor text (instead of anchor text such as "click here") is so important:

```
html, body {
  background-color: #fff;
  background-image: none;
  color: #000;
}
body{
  margin: 0.25in;
}
a{
  text-decoration: none;
  color: #000;
}
```

Notice that these CSS rules are overriding only what we have to from the previous rules, and they are ignoring the declarations that we want to keep, such as font sizes and font faces. Also note that, because we are now working on physical media, it makes sense for us to use length values that are native to physical spaces (such as inches).

Next, let's clean up our header a bit, so that we don't end up with a big, dark stripe on the page. We can keep the character of our font, but let's change it over to black text on a white background instead:

```
header{
  background-color: #fff;
}
header h1, header p {
  color: #000;
  text-align: left;
}
```

Now let's clean up some of our blocks and remove the sidebar and the footer from the page—they're not really necessary for a printed registration form:

```
div#pagewrap{
  width: 100%;
}
aside, footer {
  display: none;
}
section#main{
  float:none;
}
section#registration_form{
  width: 100%;
  float:none;
}
```

Last but certainly not least, those dark gray boxes are going to be a little hard to write on. Usually, paper forms just have solid lines where you're supposed to write in your answer—that makes better sense here, too.

```
input[type="text"], input[type="number"], input[type="tel"], input[type="email"],
input[type="date"] {
  background-color: #fff;
  border-bottom: 1px solid #000;
  font-size: 1.3em;
  -webkit-border-radius: 0;
  -moz-border-radius: 0;
  -o-border-radius: 0;
  border-radius: 0;
  width: 100%;
}
input[type="submit"]{
  display: none;
}
```

We made the background color white, put a black border on the bottom, increased the font size (which makes the lines bigger so that somebody has more room to write), turned off the rounded corners, and set the width of the fields to 100%. We also took the opportunity to hide the submit button—that's really not going to do any good on a printed copy:

```
html, body {
  background-color: #fff;
  background-image: none;
  color: #000;
}
body{
  margin: 0.25in;
}
a{
  text-decoration: none;
  color: #000;
}
header{
  background-color: #fff;
}
header h1, header p {
  color: #000;
  text-align: left;
}
div#pagewrap{
  width: 100%;
}
aside, footer {
  display: none;
}
section#main{
  float:none;
}
section#registration_form{
  width: 100%;
  float:none;
}
input[type="text"], input[type="number"], input[type="tel"], input[type="email"],
input[type="date"] {
  background-color: #fff;
  border-bottom: 1px solid #000;
  font-size: 1.3em;
  -webkit-border-radius: 0;
  -moz-border-radius: 0;
  -o-border-radius: 0;
  border-radius: 0;
  width: 100%;
}
input[type="submit"]{
  display: none;
}
```

Our completed print style sheet is only 45 lines long, but it drastically changes the appearance of our registration form when you print it. And wait! Don't forget to put that media="print" attribute back in, or this style sheet will drastically alter the look of our form everywhere! We should see something similar to Figure 6-7 when we print our registration form.

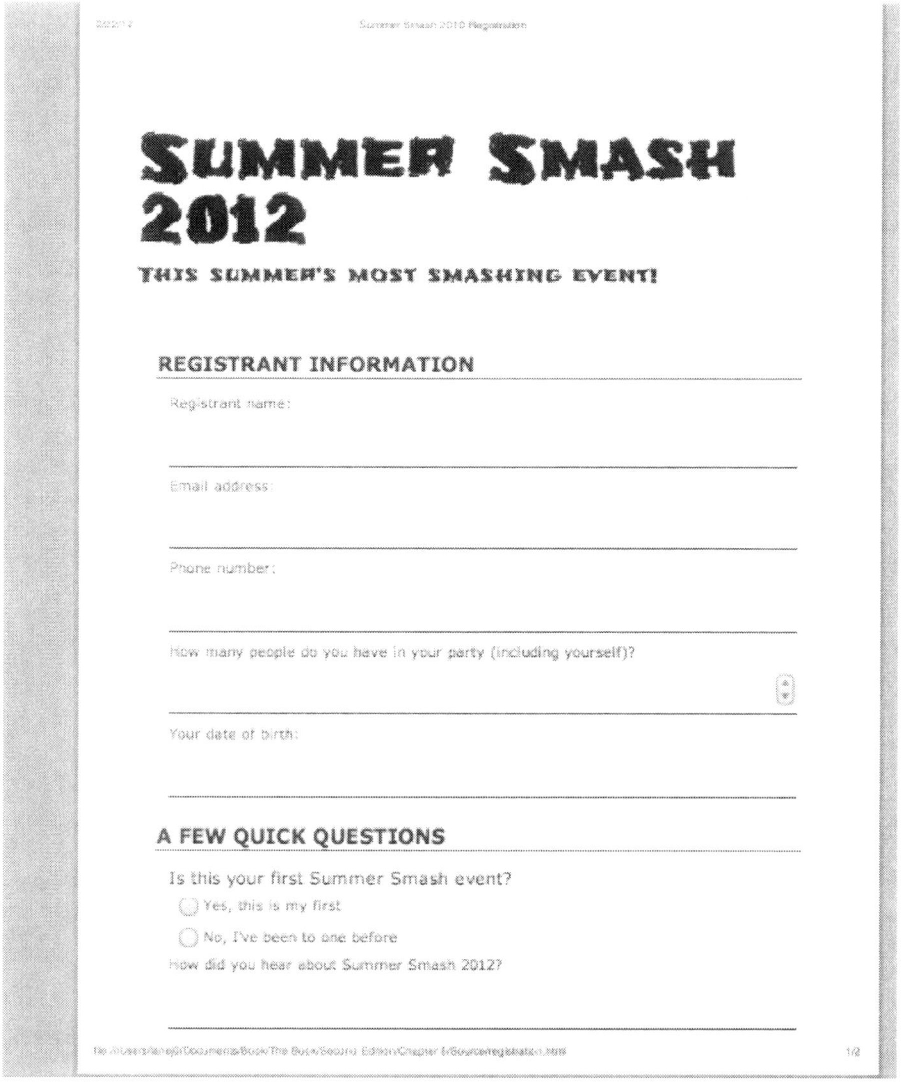

Figure 6-7. A print preview of our registration form

145

Designing for other media types and devices

As you can see, creating new style sheets for different media types is fairly painless. All it really requires is an understanding of the destination media and how it works. For printed pages, this should be easy because most, if not all of us, are intimately familiar with what printed pages can and can't do. It's the other media types—most notably the handheld media type—that are trickier.

Luckily for us, we've been styling a lot of our elements using proportional units (ems and %) as opposed to absolute units. We'll kick this up a notch in the next chapter as we transform our registration form from one that looks fine on a computer screen to one that "responds" to the device it's being viewed on. We'll convert our humble registration form to a registration form that functions perfectly on an iPhone, an Android device, and a tablet (like an iPad or Kindle Fire). It will also continue to keep looking great on a traditional screen.

We won't develop separate style sheets for each of these devices; instead, we'll put in a few exceptions here and there to make things look and work great at any resolution. Trust us: we're already well on our way there.

Summary

As we've now seen, the implementation of a design in a CSS style sheet is relatively straightforward, but it can be complicated by numerous factors, such as browser bugs or natural differences in the display medium. With the simple design for Summer Smash 2012, we saw numerous examples of how designing for the web page is drastically different from designing for the printed page. We also saw some examples of common techniques used to leverage the flexibility and fluidity of web pages to maximize the usability of our web pages.

By using dynamic pseudo-classes, we added interactivity that would not have been possible on a printed page. We laid out our page using floated blocks, and further styled our form using CSS rules that aren't fully implemented by all browsers at this point. Finally, we learned how to take the original style sheet and modify it to create a print-ready version of our page in mere minutes.

Clearly, there's plenty we can accomplish just by utilizing what HTML and CSS have to offer. However, there's much more that the web browser has to offer in terms of creating dynamic effects that far exceed the modicum of interactivity that CSS's dynamic pseudo-classes provide. In later chapters, we'll cover how to harness the full power of JavaScript, a standards-based, full-fledged programming language that's embedded directly inside web browsers. This will enable us to take our web pages to a whole new level.

Chapter 7

Responsive Design

Responsive design is a new name for an old concept. The term *responsive* used to be applied mainly when talking about a website's speed (i.e., if a website was fast, it had a good response time). Lately, the term has been co-opted for a different purpose. A responsive website now refers to a website that responds to its viewport. It used to be that web designers had to concern themselves only with a minimum screen resolution of 640 pixels by 480 pixels and a maximum resolution of 1280 by 1024 pixels. Two factors have led to both the floor being dropped and the ceiling being raised. First, the sharp rise in mobile and tablet devices used to access the web has dropped the floor all the way down to 240 by 320 pixels. Second, a sharp increase in screen resolutions coupled with the introduction of widescreen monitors has raised the resolution ceiling to 2560 by 1440 pixels (and possibly even larger than that). How are we expected to produce a website that looks good given such a range of devices?

Why bother?

The first question worth asking is, "Should I even bother?" The very simple answer is that you may not have a choice. A lot of clients these days are asking that their websites work on an iPhone. You can go a couple of ways if that's the case: build a responsive website, or duplicate your efforts and build two parallel websites for the exact same content.

If that isn't specified as a requirement, though, how do you decide whether a responsive website makes sense? Begin by putting yourself in your visitor's shoes. Depending on the type of website you're working on, it may not be worth the added trouble. Are people going to be accessing this site frequently when they're on the go? What sort of actions will they need to take?

For certain sites, the decision is obvious: anything that's related to travel and tourism would likely benefit from a mobile-friendly view. How much do you wish that your favorite restaurant would allow you to view its menu on your cell phone? Maybe it does, and that's why it's your favorite!

Here's another great example: where we live, there can be some really great windstorms in the winter, and the power goes out often. The local power company has a wonderful mobile-friendly (albeit not responsive) website that allows you to view the status of the power outage affecting your area and see when it estimates that it'll have service restored. During an outage, not many folks will be able to power up their desktop computers and connect to the Internet, so a cell phone is their lifeline to the outside world.

Now that we've (hopefully) made the case for building a responsive design, how do we go about taming this beast?

Strategy and Practice

The good news is that, nothing is really different from what we designers have had to deal with since the beginning of the Web. In this case, the technology has just improved and made it easier for us to deal with these variations.

The first step in developing a responsive website (and one that can take place during your early discussions with your client) is determining which device(s) you're designing for. Will this website benefit from being mobile-phone friendly? The argument can be made that any website benefits from being mobile-friendly. For example, if you have a mobile-friendly shopping site, people will buy when they're on the go. If you have a mobile-friendly news site, people will read it when they're commuting to and from work. And if you have a mobile-friendly event-registration website, people will be able to sign up for your event anytime and anyplace!

We might be going overboard here; but honestly, you should think about whether there's any benefit to making your website iPhone and Android-compatible. Are tourists likely to reference your site while on vacation? It's far more likely that they'll be looking for local information using a mobile device than a desktop computer. Also, think about the scenarios where you use a mobile device; does this business/organization/individual's website fit into one of those scenarios. If you reach an impasse here and just can't decide, do a quick estimation of how much added time "going responsive" will take and present your client with a dollar figure. How long will it take to recoup that cost based on the perceived benefits of a mobile site?

Using the prior power company example, the financial benefit of a mobile site lies in the savings achieved by not having to have as large a call center answering calls that revolve around, "When will my power be back on?" Instead, folks can access that information themselves online. It's not hard to appreciate that such a website would pay for itself pretty quickly.

Other considerations

Screen size isn't the only limitation of a mobile device, however; bandwidth is also a concern. Despite the rapid pace of development in cell phone networks, they do still lag behind the fastest home and business connections available. Compound this with the issue of coverage being inconsistent in all areas, and you could find that some visitors are having to view your website at speeds that are much lower than what you originally planned for (most websites aren't designed with dial-up Internet access in mind these days).

There are a few really simple things you can do with speed in mind: serve up alternate, smaller images for mobile devices or eliminate some images altogether. But we're getting ahead of ourselves here!

What's next?

Making the decision early on in the process makes it easier on you, the developer, to produce a website that will work at a range of resolutions. You can opt to either design from the top down (highest resolution to lowest) or from the bottom up. We would argue that taking the bottom up approach is actually better because you've got the largest number of constraints in mind from the start.

Unfortunately, decisions aren't always made early on. We're going to continue with our project from the previous chapters; the difference is that now we've made the decision to produce a website that works on the following:

- desktop machines
- tablet devices
- mobile phones

We've made it this far, so we need to do just a little added legwork. For example, do we have to produce separate style sheets for each device, and do we have to produce separate websites for each device? There's really good news on this front: by making use of the "cascade" part of Cascading Style Sheets (that we discussed in our chapters on CSS), we can reuse the majority of the style information we've already got and override only those parts that we need to (like font sizes and margins).

So, we're already off to a good start on this front. Thus far, all of our development work has been specified in proportional units (ems and %) instead of fixed units (pixels). This means, in its current form, the Summer Smash 2012 website will scale somewhat. Check out Figure 7-1 to see how we're currently doing on a 320 by 480 display. It's definitely legible, but we can do better. Had we used fixed units, things could be way worse though.

Figure 7-2 shows the same website implemented using fixed widths and pixel sizes for text. Note that we'd have to scroll to the right to see the rest of the site.

Introducing the @media query

We talk a lot about the old days, and we'll just take one more step back. Detecting specific browsers or devices isn't a new idea; in fact, during the browser wars of the 90s, it was considered an almost essential survival tool. If you wanted to do anything other than display a simple, table-based page, you were left using JavaScript to sniff out which *useragent* (i.e., which web browser) was accessing your page.

Useragent sniffing isn't a foolproof way of operating, though. It's really easy to spoof a specific useragent, and it actually became common practice because some websites would shut out or deny access to you if you weren't using their preferred browser (e.g., Internet Explorer or Netscape Navigator). As a result, you

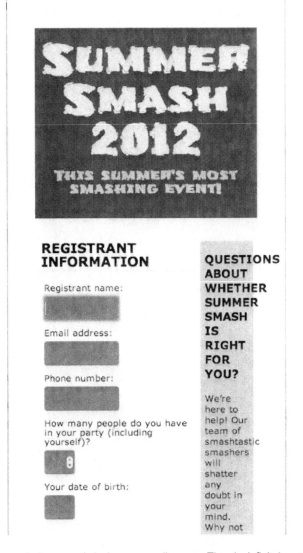

Figure 7-1. This is how our website currently looks on a small screen. There's definitely some room for improvement in our margins and in the sizes of things!

just can't trust the self-reporting that goes on. Think of it this way: you're familiar with those stickers that say "Hello, my name is" where a person writes in his name. How can you be sure that this person wrote in his real name? And how do you know that the Reillys aren't impersonating the Parkers (by the way, this can be a really fun thing to do, depending on the situation!).

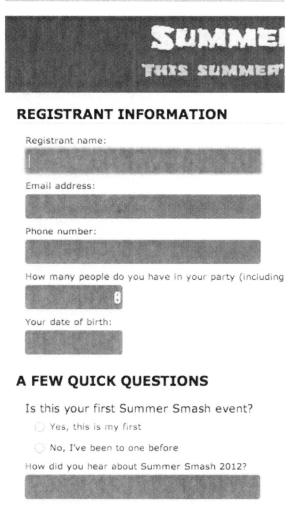

Figure 7-2. Things could be far more dire—if we hadn't used proportional units in our original design, this is what we'd be looking at right now.

Thus it would be better to be able to sort things out based on certain characteristics instead of a name. Similarly, it would be better to look for a 480 by 320 screen instead of the following:

```
Mozilla/5.0 (iPhone; CPU iPhone OS 5_0_1 like Mac OS X) AppleWebKit/534.46 (KHTML, like
Gecko) Version/5.1 Mobile/9A405 Safari/7534.48.3
```

That's where the @media query comes in; it lets you specify one or more properties of the target device in order to apply one or more rules specifically to that device.

In our case, we're looking specifically at the screen medium (we can also use media queries to specify print styles). We also want to target specific *breakpoints*; that is, we want to identify certain resolutions where we're likely to be transitioning from one device to another. This will enable us to make our site display perfectly on each of the three devices that we've identified:

```
@media screen and (max-width: 520px) {
  ...
}
```

This little snippet says that, for any screen with a width up to 520 pixels wide, we need to apply the rules that follow. This rule targets all of our small-scale devices, but not tablets—those devices start at resolutions higher than that.

Adding phone-specific rules

Let's jump right in and add a few phone-specific rules to our style sheet:

```
@media screen and (max-width: 520px){
  div#pagewrap {
    width: 100 %;
    margin: 0;
  }
  header {
    padding: 0.5em;
  }
  header h1 {
    font-size: 1.5em;
  }
  header p {
    font-size: 0.7em;
    font-family: Verdana, Arial, sans-serif;
    font-weight: bold;
  }
}
```

There are a few tweaks, here. First, the page takes up the entire screen width. There's no reason to narrow it down and center it on such a small screen, so we've set the width to 100 % and removed the margins. We've also decreased the padding on the header and shrunk the header text down a bit. At 0.7em, the tagline is a bit difficult to read in the Frijole font-face, so we've also changed the font to Verdana (but still made it bold). Our header is looking pretty good now (see Figure 7-3); however, our content still needs some work:

```
section#registration_form{
  float:none;
  width: 100 %;
}
aside{
  float:none;
    width: 100 %;
}
```

Figure 7-3. We've cleaned up the size and padding on our header and made our layout use the entire width of the screen.

We've removed the floats here and placed our content in a more linear format. Small screens aren't too conducive to having multiple columns of text, so we've also taken out our sidebar and placed it after our registration form. We've got things looking acceptable now, but let's do a few more tweaks to improve readability and make the best use of the little screen real estate we have. Here's the completed media query for this screen width (see Figure 7-4).

```
@media screen and (max-width: 520px){
  div#pagewrap {
    width: 100 %;
    margin: 0;
  }
  header {
    padding: 0.5em;
  }
  header h1 {
    font-size: 1.5em;
  }
  header p {
    font-size: 0.7em;
    font-family: Verdana, Arial, sans-serif;
    font-weight: bold;
  }
  section#registration_form {
    float: none;
    width: 100 %;
    margin-bottom: 1em;
  }
```

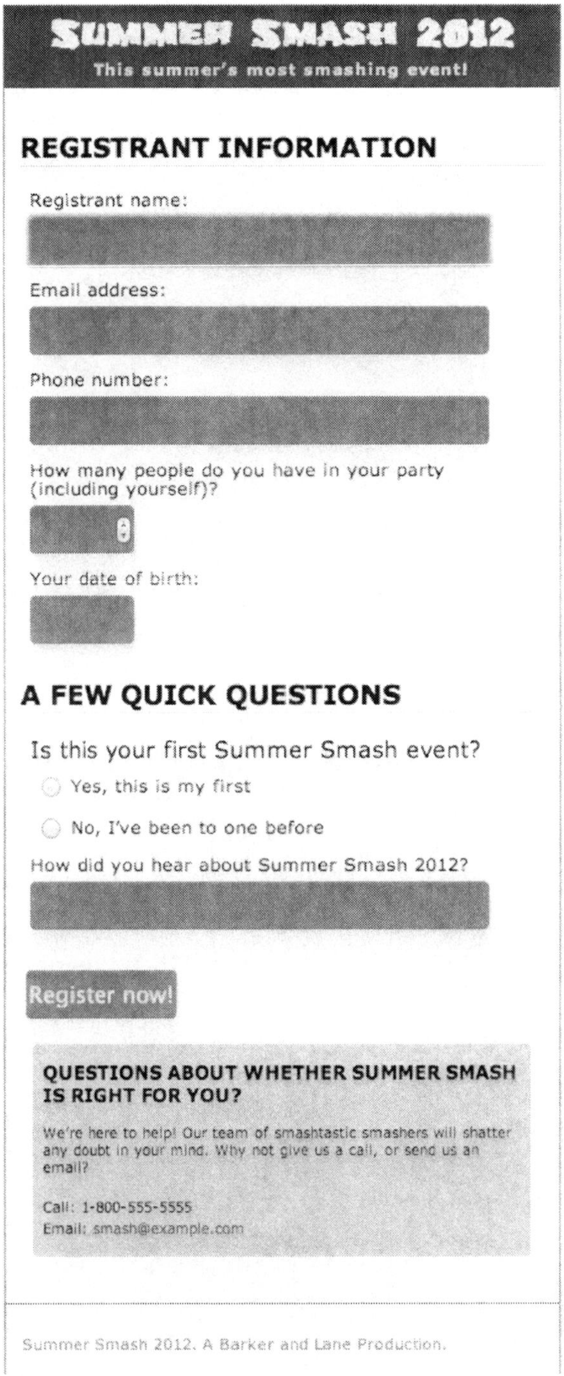

Figure 7-4. Our completed smartphone-friendly layout. The most notable changes: We've moved our sidebar down below our registration form and gone to a one-column layout.

```
  aside {
    float: none;
    width: 90 %;
    font-size: 0.8em;
    margin: 0 auto;
  }
 input[type ="text"], input[type ="tel"], input[type ="email"]{
    width: 90 %;
  }
  footer {
    font-family: Verdana, Arial, sans-serif;
    font-size: 0.7em;
  }
}
```

Because we're using max-width, testing is really easy. We can just resize our browser window down to view our narrow version, and then resize it up to see it snap back to our regular layout. That's not to say that we shouldn't also test it on iPhones/Android phones, especially if we've got some advanced formatting, or we're using complex JavaScript. But a simple browser resize is just fine to help us check over things quickly.

Adding tablet-specific rules

We've got one more stop to make on the road to device nirvana—let's see how things would look on a tablet screen (like an iPad). Whereas our phones have a maximum width of 520 pixels, our tablets have a maximum width of around 768 pixels (and really, on anything wider than that our site just looks normal). So let's give our window a quick resize and see how we're looking at 768 pixels, as seen in Figure 7-5.

All in all, it's not too bad. There are a few issues we want to address here, though. For example, let's reduce the whitespace around the header a bit and clean up that sidebar. We can also widen the form fields a bit. To do this, we'll create an @media query that looks for a max-width of 768px and... hey, wait a minute! If we're looking at a max-width of 768px, won't anything written here also apply to our smaller-screen devices?

Yes, absolutely! What we want to do here is make these style declarations above our 520 media query in the style sheet, so that any declarations we make in that @media query will override the declarations in the 768 media query. We can also take advantage of this to simplify things. For example, we can move our form field's width declaration up (and a few other things):

```
@media screen and (max-width: 768px){
  div#pagewrap {
    width: 95 %;
    margin: 1em auto;
  }
  aside {
    font-size: 0.8em;
  }
 input[type ="text"], input[type ="tel"], input[type ="email"]{
    width: 90 %;
  }
}
```

Figure 7-5. The current state of affairs on tablet devices. It's definitely not too dire, but there are still some things we can clean up here to make it look great on a medium-sized screen.

In the preceding snippet, we've widened the page, reduced the margins, and decreased the size of the sidebar a bit (this rule was moved from our 520 media query). Now our page looks as it does in Figure 7-6. At smaller screen sizes, everything still looks as it did before, but we've prevented duplication in our rules.

Pulling it all together

Here's our completed source code:

```
/* Tablet styles */
@media screen and (max-width: 768px){
  div#pagewrap {
    width: 95 %;
    margin: 1em auto;
  }
```

REGISTRANT INFORMATION

Registrant name:

Email address:

Phone number:

How many people do you have in your party (including yourself)?

QUESTIONS ABOUT WHETHER SUMMER SMASH IS RIGHT FOR YOU?

We're here to help! Our team of smashtastic smashers will shatter any doubt in your mind. Why not give us a call, or send us an email?

Call: 1-800-555-5555
Email: smash@example.com

Figure 7-6. Our tablet-friendly view

```
aside {
   font-size: 0.8em;
}
input[type ="text"], input[type ="tel"], input[type ="email"]{
   width: 90 %;
   }
}
/*Phone-speci ficstyles*/
@media screen and (max-width: 520px){
  div#pagewrap {
    width: 100 %;
    margin: 0;
  }
  header {
    padding: 0.5em;
  }
  header h1 {
    font-size: 1.5em;
  }
  header p {
    font-size: 0.7em;
    font-family: Verdana, Arial, sans-serif;
    font-weight: bold;
  }
```

```
section#registration_form {
  float: none;
  width: 100 %;
  margin-bottom: 1em;
}
aside {
  float: none;
  width: 90 %;
  margin: 0 auto;
}
footer {
  font-family: Verdana, Arial, sans-serif;
  font-size: 0.7em;
}
}
```

Summary

Using the cascade in CSS has allowed us to progressively enhance our site and offer a range of display formats to a range of devices. Because styles can be globally applied, and then overridden based on screen-sizing criteria that we specify, we can avoid doing a lot of extra work and duplicating style sheets for different versions.

It's important to identify what device(s) we're targeting early in the process and to start at the bottom (the smallest device). Also, we should use proportional units instead of absolute units and identify the maximum-width breakpoints where we need to tweak the display for a particular device. Next, we need to optimize our design for the device. A two column layout isn't the best plan for a smartphone, whereas a single column of text is just too much for a widescreen display. We need to plan accordingly.

Chapter 8

JavaScript Primer

In this chapter, we will start to talk about JavaScript and programming in general. Along the way, we will explore the building blocks of programming logic as they exist in JavaScript. But before we do this, let's look back at the history of JavaScript, so as to get the full context of what has gone before and to see the bigger picture of the major events that have shaped the modern landscape of JavaScript.

Since the goal of this chapter is to give an introduction to JavaScript, you can skip this chapter if you already have a passing knowledge of JavaScript. You can also skip it if you know what variables are or how to construct a conditional statement or loop. On the other hand, you should definitely read this chapter if you've ever edited someone else's code, but weren't sure about what it did, line for line. This chapter will help you ensure you are well versed in the basics of the language.

What is JavaScript?

JavaScript is the scripting language of the Web. It is embedded in our HTML pages, executed by an interpreter that is built into the browser, and has access to all of the HTML elements on the page. As such, we can use it to add interactivity to our pages. We can also use it to load and parse information from external sources or even from our end users. Modern JavaScript is sleek, nuanced, and an integral part of any web developer's skill set.

A brief history of JavaScript

Before we dig into the specifics of JavaScript, let's look back a little on the history of the language and how its usage has evolved over time (see Figure 8-1).

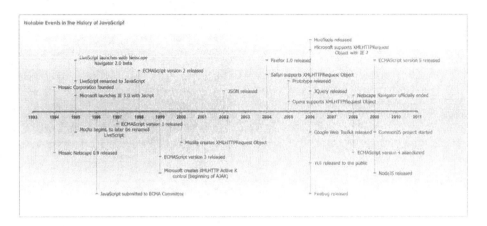

Figure 8-1. Notable events in the history of JavaScript

Early history

Brendan Eich created JavaScript while working at Netscape. The language was intended to serve as the glue language of the company's browser, so he added scripting capabilities to the front-end. By his own account[1] he was recruited to work at Netscape with the intent of implementing a Scheme interpreter in the browser. The language was initially codenamed Mocha, then called LiveScript when it was first released in Netscape version 2.0 beta. Finally, it was renamed to JavaScript in 1995 with the release of Netscape Navigator version 2.0B3.

Keep in mind that it was a different world in 1995. The two main browsers on the market were Netscape Navigator and Internet Explorer. Internet Explorer was not yet integrated into the operating system, and neither browser was free, let alone open source.

JavaScript was clearly well received because within a year it was reverse-engineered, rebranded as JScript, and included in Internet Explorer along with what Microsoft hoped would be a direct competitor to the JavaScript language: VBScript.

As a side note: While VBScript went on to have success in other domains—as the language of choice for ASP and as the glue language within Microsoft Office products—it was never embraced by the web development community as a client-side scripting language. This was mainly because only IE supported it, while JavaScript was supported in every browser (even if it was sometimes, unfortunately, called JScript).

It was in this climate—and perhaps partly as a result of the attempt to dilute the brand—that Netscape submitted JavaScript to the ECMA Committee (later to be known as Ecma International) to be standardized as ECMAScript.

---

[1] http://brendaneich.com/2008/04/popularity/

For context, Ecma International is a non-profit international standards organization. ECMA is an acronym that stands for European Computer Manufacturers Association. Ecma International is also responsible for many other standards, including the C# language specification, the FAT file system, and the Eiffel language.

Modern JavaScript

In this way, JavaScript continued to grow in adoption and popularity in tandem with the expansion and growth of the Web and the refinements of the browsing experience. ECMA continued to release new updates to the standard, and the browsers themselves added their own improvements via localized dialects.

Easily the most notable localized improvement was the XMLHttpRequest object (XHR), which led to the innovation of Ajax (Asynchronous JavaScript and XML). Interestingly, XHR started life as an ActiveX Control in IE 5 before being adopted as a JavaScript object in localized browser dialects.

With the introduction of XHR, web developers could finally, from the client-side, send data to or receive data from a web server either synchronously or asynchronously. This innovation expanded the scope of what could be done with web applications, but it also increased the complexity of web development in general.

To keep up with the higher level of demands that this new complexity put on their products, the browser makers—of which there were many more of by now—were putting considerable effort into refining and streamlining their own proprietary JavaScript interpreters (or JavaScript engines, as they are sometimes called). As of this writing, there are five mainstream JavaScript engines:

- Nitro for Safari
- V8 for Chrome
- SpiderMonkey for Firefox
- Carakan for Opera
- Chakra for IE

With all of this increased complexity, both in the capabilities of the technology as well as the potential for efficiency in the browsers, web developers also had to level up their own skills. Think about it: it was now possible to load new content into a page at run time, but this introduced new issues. What happens to the current state of all the information currently stored on the page when it is updated or replaced with the new content? If the new content is loaded asynchronously, what is the state of the page while you're waiting for the data? What happens if the data never loads? And will the new data stomp all over the existing data?

With the greater demand for code craftsmanship in web development, the best parts of the language were being mainstreamed, and the flaws were getting workarounds.

And while web developers were getting more and more adept at using the intricacies of JavaScript, they were also developing frameworks and libraries to speed up development and take care of the lower level functionality. Prototype, JQuery, and a host of other JavaScript frameworks emerged. Each allowed web developers to achieve more and do it faster, but at the cost of learning a new way to do things.

That brings us to the current day. There continues to be new innovation with JavaScript, most recently with frameworks such as Jasmine and QUnit to facilitate unit testing for test driven development (TDD), which we will get to in Chapter 10. You can also see this innovation in new frameworks such as Node.js, which enables server-side development in JavaScript.

JavaScript the basics

OK, now that we have the full context for how JavaScript came to be, let's start exploring the fundamentals of the language.

Code placement

JavaScript can be included in a document either by placing script tags inline in the document or by linking to an external JavaScript document. Whichever way you choose to include your JavaScript, it can only be included either in the head or body section of the page.

Inline JavaScript looks something like this:

```
<script>
//some javascript here ...
</script>
```

When including JavaScript externally, you put the URL to the external file in the src attribute of the script tag and set the type to "text/javascript" so that the browser knows how to interpret the new data being loaded in:

```
<script src="[url to external js file]" type="text/javascript"></script>
```

The external file should be named with a .js extension and have just pure JavaScript in it, without any script tags or any HTML tags at all.

How you include your JavaScript is up to you. You may choose to include JavaScript externally to share core functionality across your entire web application. But doing that means that the browser must make an HTTP call for each file included. This can increase the amount of time needed to load the JavaScript. You may choose to include all of your JavaScript inline on your page to reduce the amount of HTTP calls, but doing this will increase the overall size of the page that your browser has to download and interpret. There is no single right answer; it's up to you to determine what is best for the functionality of your web application, how large your pages are, and what your target audience is using to access your site.

> *Tip: It is sometimes useful to have all of your JavaScript loaded at the bottom of the page. This is because the browser interprets the page top down. Putting the external scripts at the bottom allows the page be rendered to the end user first, before it begins interpreting the JavaScript. This creates the perception of a faster loading page. If you do this, however, make sure that nothing on the page is dependent on objects in JavaScript being present on page load.*

Code execution

Code placed at the root level of the `script` tag or at the root level of the JavaScript document will execute as soon as it is loaded. The only way to delay this execution is to wrap the code in a function, since a function will not run until it is invoked:

```
<script>
// this will run as soon as it is read by the browser
var userMessage="hello, world!";

//this will run only when it is invoked
functioninitialize(){
 var msg = "hi there";
}
</script>
```

Commenting your code

The preceding example includes lines beginning with two forward slashes. These lines are commented out. Comments are lines in your code that are not executed by the interpreter. Usually you put comments in your code to leave notes about the code, for yourself and for whoever is going to read the code after you.

There are two kinds of comments in JavaScript: single line comments and multiline comments.

Single line comments begin with two forward slashes. Anywhere you insert these two forward slashes begins a comment, and the interpreter will ignore everything that follows them until it hits a new line. The following snippet shows valid examples of single line comments:

```
<script>
// this is a comment

var tempData = "" // this is a comment, probably about tempData
function initialize(){ // this is a comment, probably about the initialize function

}
</script>
```

Multiline comments begin with a forward slash and an asterisk (/*), and they end with an asterisk and another forward slash (*/). Anything between the opening and closing of the comment is ignored by the interpreter. What follows is an example of a multiline comment:

```
<script>
/*
 this is a multiline comment
 used to denote blocks of
 comments across multiple lines
*/
</script>
```

Why would you want to comment your code? Commenting your code makes it more readable, in that you and others can easily tell what is happening on the page. This will benefit you when you return to the code after days, months, or even years of working on other things. It will also help the next developer that takes on your code. This second part is very important; the world is becoming increasingly smaller, and the reputation that you build in your peer community around the code that you leave for the next person to pick up can have an impact on you in the future. There are many ways to make your code readable, and commenting is just one of them. We will point out additional ways to make your code more readable as you progress through the book.

Expressions, white space, semicolons, and minification

Every language, including spoken and written languages, has syntax. Merriam Webster[2] defines *syntax* as follows:

> *the way in which linguistic elements (as words) are put together to form constituents (as phrases or clauses).*

To apply this to JavaScript, sentences are called expressions. Expressions are composed of keywords, variables, and values.

Keywords, or reserved words, are words that have special meaning in the language because they are used to define the native functionality. *Variables*, which we will explore in much more detail very soon, are words that we create to hold data, or *values*.

Expressions end in semicolons, and words in expressions are separated by white space. The following snippet shows several examples of expressions:

```
<script>
var expressionExample = "";

sum = 421 + 42;
var anonFunction = function(){
 //some functionality
};
</script>
```

Expressions also evaluate to values.

> **Tip:** *The JavaScript interpreter ignores unneeded white space (spaces, tabs, and new line characters), so you can reduce the size of your JavaScript files by minifying them. Minification removes the unneeded white space, as well as comments, from your code. A couple of popular minification tools are JSMin* (http://crockford. com/javascript/jsmin) *and YUI Compressor* (http://developer.yahoo.com/yui/ compressor).

Variables

Variables are blocks of memory that you can assign a name to. You use them to store, update, and retrieve data. Think of it like this: your computer—or phone or device or whatever—has a finite amount of resident memory. Resident memory is RAM, and it loads up and is available for storage at run time. The browser

---

[2] www.merriam-webster.com/dictionary/syntax

you have running has a footprint in resident memory, and this is the amount of memory the browser takes up and has allocated for its usage. When you create variables in your code, the browser—via the JavaScript interpreter—allocates a chunk of memory from this footprint and gives it the name that you assigned to it, allowing you to use that chunk of memory (see Figure 8-2).

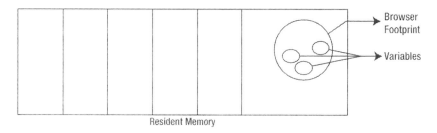

Figure 8-2. Resident memory

You create variables in JavaScript using the var keyword:

```
<script>
var newVariable = "";
</script>
```

When creating multiple variables, you can queue their initialization up in one expression, separated by commas. This saves you the trouble of typing var over and over again, and it reduces the amount of characters in your JavaScript files. Consider the following example:

```
<script>
// this is grossly inefficient, 30 characters in total not counting new lines
var a = 1;
var b = 2;
var c = 3;

// this is more streamlined, minified it only takes 16 characters, 53% the size of the ➡
  above example
vara=1,b=2,c=3;

/* this makes it more readable, and if you automate minification before releasing to ➡
  production you still get the improvement from the above example*/
var a = 1,
  b = 2,
  c = 3;
</script>
```

You use variables to store data that you can evaluate and execute on, but what kind of data can you store in variables? JavaScript supports several data types, including String, Number, Boolean, Undefined, and Array. It also supports function and object datatypes. Let's take a look closer look at each of these datatypes.

The String data type is any alphanumeric character surrounded by single or double quotes:

```
<script>
var myString = "this is a string";
</script>
```

The Number data type is any numeric value, including negative numbers, zero, and floating point numbers:

```
<script>
var myNumber = 34;
</script>
```

The Boolean data type is named after a 19th century mathematician and philosopher who was also one of the founding fathers of computer science: George Boole. It represents the value of either true or false.

```
<script>
var myBool = true;
</script>
```

The Undefined data type is used to represent a variable that has been named, but has had no data assigned to it. It is the lack of data type.

The Array data type indicates that the variable contains an array. Arrays are vector data types in that they contain multiple values. Since JavaScript is a loosely typed language, you can store data of any type in an array, even other arrays. When arrays contain other arrays, they are considered multidimensional arrays.

You instantiate a new array either by using the Array constructor or by simply assigning data to a variable in array format; that is, to a variable wrapped in square brackets with a comma separating each value:

```
<script>
var first_list = new Array(); // using array constructor
var second_list = [583, 103, 902]; // assigning value implicitly creates a new array
var multidim_list = [ [34, 21, 10] , [88, 310, 34] ]; // a multidimensional array, an array
➡ of arrays
</script>
```

You retrieve and set values from arrays via their index number, which is the number in sequential order that they are stored in. Note that all arrays are zero-based, in that the number ordering for arrays starts at zero.

```
<script>
var ind = second_list[0]; // retrieves 583 from the array and stores it in ind
second_list[2] = 20; // overwrites the previous value with 20
</script>
```

The other data types that JavaScript supports are functions and objects, both of which we will talk about at length next.

Data types define the kinds of data that you can store in variables, but JavaScript is a loosely typed language (another term for this is *weakly typed language*). This means that, when you declare a variable and assign data of one type to it, you can then go and assign data of a completely different type to that same variable. The example that follows is perfectly valid JavaScript:

```
<script>
var userName = "tom@tom-barker.com";

userName = 21; // userName was a string, now it's a number
//the below code shows that arrays can hold data of different types
var myCollection = [23, "test data", true, true, false, -120, [20, "user@tom-barker.com"]];
</script>
```

This approach is in contrast to languages that are strictly typed (another term for this is *strongly typed*). With strictly typed languages, you must declare the data type of a variable when you create it, and that variable can only hold that type of data.

This has implications for how you can safely code. With loosely typed languages, you don't need to cast (i.e., convert) your variables to different types, and your arrays are much more flexible. But with loosely typed languages, you can never assume you know what the data type of your variable is.

JavaScript has the typeof operator, which allows you to inspect a variable to see what data type it contains:

```
<script>
var myVar = "";
alert(typeofmyVar);
</script>
```

Now that we know what variables and expressions are, let's look at how we can take action on variables to create more complex expressions.

Conditionals and operators

You can control the flow of logic in your applications by testing the value in your variables or testing what expressions evaluate to. You perform these tests in conditional statements. JavaScript supports the following conditional statements: if, else, and else if.

Using conditional statements

You structure if -else statements like this:

```
if([somecondi tiontotest]  ){
    //execute this block if condition evaluates to true
}else{
    //execute this block if condition evaluates to false
}
```

You may also follow an if with an else if; such a statement would be structured like this:

```
if([somecondition]  ){
}elseif ([somedifferentcondition]  ){
    //execute this block if the second condition is true
}
```

The preceding examples use the if keyword to test a condition; that condition is wrapped in parentheses. Conditions usually evaluate a variable, and they might test an upper limit of a list, check whether a variable contains the expected type of data, or examine something similar. Curly braces surround blocks of code, which are just groups of expressions, as shown in the following example:

```
<script>
var userName = "tom@tom-barker.com",
 passWord = "test123";
if(passWord.length > 0){ //if the variable has data in it
    submitCredentials();
```

```
}else{ //if the data does not have data in it
    promptForCredentials();
}
</script>
```

The preceding example is ludicrously simplistic, but with it we can start to see how the concepts we've learned so far work together. We create two variables, and then we test that one of the variables—the password—has data in it. If it does, then we submit the variable for further execution. If it doesn't, then we prompt the user to enter new credentials.

This technique controls the flow of logic with a conditional statement.

Using operators

You use operators to test conditions. JavaScript supports the following operators: comparison, arithmetic, assignment, logical, and ternary. The upcoming sections examine these operators in greater depth:

Comparison operators

`==`	This is the equality operator; it tests whether values on either side of it are equal. This operator tests the values, but not the data types:
	
	`if ( sum == 10){`
	
	`}`

`===`	This is the strict equality operator; it tests whether both the values and the data types on either side of the operator are equal:
	
	`if(sum==="10"){`
	`  // this is only true if sum is a string`
	`  // that is equal to "10"`
	`}`

`!=`	This is the inequality operator.
`!==`	This is the strict inequality operator.
`<=, <, >, >=`	These operators are less than, less than or equal to, greater than, and greater than or equal to, respectively.

Arithmetic operators

+	When used on numbers, this is the addition operator:
	
	`var sum = 45 + 19;`
	
	When used on strings, this becomes the concatenation operator, joining together two or more strings into a single string:
	
	`varusername="tom@tom-barker.com";`
	`var msg = "Welcome, " + username; //produces Welcome, tom@tom-barker.com`
	
	Note that when this is used on a combination of strings and numbers, the numbers get converted to strings and string concatenation is performed, instead of numeric addition.

-	This is the subtraction operator.
/	This is the division operator.
*	This is the multiplication operator.

++	This is the increment operator; it adds one to the value that it is used on:
	
	`varrunningTotal=1;`
	
	`runningTotal++; //now contains 2`

--	This is the decrement operator; it subtracts one from the value that it is used on.
%	This is the modulus operator. When used with two numbers, it performs division and returns the remainder of that calculation. This is most useful when programmatically drawing out a grid or when figuring out alternating rows. • In the case of drawing a grid, when iterating you simply get the modulus of the current iteration and the number of columns in the row. When the modulus is zero, you start a new row. • In the case of alternating rows, you do the same as above, but you get the modulus of the current iteration and learn whether the current row is an odd or even row number. We will talk more about iterations soon.

Assignment operators

=	This is the assignment operator; it is used to assign value to variables.

+=, -=, *=, /=	These operators are all shorthand to perform arithmetic and assign values at the same time:
	
	`sum += 3; // adds 3 to the value of sum`
	`diff -= 1; // subtracts 1 from the value of diff`
	`prod *= 2; // multiplies the value of prod by 2`

Logical operators

&&	This is the logical AND operator. This groups together two or more conditions, and all must equate to `true` for the overall aggregate to equate to `true`:
	
	`if((x >0) && (x <=10)){`
	`    // x must be both greater than 0 and less`
	`    // than or equal to 10 in order for`
	`    // this condition to be true`
	`}`

||	This is the logical OR operator. Like the logical AND operator, this groups together two or more conditions, but only one of the conditions must be `true` for the overall aggregate to equate to `true`.
!	This is the logical NOT operator. This tests the inverse of what is in the condition: `if !(x < 10){} // this is true if x is not less than 10`

Ternary operator

You can use a ternary operator to replace an `if else` statement. This is eminently less readable, but will use fewer characters, which technically will equate to a smaller byte size for your JavaScript files. The trade off is up to you and the standards that you adopt in your organization.

The ternary operator is ? : and is structured like this:

`[condition to evaluate] ? [if condition is true] : [if condition is false]`

The ternary operator returns a value, so it can be used in variable assignment. Consider the following code example, which creates three variables:

- A maximum amount

- A random amount up to that maximum amount

- A string to demonstrate if the random amount is above or below the midpoint to the maximum amount:

The ternary operator code looks like this:

```
<script>
var ceiling = 100,
 random = Math.random()*ceiling,
 returnValue = (random <= (ceiling / 2)) ? "less than halfway there" : "over halfway there";
alert(random + " " + returnValue);
</script>
```

Iterations

So far we've learned to create expressions by declaring variables, assigning values to them, and testing them with operators and conditional statements. But let's say we want to repeat the same expression or group of expressions multiple times, or step programmatically through each index in an array—this is when we need to use loops, which also called *iteration statements*.

JavaScript supports several types of loops; the first loop type we'll talk about is the for loop.

The for loop is composed of three parts:

- the initializer
- the condition
- the incrementor

Each part is separated by a semicolon, and all three are wrapped in parentheses and preceded by the for keyword. The block of expressions that you wish to repeat is wrapped in curly braces. Its structure looks like this:

```
for ([initializer] ; [condition] ; [incrementor]) {
    // block of expressions to repeat
}
```

Each part of the for loop does exactly what it sounds like it does:

- The *initializer* initializes a variable.
- The *condition* tests a condition—presumably the variable and the loop will continue to iterate as long as the condition is true.
- The *incrementor* increments the variable.

The general idea is to increment (or decrement) the variable to eventually make the condition no longer equate to true, so that the loop eventually ends (see Figure 8-3).

If you play with each part, you can test the boundaries of what the language will support with for loops. For example, you might try declaring and testing multiple variables. You might also try initializing your variable to a high value and then decrementing it to make a countdown, and so on.

Now just mechanically repeating the same thing over and over again is only so useful. It's the fact that the incrementor changes the value each step through the loop (and we can access its value) that makes the loop so much more interesting.

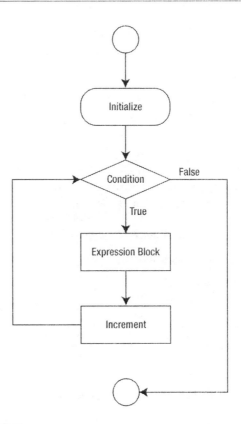

Figure 8-3. Implementing a for loop

Let's say you want to step through each index in an array. To do so, simply use the iterator variable as the index, as in this example:

```
<script>
var my_list = [20, 1003, 394, 2];
for (var x = 0; x < my_list.length; x++){
    alert(my_list[x]); // using x as the index number
}
</script>
```

JavaScript also supports the while loop, which is structured like this:

```
while([condition]){
    //block of code to execute
}
```

It also supports the do while, which is structured like this:

```
do{
}while([condition])
```

A word of caution: The `for` loop declares an iterator that you test against to end your loop, but the `while` and `do while` loops have no such iterator. You must keep track of what you are testing in the condition and make sure this test will eventually evaluate to false; otherwise, your loop will never end (that is, it will become an *infinite loop*). An infinite loop will cause your application to fail, and most likely cause your browser to crash (more modern browsers have begun to wise up to this issue, and may give the user a chance to kill code that is taking too long to run).

Though they technically do the same thing—repeat a set number of times—the `for` loop and the `while` loop are philosophically different. Since the `for` loop has its termination built in, it is best suited for iterating over a known quantity like an array or properties in an object. The `while` loop has no built-in terminator, so it will continue to loop while its test condition is `true`. Therefore, it is best saved for things like a game engine loop where the status is maintained in the loop until user or system events fire to update the status, thus stopping the loop.

Summary

In this chapter, we explored the history of JavaScript and talked about some of the events that shaped and influenced its rise in popularity and complexity. We also dipped our toes into the basics of the language, from creating variables to testing conditions and looping.

These are the building blocks of programming logic. In the next chapter, we will take these concepts and begin to think abstractly in JavaScript with them, using metaphorical concepts like objects and functions—and even delving into the beautiful world of functions as first-class objects.

Chapter 9

A Deeper Dive Into JavaScript

Now that we can construct more complex logic with loops and conditional statements, let's take our knowledge of JavaScript to the next level.

In this chapter, we'll cover some of the more advanced concepts in JavaScript. For example, we'll look at object-oriented design—from the strategy of *why* you would use objects to the tactics of *how* you would use them. Understanding object-oriented design is a vital skillset that will apply to most other languages that you will learn.

We'll also learn about functions, from introductory concepts such as how to construct a function to advanced concepts like lambda calculus, or the art of using functions as variables. Using functions as variables is a key concept in functional programming, which is a very fluid and extensible programming philosophy that is embodied in other languages like Scala, Clojure, and Lisp.

Next, we'll talk about events, the glue that allows your code to react to actions taken by the user. And finally, we'll look at interacting with the DOM—the API that the browser exposes to JavaScript to interact with HTML elements on the page—and tying everything that we've learned so far into a comprehensive example.

Philosophy of object-oriented design

When talking about objects, the first question we need to address is this: what are objects? At an abstract level, objects are metaphors that represent ideas.

Maybe these are metaphors for high-level business concepts like the idea of a user of a system. Or perhaps these are metaphors for the parts of a system, like a directory watcher. Whatever idea they represent, objects should encompass everything about the concept, including what defines the idea (values of properties) and what the concept does (methods of the object).

For example, if an object represents a user, then the *properties* of the user are things that define the user. Consider what happens when you fill out a registration form online. You usually enter your name, email address, a password, and maybe your street address. These are all properties that define you in a given system.

Continuing with the same analogy, *methods* are actions that a user can make. In the case of an online shopping cart, a user could add an item to her cart. Or, a user could log in and out of the site. Those are all actions—represented by methods—that a user can take.

But at its most concrete level, an object is a collection of functions (i.e., methods in the context of objects) and variables (i.e., properties in the context of objects).

Why would we want to use objects? Objects allow us to encapsulate all of the information that pertains to a given idea in one neat and easy-to-understand variable. They allow us to construct the logic of our applications using the language and terminology of business cases.

In JavaScript, we can create objects a couple different ways:

- Using an object constructor

- Using object notation

Object constructor

The first way we will explore creating objects is with an object constructor. Object constructors are functions (and we will explore functions in much more depth in the next section) that accept parameters and populate the properties of the object with the passed in values. We *instantiate* new objects from object constructors with the new keyword:

```
<script>
  function user(fname, lname, emailaddress){
    this.firstname = fname;
    this.lastname = lname;
    this.email = emailaddress;
  }
  var tom = new user("tom", "barker", "tom@tom-barker.com")
</script>
```

In the preceding example, we created a new object constructor called user that accepted three parameters:

- first name (fname)

- last name (lname)

- email address (emailaddress)

Note that the property names are firstname, lastname, and email, yet the variables defined in the signature of the function are fname, lname, and emailaddress. This is because these are different variables. The properties are variables that are referenced through the object (user.firstname), but the variables in the signature are parameters, and we don't want to mix up the two. We will talk more about parameters later in the chapter.

The constructor took those passed in values and stored them in variables. Note that the variables are scoped using the this keyword. The this keyword exposes the variables as properties of the object; if we didn't use that keyword, we would not see the values stored when we create an object from the constructor.

To create a new object, we simply create a new variable. For example, we might create a tom object and assign to it the object constructor. This creates a new object named tom with its properties set to the values we pass into the constructor.

We can access the properties and methods of the object using dot notation. This means that we reference properties and methods like [object name].[object property]. So, for the preceding example, we could use this syntax to access the firstname property of the tom object:

```
<script>
log(tom.firstname);
</script>
```

But objects also have methods, so let's update this example to give the user object some actions to perform:

```
<script>
  function user(fname,lname, emailaddress){
    this.firstname = fname;
    this.lastname = lname;
    this.email = emailaddress;
    this.whoami = function(){
      alert(this.fname);
    };
  }
  var tom = new user("tom", "barker", "tom@tom-barker.com")
  tom.whoami();
</script>
```

In the preceding example, we added the whoami() method to the constructor—again, note that it is prefaced with the this keyword. Once again, we access the whoami() method via dot notation.

Object notation

Another way to create objects in JavaScript is with straight object notation. When creating an object via object notation, objects are wrapped in curly braces, and methods and properties are comma-separated name-value pairs. This is also called creating an *object literal*. To reproduce the preceding functionality with object notation, we would do the following:

```
<script>
var newuser = {
  firstname:"t om",
```

```
  lastname: "barker",
  email: "tom@tom-barker.com",
  whoami: function(){
    console.log(this)
  };
}
newuser.whoami();
</script>
```

Inheritance

You gain many benefits by using objects. Objects encapsulate all of the data and functionality associated with a given concept, which saves you the trouble of keeping track of and associating many disparate variables. This wraps all of the relevant information about a given subject and allows you to check and update that information in a single variable. It also allows you to reuse that aggregation and structure to create subclasses.

You can also create subclasses from existing classes that derive their functionality from the original object, but allow you to expand on that functionality for different use cases. This is called *inheritance*.

What does this mean, exactly? Let's take a closer look at the preceding example. We created a user object that contained the first name, last name, and email address of a user. The user object also had a method called whoami that output the object to the console (assuming Firebug is installed; learn more about Firebug in Chapter 10).

But let's say we want to create a special user—a super user—who can modify other users. We could create a new object called admin that is derived from the user object, as in this example:

```
<script>
  function user(fname,lname, emailaddress){
    this.firstname = fname;
    this.lastname = lname;
    this.email = emailaddress;
    this.whoami = function(){
      alert(this.fname);
    };
  }
  function admin(){
  //do some initialization here
  };
  admin.prototype = new user;
  admin.prototype.constructor = admin
  admin.prototype.editUser = function(usr){
    //update user properties or permissions
    console.log("editing properties of " + usr.firstname)
  };
  var su = new admin();
  su.whoami(); //shows object in object notation
  su.editUser(tom) // assumes that object tom from previous example exists

</script>
```

Now let's carefully walk through the preceding example.

First, we created a constructor function called admin. Note that we didn't include any parameters when we created the admin constructor. This is purely because, in this example, we just created a stub for the admin constructor; it has no real functionality in this case. However, depending on what we want it to do, we could pass in arguments that will initialize properties on startup, just as we did with the user constructor. We could then set the prototype of admin to be the user object.

This is a key part of the philosophy behind JavaScript: it is a prototype-based language. What this means at a tactical level is that objects can be linked together via their prototype property, forming a prototype chain. When you reference a method or a property of an object, and it doesn't explicitly have that property or method defined, it looks to its prototype property to see whether the object stored there has that property or method. And this searching up the chain continues until one of the objects has the property or method—or until JavaScript reaches the top of the chain, at the Object object. The Object object sits at the very top of the prototype chain, and it is the base object that all objects in JavaScript inherit from (see Figure 9-1).

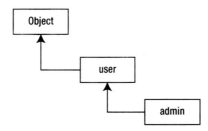

Figure 9-1. The JavaScript prototype chain

What that means for our example is that, by making the user object the prototype of the admin object, we can then call methods or properties of the user object from the admin object.

So, after we set the prototype of the admin object, we then set the constructor property of the admin object to be the admin constructor. Doing this ensures that any instances we create are of the admin type.

Next, we create a new method called editUser(). This method exists only in the admin object, not the user object. In this way, we have extended the user object to create a special user—admin—that has augmented functionality.

We can see this in action by calling the whoami() method of admin; which works the same way as the user object.

Functions

Functions are a way to meaningfully aggregate and name expressions. By giving a function a name, we can invoke the function by its name, and it will execute all of the expressions that it contains. Functions are structured as follows:

```
function [function name] (){
//expressions to execute
}
```

We can name functions just as we would name any other variable. For example, assume we wanted to have a function that messaged the user. We might make something like this:

```
<script>
functionmessa geUser(){
  alert("hello, world!");
}
</script>
```

This creates a function called messageUser. Every time we call the function, it pops open an alert with the string, "hello, world." We invoke the function by calling its name, followed by open and closed parentheses:

```
messageUser();
```

Parameters and arguments

By itself, this approach would only be so useful; however, we can also pass data in to be used by the function. When creating a function, we can allow for one or more arguments to be passed into the function. The data from these arguments are temporarily stored as parameters, which are local variables in a function that exist only as long as the function is running. It would be structured as follows:

```
<script>
functionmsgUs er(msg){
  // now do an alert, using the string passed in and stored in the parameter msg
  alert(msg);
}
msgUser("hello,world!");
</script>
```

When we invoke a function, we pass in data (one or more arguments) to be stored in the parameter(s). To be clear, when we call the function, the data being passed in is called the *argument*. When the function is defined, the local variable that is created to hold the passed in data is called the *parameter*.

So, in the preceding example, the msg variable in the function signature is the parameter, and the "hello, world" string is the argument being passed into the function.

Pardon the tangent—I'm sick of writing alerts! In real production code, we never pop open alerts to the end user. So, for the next example, let's create a log function. This will be a function to which we pass in a string, and it will write that string to a div on the page, followed by a line break. From this point on, all of our examples where we want to display data will use our log function. The log function assumes that a div with the id of log exists on the page:

```
<body>
<divid="log"> </div>
<script>
functionlog(m sg){
  document.getElementById("log").innerHTML += msg + "<br/>";
}
log("hello, world!"); // invoking the function, passing in the string hello, world
</script>
</body>
```

Return values

Functions also return values. In strictly typed languages, functions are declared with a return type. Even when there is no value returned, we would need to declare that as a void type. But since JavaScript is loosely typed, we don't have to worry about that.

We use the return keyword to exit the function with a returned value.

Return values allow functions to output the result of their processing. This output can be stored in variables or tested in conditions.

In the next example, we create two functions, one called sum and one called avg. The function called sum receives an array as a parameter, loops through the array, and adds up the values it contains (only if the value at a particular index is a number). Finally, it returns the total.

The function called avg also receives an array; calls the sum function passing in the array; stores the value returned from sum; and finally, returns that total from sum divided by the length of the array, which is the average value in the array:

```
<script>
functionsum(vals){
 var summed_value = 0;
 for(var x = 0; x < vals.length; x++){
   summed_value += vals[x];
}
return(summed_value);
}
functionavg(vals){
 var total = sum(vals);
 return(total / vals.length);
}
var test_scores = [90, 94, 88, 56, 100, 81];
var grade = avg(test_scores);
</script>
```

Note that using the return keyword does more than return a value; it also exits the function. If you load up your function with many different return paths—for example, if you have multiple if statements where each branch returns a different value—then you will have a harder time debugging your application. It's generally a best practice to have only one way to exit your functions. If you do have multiple if statements, you should set a variable in the body of the if statements and then return the variable after the if statements, as in this example:

```
<script>
functiondosomething(){
 var returnValue = 0;

if(somecondition){
   returnValue = 1;
}else{
   returnValue = 2;
}
```

```
 return returnValue;
}
</script>
```

Functions as first class objects

In the last chapter, we said that functions are a data type. That's a hugely important point to effectively use some of the more interesting features of JavaScript. While we can store return values from functions, those return values are of the type that is returned. In the preceding example, both sum and avg return numbers.

But we can also store the functions themselves in variables! This means that we can pass functions into other functions and return functions from functions. This is what is meant when we say that functions are first-class objects, and this opens up a huge amount of things that we can do with functions.

Again, consider the previous example with the avg and sum functions, but this time assume we will be a professor who wants to create a script to calculate semester grades based on input test scores. As a professor, we will want to change our business logic to drop the lowest grade from the semester, as in the following example:

```
<script>
var LOGIC_TO_USE = "adjusted",
 semester_data = {
 test_scores:[90, 94, 88, 56, 100, 81],
total:0,
grade:0
};
if(LOGIC_TO_USE === "adjusted"){
 avg(semester_data, sum_drop_lowest); // this will return average
 // based on dropping the lowest score
}else{
 avg(semester_data, sum); // this will return average of all test scores
}
log(semester_data.grade);
//this begins the engine that drives the business logic
functionsum(semester_object){
for(var x = 0; x < semester_object.test_scores.length; x++){
 if(typeof semester_object.test_scores[x] == "number"){
 semester_object.total += semester_object.test_scores[x];
}
}
return(semester_object);
}
function avg(semester_object, sum_function){
 semester_object = sum_function(semester_object);
 semester_object.grade = semester_object.total/ semester_object.test_scores.length;
return(semester_object);
}
```

```
functionsum_d rop_lowest(semester_object){
 semester_object.test_scores = semester_object.test_scores.sort(function(a,b){return a -
b});
 semester_object.test_scores = semester_object.test_scores.slice(1,↳
semester_obje ct.test_scores.length)
 for(var x = 0; x < semester_object.test_scores.length; x++){
  if(typeof semester_object.test_scores[x] == "number"){
  semester_object.total += semester_object.test_scores[x];
}
}
return(semest er_object);
}
</script>
```

OK, this is a fair bit of refactoring; however, don't be intimidated because we'll walk through the example a little at a time. First, we created an object to aggregate the semester data, so that we could pass it around and not have the functions dependent on each other. The semester object has test_scores, total, and grade as its properties. We can access these properties via dot notation, such as obj.grade and obj. total.

Next, we created three functions. We've already seen the function sum. In this case, we just updated the function to use the object that holds the array; instead of returning the sum, the function updates the total in the object and returns the object.

Next, we created a new function, sum_drop_lowest. This function takes the array of grades out of the object and sorts it. Notice that we pass a function into the sort method. Doing so makes JavaScript's native sort functionality call the passed function for each index and evaluate the index's values as parameters. This gives us a numerically sorted array. With this newly sorted array, we use the slice method to take a subsection of the array from the second to the last index (technically, it's index 1 because arrays are zero-based). This effectively drops the first value because that is the lowest grade. The function then returns the object.

And finally, we updated the avg function, which now accepts two parameters: the object and a function to sum the grades. Depending on what we pass into the avg function, it will do different things. If we pass in the regular sum function, it will work as it did before, giving us a result of 84.8; however, if we pass in the sum_drop_lowest function that drops the lowest grade, the avg function will give us a result of 90.6.

We created a variable called LOGIC_TO_USE that we will treat as a constant—the const keyword does exist, but it isn't yet supported by IE, so we'll continue to use var. Constants are variables that cannot have their value changed once they are declared. We test the value of this *faux* constant and pass in the appropriate function to the avg function.

Anonymous functions

JavaScript supports *anonymous functions*, which are functions that don't have assigned names. Anonymous functions can be assigned to variables, returned from functions (most likely to be stored in a variable), stored (in a property) as a callback function, or be a self-invoking function, usually to namespace variables on a page (see the next section).

Anonymous functions are typically formatted as follows:

```
function(){
//code to execute
}
```

When storing them in a variable, you would format them like this:

```
var func = function(){
  //code to execute
}
```

If you store the function in a variable (or property of an object, or pass around as a parameter), you can invoke the function using the variable name as if the function had a name, as in this example:

```
func();
```

When returning an anonymous function from a function, you would format it like this:

```
functionx(){
  return function(){
    //code in the returned anonymous function
  }
}
```

To store and execute a returned anonymous function in a variable, you would do the following:

```
functionretur nAnonFunc(){
  return function(){ // returned anonymous function
   alert("anonymous function!")
};
}
```

```
var f = returnAnonFunc(); // anonymous function stored in this variable
```

```
f(); //we can invoke the stored anonymous function
```

Self-invoking functions

Self-invoking functions are functions that are executed as soon as they are defined. They are formatted the same as any other anonymous function, except that they are followed by open and closed parentheses:

```
function(){
  //code to execute
}();
```

You might wonder why you would ever want to use a self-invoking function because code defined at the root level of the script tag automatically executes anyway. The answer: Such a function limits the scope of the variables and functions that you define. Let me explain:

A variable that is defined at the root of the script tag (or outside of a function or object) will be placed in the global scope; this is called a *global variable*. Such a variable is available everywhere in the current page, and it can be accessed by code in other script tags or code imported externally. Most importantly, a global variable can accidentally be overwritten by the code in other script tags, as well as by the code imported externally.

To demonstrate why this is dangerous, consider the following scenario.

Assume you have ad tags on your site that allow JavaScript to be included on your page from a third-party ad server. You have a function that you have written called `log()` that logs errors and other issues to your server for analysis. Your `log()` function exists at the global scope because you defined it at the root of a `script` tag on your page.

The ad code that is running on your page also has a `log()` function, which it uses to report back to the ad server that the ad has been displayed, so you can be paid for this ad view. The ad code's `log()` function also exists at the global scope.

If your code is loaded and interpreted first, then the ad code will overwrite your `log()` function when it is loaded, and you'll never get the messaging on your server for that page load. At the same time, you'll be making fraudulent ad calls to the ad server and that could have legal and financial repercussions for your company. If the ad code loads first, then you will overwrite it when your code loads, the ad impression will never be recorded, and you won't be paid by the ad company for that page load.

And if other functions or objects depend on the `log()` function, the repercussions could just ripple outward.

Fortunately, we have a work around for this: *namespacing.*

Variables that are defined within functions are locally scoped, which means that they exist only as long as the function is running and can only be accessed by code within the function. Once the function runs to completion, the variable is destroyed and the space in memory allocated to it is scheduled for garbage collection. This is called *local scope.*

However, through a concept called a *closure*, we can bind the locally declared variables and functions to a returned object, as in this example:

```
<script>
var myPage = function(){
  return {
    log : function(){
      //logs data to my server
    }
  };
}();
</script>
```

In the preceding example, we declared a variable called myPage. This variable holds the returned object from the anonymous function. This is our namespace, and it protects all of the functions and variables that we will write for our page or web application. To invoke the `log()` function (or any other function that we will namespace), we go through the myPage object, like so:

```
myPage.log();
```

If we want to take the preceding example a step further, we can create variables and functions inside the anonymous function (but not inside of the returned object), and these variable and functions will be accessible to the returned object, but not anywhere else:

```
<script>
var myPage = function(){
var runtime = "production"; //locally scoped
```

```
function _logtopage(msg){ //privately scoped
 //writes msg to page
}
function _logtoserver(msg){ //privately scoped
//sends msg to server
}
return{
  log : function(msg){
  if (runtime === "production"){
      _logtoserver(msg);
  }else{
      _logtopage(msg);
  }
}
};
}();
</script>
```

In this code snippet, we created a namespace called myPage that has an exposed log() method. The log() method will either send a message to the server or write to the page, depending on the value of the runtime variable.

This example illustrates how the runtime variable and the _logtopage() and _logtoserver() functions are locally scoped inside the anonymous function. However, they are accessible to the function inside the returned object. This is a closure, as described previously; it is the context that keeps the locally scoped variables available to the functions that were created in the same context—the anonymous function, in this example.

Events

Events are actions that occur during the lifetime of the page. These can be actions that the end user fires off by clicking a button or moving the mouse, or they can be caused by other DOM- or UI-related actions. They can also be actions that happen on the page (e.g., the document loading) or on the network (e.g., the HTTP status changing in an Ajax call). Chapter 10 discusses Ajax in greater depth.

JavaScript responds to events with *event handlers*, or functions that are called when an event is fired. Event handlers can be called by name or defined as function literals.

When binding an event to a DOM element—remember that the DOM is the API through which the browser allows JavaScript to access the HTML elements on the page—you can include the event handler in the DOM element referenced in the event attribute. It is structured like this:

```
<element [event attribute] = "[javascript function]"/>
```

A more specific example would involve adding the onmousemove event attribute to a div to fire an event every time the mouse moves over the div. That would look like this:

```
<div onmousemove = "trapMouse()"></div>
```

Now let's flesh this idea out with a longer and more involved example:

```
<body>
<div id="content" onmousemove="trapMouse(event)">
```

```
<p>Show the mouse location.</p>
<divid="log"> </div>
<script>
functiontrapM ouse(event){
  log("mouse X: " + event.clientX + " mouse Y: " + event.clientY)
}

functionlog(m sg){
  document.getElementById("log").innerHTML += msg + "<br/>";
}
</script>
</div>
</body>
```

In the preceding example, we added the onmousemove event attribute to the content div. The onmousemove event attribute points to the trapMouse() function. It passes in a reference to the event that was fired in the form of an event object.

The trapMouse() function receives the event object and calls our existing log() function, passing in a string that contains the x and y coordinates of the current mouse location.

The downside to using event attributes inline in your HTML is that you have now coupled your functionality with your presentation. To make your code more flexible, you can programmatically assign event handlers to elements.

The next example has two files. The first is an HTML file (chapter9_example.html) that contains only the layout of the page (see Listing 9-1), and the second is a JavaScript file (chpt9_engine.js) that contains the functionality; make sure that these files are in the same directory (see Listing 9-2).

Listing 9-1. The Page Layout File

```
<html>
<head></head>
<style>
#content{
  border:2px solid;
}
</style>
<body>
  <div id="content"></div>
  <div id="log"></div>
  <script src="chpt9_engine.js"></script>
</body>
</html>
```

Listing 9-2. The JavaScript File that Contains the Functionality

```
var myApp = function(){
  return{
    log:function(msg){
      document.getElementById("log").innerHTML += msg + "<br/>";
    },
```

```
    registerEventHandlers:function(){
      document.getElementById("content").onmousemove = function(){
        myApp.log("mouse moving!")
      }
    }
  };
}();
myApp.registerEventHandlers();
```

In the preceding example, we pulled together a lot of what we've been talking about. We created a self-executing anonymous function to namespace all of the objects on the page. The namespace is called myApp. The myApp object has a function called registerEventHandlers() that assigns an anonymous function to the onmousemove event of the element on the page that has an id of content.

The beauty of this method is that we can apply this to whatever HTML page we want, and it will work, as long as the page has an element with an id of content.

For a full listing of events and what each event is, see the W3C's list of events here at www.w3.org/TR/DOM-Level-3-Events.

Interacting with the DOM

At this point, we have a much better grasp of JavaScript, so let's start to add some scripting to the running example that we've been working with. The first thing we want to do is to create an external JavaScript file that our Summer Slam form will link to. We'll call the file javascript.js, and we'll put it in the js directory.

Let's start by creating a namespace. First, we create an object called summerSlam that is returned from a self-executing function. In this object, we create a method called formValidate(). For now, this method just pops up an alert; this is so that we can make sure that we are linking to the .js file, creating the object, and invoking the method without issue. It's always best to make sure your code is wired up correctly before you start layering in the functionality because it will only get harder to debug any issues as you add more code:

```
var summerSlam = function(){
    return{
        formValidate: function(form){
            alert("hello there");
            return false;
        }
    };
}();
```

To test this, we can update the form element in the HTML page:

```
<form action="/registration/" onsubmit="return summerSlam.formValidate(this);">
```

So far, we have hooked into the onsubmit event in the form and invoked the formValidate() method of the summerSlam object.

There are a couple of things to note here. First, we pass this to the formValidate() event handler; in this context, the this keyword refers to the form element and gives our JavaScript direct access to the elements in the form and their values.

The other thing to notice is that, in the event handler, we are specifically returning the result of the formValidate() function. If we have formValidate() return false, then this cancels any further submission of the form; however, if it returns true, then the form will successfully submit.

If we've successfully wired everything up correctly, then filling out the form and hitting submit should raise an alert. The next step is to actually do something on hitting submit.

We have some very cool HTML5 validation in the form elements to make sure that they are filled in; however, let's code some JavaScript fallbacks, just in case our end user has a browser that doesn't support that feature.

Let's start by updating formValidate(). First, we will create an array to hold the ids of all of the fields that are required fields:

```
var requiredFields = ["name", "email", "party" ]
```

Next, we'll loop through all of the form's elements via the passed in data from the form object. They are stored as an array in the elements property:

```
for(var x = 0; x < form.elements.length; x++){
}
```

For efficiency's sake, we'll make sure that we only reference elements that are in our required list. To do that, we make an if statement that, as we loop through the form elements, checks with the indexOf() method to see if each element is in our array of required fields. The indexOf() method returns an index number that you can use to find the value you are searching for. If the array does not contain that value, then indexOf() returns a value of -1.

```
if(requiredFields.indexOf(form.elements[x].id)>-1){
}
```

Within that if block, we'll then test whether the element has any sort of value assigned to it. We're pretty much just interested only in the text boxes in the form, so we'll test the value property—that's where the data that gets typed into the text box gets stored. We'll test whether the value property has no value or has an empty string for a value. If either of those conditions are true, then we'll send the user back to the input element in question by calling the focus() method of that element. Next, we'll instruct the user to please complete all of the required fields; and finally, we'll return the value, false.

You may remember how, in the event attribute, we set onsubmit to be the return value of this function call. Thus, returning false from the function prevents the form from submitting:

```
if((form.elements[x].value.length <=0) || (form.elements[x].value == " ") ){
form.elements[x].focus()
  alert("please complete all required fields")
  return false;
}
```

If we put all of this together, we can have the following code populate our `javascript.js` file:

```
formValidate:function(form){
  var requiredFields = ["name", "email", "party" ]
  for(var x = 0; x < form.elements.length; x++){
    if(requiredFields.indexOf(form.elements[x].id)>-1){
      if((form.elements[x].value.length <=0) || (form.elements[x].value == " ") ){
        form.elements[x].focus()
        alert("please complete all required fields")
        return false;
      }
    }
  }
}
```

Summary

We covered a lot of material in this chapter. For example, we explored the philosophy behind object-oriented design; how to create objects; and most importantly, why we would want to. Furthermore, we explored the idea of inheritance and saw how JavaScript uses prototypes to allow the creation of objects that are derived from other objects.

We also explored functions and got a taste of the flexible beauty that functional programming allows by treating functions as a first-class object that can be passed around. We also interacted with the DOM to do form validation.

Most importantly, we can now think about implementing more complex logic in JavaScript, and we should be able to solve problems with the language that we may not have been able to before.

But this is just the beginning—take what you've learned this chapter and play with the ideas. Write your own scripts to test the limits of what you think you can do with the language. I frequently challenge my own students to create applications of their own design and present them to the class, just so that they can demonstrate how they can think in the language. I now ask the same of you. Practice and play with the ideas until they make complete sense in your mind.

And when you are ready, proceed to the next chapter, where we will explore additional concepts like storing data with cookies or local storage, loading external data with AJAX, using debugging tools, and introducing test-driven methodology to our JavaScript development!

Chapter 10

Closing the Loop with JavaScript

We've come a long way already with JavaScript. We started out by understanding the roots of the language, then graduated to creating complex logic with it. Next, we began to create our own page-level namespaces; and finally, we learned how to hold all of the functionality that we need in a given page or site.

Our next step is to close the loop with the language; we will take what we've already learned and combine that with some high-level concepts that will allow us to create complete, professional applications with JavaScript. For example, we will look at the many ways to deal with data; examine how to store data for future use; learn how to load in external data; and explore the finer points of achieving and maintaining excellence in your craft, including how to debug and test your apps.

Let's begin by looking at data.

Working with data

Working with data is one of the most important things that you will be doing with JavaScript. Storing and retrieving data will comprise a large chunk of the code that you write, whether it's saving user preferences, allowing a user to vote and updating the results in real time, or looking up and displaying search data results as the user types.

Saving and retrieving client side data

First, let's ask ourselves why we would want to store data. HTTP is a stateless protocol, which means that no data is stored between sessions or requests. As such, we need to explicitly save data ourselves if we want to retain anything that happened during a browsing session. For example, we might want to save our logged-in state for a set amount of time, prepopulate a user name for the next time someone visits a site, or carry items that have been added to a shopping cart with the user from page to page. Whatever the case, we can use JavaScript for this.

Hidden form fields

The simplest way to save information from page to page is by using hidden form fields. *Hidden form fields* are exactly what they sound like: form elements that function like text boxes, but which are not displayed in the presentation of the page. They aren't exactly hidden from the end user—it's possible to view a page's source and see a given element; however, such fields they are extremely useful and lightweight if your only need is to carry information from one page to the next in the same session:

```
<input type="hidden" id="passedVal">
<script>
  document.getElementById("passedVal").value=cartItem;
</script>
```

The preceding code snippet shows a hidden form field with an id of passedVal and some accompanying JavaScript that stores the variable cartItem in passedVal. Generally, you would store data in the hidden form element before the form submission—see the previous chapter's example on how to execute code before form submission—and that value gets passed along with the rest of the form values.

The downside to this is that the information is not persistent. If you need your information to be available even after the user closes the browser and comes back the next day, then there are other options you can explore.

Cookies

Cookies have been around just about as long as the Web has, but the general public has become acutely aware of them only very recently due to the fact that the use of cookies has become more advanced and coordinated, and this has raised concerns over online privacy.

One of the founding engineers at Netscape, Lou Montulli—who is also responsible for a number of other innovations such as web proxies[1]—first created the concept of a cookie for transmission over HTTP back in 1994. Cookies are packets of data that the browser stores locally on the client machine. They are passed back and forth in the HTTP communication between client and server; and for our purposes, they are accessible to JavaScript.

Creating a cookie

You can access cookies and create new cookies with JavaScript via the document.cookie object. Essentially, cookies are just name-value pairs stored in a string. Let's code up a function in our existing page namespace to store cookies:

---

[1] www.montulli.org/lou

```
createCookie: function(cookie_name, cookie_value){
  document.cookie=cookie_name+"="+cookie_value;
}
```

Remember: We're using object notation here. This function accepts two arguments— `cookie_name` and `cookie_value`—and it simply sets a cookie (named whatever string value is in the variable `cookie_name`) with the value of `cookie_value`.

We can test this out with the following call:

```
summerSlam.createCookie("sslam","my firstcookie");
```

This creates a cookie named `sslam`, and it has the value of `myfirstcookie`.

This is a good start, but let's flesh this out a bit more and make it more useful for us. Let's update our existing code, the code that does form validation, and have it also save the form values in a string of name-value pairs. Next, we will pass the saved name-value pairs to our cookie once the form is successfully submitted.

Let's begin by adding a new variable called `storedValues` in the `formValidate()` function:

```
//snippet…
formValidate:function(form){
    var requiredFields=["name", "email", "party" ];
    var storedValues="";
//snippet…
```

`storedValues`is the variable that we will *concatenate*, or append, all of the form values to; and we will ultimately pass it to our `createCookie()` function.

Next, let's add the following lines of code in the `for` loop, after the `if` statement that checks for required fields:

```
if(form.elements[x].id){
  storedValues+= form.elements[x].id+"="+form.elements[x].value+",";
}
```

The preceding code first checks to make sure that the form field we are currently on actually has an id—we don't want to capture the fieldsets in there. If it does, we then append a string with the form element's id and value to the end of `storedValues`. We also store a comma at the end of each id-value pair.

Next, we will add the following code after the `for` loop:

```
this.createCookie("sslam",storedValues);
```

This snippet calls our `createCookie()` function and passes in the form's id-value pairs as the cookie value.

We can now successfully store all of the form names and values in a cookie! The only catch? The cookie has no expiration explicitly set, so it will expire at the end of the current browsing session. To get around this, let's set an expiration date.

Let's update the `createCookie()` function to accept another parameter that will be the number of days to keep the cookie:

```
createCookie: function(cookie_name,cookie_value,daysToExpire ){
  var expirationDate=new Date();
  expirationDate.setDate(expirationDate.getDate()+daysToExpire);
  cookie_value+= ";expires="+expirationDate;
   document.cookie=cookie_name+"="+cookie_value;
}
```

Here we pass in a third parameter that signifies the number of days in the future that the cookie will expire. We also append that date to the cookie value, in the format of `expires=[date to expire]`.

Our namespace should now look like this:

```
varsummerSlam =function(){
   return{
    formValidate: function(form){
      var requiredFields=["name", "email", "party" ]
      var storedValues="";
      for(var x=0; x<form.elements.length; x++){
        if(requiredFields.indexOf(form.elements[x].id)>-1){
         if((form.elements[x].value.length<=0) || (form.elements[x].value == " ") ){
            form.elements[x].focus()
            console.log(form.elements[x].value.length)
            alert("please complete all required fields")
            return false;
         }
        }
        if(form.elements[x].id){
           storedValues+= form.elements[x].id+"="+form.elements[x].value+",";
        }
      }
      this.createCookie("sslam", storedValues, 30)
      return false;
    },
    createCookie: function(cookie_name,cookie_value, daysToExpire){
      var expirationDate=new Date();
      expirationDate.setDate(expirationDate.getDate()+daysToExpire);
      cookie_value+= ";expires="+expirationDate;
      document.cookie=cookie_name+"="+cookie_value;
    }
  };
}();
```

Excellent! Now whenever a user submits our form, we save her data in a cookie that expires in 30 days.

Now that we can store data on the client side, let's retrieve it.

Retrieving data from a cookie

Remember that the cookie is stored as a string in the document.cookie object; for our purposes, it has a value formatted like this:

```
sslam=name=[value],email=[value],phone=[value],
party=[value],dob=[value],yes_first=[value],no_first=[value],
how_hear=[value],
```

In this case, [value] is the value that the end user entered into the form fields. Let's think about how to intelligently parse this out.

First, we'll need to strip out the cookie name from the cookie value. We'll do this by splitting the string using sslam= as the delimiter. To do this, we'll use the split() method, which takes a string, breaks it apart into smaller strings, and returns these in an array. It breaks the string up at every instance of the delimiter, which is a variable that you pass in. So, if you took a string that held a sentence and passed in an empty space as the delimiter, split() would return an array containing each word in the sentence. In our case, we'll pass in sslam=, so that we can strip that out of the stored cookie data.

```
varcookieVal= document.cookie.split("sslam=")[1]
```

We can create a variable that will hold the second index in the returned array: the first value will be an empty string, and the second will have our name-value pairs in the cookie data, separated by commas. At this point, cookieVal should look like this:

```
name=[value],email=[value],phone=[value],party=[value],
dob=[value],yes_first=[value],no_first=[value],how_hear=[value],
```

Next, we want to split cookieVal at the commas, to give us an array of strings that are just name-value pairs.

```
namevalueArray=cookieVal.split(",")
```

Essentially, we'll create an array of name-value pairs that look like this:

```
"[name]=[value]"
```

And finally, we want to iterate through namevalueArray and split each index on the assignment operator (=). To be really efficient, let's create an object, adding the name as a property of the object and the value as that property's value:

```
varformdata={ };
for(ind in namevalueArray){
    namevalHolder=namevalueArray[ind].split("=")
    formdata[namevalHolder[0]]=namevalHolder[1];
}
```

Oh, but what if there is no cookie saved yet when we try to access this? For the bare minimum in safe coding, let's wrap our logic in an if statement that tests to see whether document.cookie has data. Next, we'll encapsulate that functionality in a function called parseCookieData() and have parseCookieData() return the formdata object:

```
parseCookieData:function(){
    var formdata={};
  if(document.cookie.length>0){
```

```
    var cookieVal=document.cookie.split("sslam=")[1]
    namevalueArray=cookieVal.split(",")
    for(ind in namevalueArray){
      namevalHolder=namevalueArray[ind].split("=")
      formdata[namevalHolder[0]]=namevalHolder[1];
    }
  }
  return formdata
}
```

Populating a form with cookie data

OK, so let's take that object and prepopulate the user's form with the data if he comes to our site with the cookie. First, we'll create a function, populateForm(), and have it accept an object as a parameter. In populateForm(), we'll loop through each key-value pair in the passed in object:

```
populateForm: function(data){
   for (var key in data) {
   }
}
```

In this case, the key variable holds the name of the property.

Next, we need to make sure that each property that we are looping through belongs to the current object—we do this so that we don't reference properties that could be inherited down the prototype chain (see the last chapter for more information on this). To do this, we test the hasOwnProperty() method of the object:

```
if (data.hasOwnProperty(key)) {
}
```

So, as we are looping through each name-value pair, we'll need to test what the form element type that we are dealing with is. We know from looking at our form that we'll mainly need to deal with text boxes and HTML5 text box derivations like tel and date that, for our purposes in JavaScript, work just like text boxes and radio buttons. So, let's do the following:

```
if(currentElement.type === "radio"){
   if(data[key] === "1"){
      currentElement.checked=true;
   }
}else{
   currentElement.value=data[key];
}
```

As we loop through the properties of the object, we reference the corresponding element on the page (i.e., we get the element on the page that has the id that matches the name of the object property) and test what the type of the element is (e.g., is the element a radio button?).

If it is a radio button and if the value of the corresponding property is the string, "1"—then we set the checked property of the element to true. This selects the radio button for the user.

If it is not a radio button, for our purposes we can assume it is a text box of some sort. Therefore, we set the value property of the element to the value of the object property.

Our complete function should look like this:

```
populateForm: func tion(data){
for (var key in data) {
  var currentElement=document.getElementById(key)
  if (data.hasOwnProperty(key)) {
    if(data[key] !== undefined){
      if(currentElement.type === "radio"){
        if(data[key] === "1"){
          currentElement.checked=true;
        }
      }else{
        currentElement.vsalue=data[key];
      }
    }
  }
 }
}
```

To tie it all together, we can create a function that we'll call setFormData() that will call populateForm() and pass in the return of the parseCookieData() function. We will also create an init() function that kicks this all off:

```
setFormData:function(){
    this.populateForm(this.parseCookieData());
}
init:function(){
    this.setFormData();
}
```

And finally, we'll call the init() function from the body onload event in the HTML page.

```
<bodyonload="summerSlam.init();">
```

At this point, our namespace—the place where we capture submitted form data in a cookie and use the cookie to prepopulate the form when the user returns—should look like this:

```
varsummerSlam=function(){
    return{
      init: function(){
        this.setFormData();
      },
      formValidate: function(form){
        var requiredFields=["name", "email", "party"]
        var storedValues="";
        for(var x=0; x<form.elements.length; x++){
          if(requiredFields.indexOf(form.elements[x].id)>-1){
            if((form.elements[x].value.length<=0) ||
               (form.elements[x].value == " ") ){
              form.elements[x].focus()
              console.log(form.elements[x].value.length)
              alert("please complete all required fields")
```

```
            return false;
          }
        }
        if(form.elements[x].id){
          storedValues+= form.elements[x].id+"="+form.elements[x].value+",";
        }
      }
    }
    this.createCookie("sslam", storedValues, 30)
    return false;
  },
  createCookie: function(cookie_name,cookie_value, daysToExpire){
    var expirationDate=new Date();
    expirationDate.setDate(expirationDate.getDate()+daysToExpire);
    cookie_value+= ";expires="+expirationDate;
    alert(cookie_value)
    document.cookie=cookie_name+"="+cookie_value;
  },
  setFormData: function(){
    this.populateForm(this.parseCookieData());
  },
  parseCookieData: function(){
    var formdata={};
    if(document.cookie.length>0){
      var cookieVal=document.cookie.split("sslam=")[1]
      namevalueArray=cookieVal.split(",")
      for(ind in namevalueArray){
        namevalHolder=namevalueArray[ind].split("=")
        formdata[namevalHolder[0]]=namevalHolder[1];
      }
    }
    return formdata
  },
  populateForm: function(data){
    for (var key in data) {
      var currentElement=document.getElementById(key)
      if (data.hasOwnProperty(key)) {
        if(data[key] !== undefined){
          if(currentElement.type === "radio"){
            if(data[key] === "1"){
              currentElement.checked=true;
            }
          }else{
            currentElement.value=data[key];
          }
        }
      }
    }
  }
};
}();
```

While cookies are useful, they have certain issues. They are included in the HTTP transmission, so they add to the total payload of the page. Browsers apply certain limitations to cookie usage, such as setting a potential cap of 300 cookies in total, a 20 cookie limit per domain, and a 4 kb limit per cookie[2].

Web storage

HTML5 has brought with it a new API for storing client-side data: web storage. Web storage has two core objects that support different levels of persistence. The sessionStorage object stores data for the current session, but this is cleared when the browser is closed. The localStorage object persists even after the browser is closed and the session ends.

While cookies store data as a string that needs to be parsed, both web storage objects store data as native objects that are built-in to JavaScript. This makes it much easier to store and retrieve data from web storage objects.

Since web storage is part of HTML5, and since at the time of writing a good number of the legacy browsers in use today don't support HTML5, a professional use of web storage checks for support of the HTML5 API and falls back to cookies if that support isn't present.

The way we check that web storage is supported is to check the typeof for the Storage object. If this returns an object, we're in business. Ostensibly, we could keep checking typeof each time we need to save something, but that call would get expensive, especially for browsers that don't support web storage. Instead, let's create a boolean variable called webstoragesupport in our namespace object and do our check in the init() function:

```
webstoragesupported:false,
init:function(){
    if(typeof(Storage)){
      this.webstoragesupported=true
    }else{
      this.webstoragesupported=false
    }
    this.setFormData();
}
```

Storing data in web storage

Now let's do a bit of refactoring, so that we can use web storage when it is supported and use cookies when it is not. We'll pull all of the cookie-specific code out of formValidate() and put it in a function that we'll call saveToCookie(). Next, instead of calling createCookie() at the end of formValidate(), we'll call a function that we will define called saveData():

```
formValidate:function(form){
   var requiredFields=["name", "email", "party" ]
   for(var x=0; x<form.elements.length; x++){
     if(requiredFields.indexOf(form.elements[x].id)>-1){
```

---

[2] http://support.microsoft.com/kb/306070

```
            if((form.elements[x].value.length<=0) || (form.elements[x].value == " ")){
             form.elements[x].focus()
              alert("please complete all required fields")
              return false;
            }
         }
      }
      this.saveData(form)
      return false;
   },
   saveToCookie: function(form){
      var storedValues="";
      for(var x=0; x<form.elements.length; x++){
        if(form.elements[x].id){
           storedValues+= form.elements[x].id+"="+form.elements[x].value+",";
        }
      }
      this.createCookie("sslam", storedValues, 30)
   }
```

Next, we'll create the saveData() function. This function should simply check our webstoragesupported-boolean variable and call saveToCookie() or a new function that we'll create soon called saveToWebStorage():

```
saveData:function(form){
   if(this.webstoragesupported){
    this.saveToWebStorage(form)
   }else{
     this.saveToCookie(form)
   }
}
```

And finally, we'll create the saveToWebStorage() function. Again, we'll loop through the form, but this time we'll create new properties in the localStorage object named after the form element ids and with the same values as the form element values. Note that if we wanted to save this information only for the session (instead of in perpetuity), we would have used sessionStorage instead of localStorage:

```
saveToWebStorage:function(form){
   for(var x=0; x<form.elements.length; x++){
     if(form.elements[x].id){
        localStorage[form.elements[x].id]=form.elements[x].value
     }
   }
}
```

Our page now saves to either a cookie or localStorage! The only thing we have left to do is to refactor our code that retrieves the data. Remember that populateForm(), our function that fills in the form fields, expects an object with properties that match the ids of the form elements on the page. Also, recall that this is exactly the structure that we stored in localStorage.

Retrieving data from local storage

Accordingly, we can make a simple edit to setFormData() to pass either the output of parseCookieData() or the localStorage object to populateForm():

```
setFormData:f unction(){

this.populateForm((this.webstoragesupported)?localStorage:this.parseCookieData());
}
```

Our JavaScript file should now look like this:

```
varsummerSlam=function(){
  return{
    webstoragesupported: false,
    init: function(){
      if(typeof(Storage)){
        this.webstoragesupported=true
      }else{
        this.webstoragesupported=false
      }
      this.setFormData();
    },
    formValidate: function(form){
      var requiredFields=["name", "email", "party" ]
      for(var x=0; x<form.elements.length; x++){
        if(requiredFields.indexOf(form.elements[x].id)>-1){
          if((form.elements[x].value.length<=0) || (form.elements[x].value == " ") ){
            form.elements[x].focus()
            alert("please complete all required fields")
            return false;
          }
        }
      }
      this.saveData(form)
      return false;
    },
    saveData: function(form){
      if(this.webstoragesupported){
        this.saveToWebStorage(form)
      }else{
        this.saveToCookie(form)
      }
    },
    saveToWebStorage: function(form){
      for(var x=0; x<form.elements.length; x++){
        if(form.elements[x].id){
          localStorage[form.elements[x].id]=form.elements[x].value
        }
      }
    },
```

```
    saveToCookie: function(form){
      var storedValues="";
      for(var x=0; x<form.elements.length; x++){
        if(form.elements[x].id){
          storedValues+= form.elements[x].id+"="+form.elements[x].value+",";
        }
      }
      this.createCookie("sslam", storedValues, 30)
    },
    createCookie: function(cookie_name,cookie_value, daysToExpire){
      var expirationDate=new Date();
      expirationDate.setDate(expirationDate.getDate()+daysToExpire);
      cookie_value+= ";expires="+expirationDate;
      alert(cookie_value)
      document.cookie=cookie_name+"="+cookie_value;
    },
    setFormData: function(){
      this.populateForm((this.webstoragesupported)?localStorage:this.parseCookieData());
    },
    parseCookieData: function(){
      var formdata={};
      if(document.cookie.length>0){
        var cookieVal=document.cookie.split("sslam=")[1]
        namevalueArray=cookieVal.split(",")
        for(ind in namevalueArray){
          namevalHolder=namevalueArray[ind].split("=")
          formdata[namevalHolder[0]]=namevalHolder[1];
        }
      }
      return formdata
    },
    populateForm: function(data){
      for (var key in data) {
       var currentElement=document.getElementById(key)
       if (data.hasOwnProperty(key)) {
        if(data[key] !== undefined){
          if(currentElement.type === "radio"){
            if(data[key] === "1"){
              currentElement.checked=true;
            }
          }else{
            currentElement.value=data[key];
          }
        }
       }
      }
    }
  };
}();
```

Note that our current example could certainly be refactored in several ways, and there are many design choices open to us. For example, we could have created a completely separate namespace to handle saving data. Explore on your own how you can effectively create JavaScript libraries that you can share between pages and even between applications that you may make.

We've seen how to save client-side data; now let's look at how to load external data.

Loading external data

It was when Google started loading type-ahead data into its search box that we first saw the subtle possibilities of loading external data without interrupting the user experience. From showing real time updates, to voting results, to updating shopping cart information while the user shops—we can now reflect a greater degree of the world around our users without interrupting the user experience.

In this section, we will look at how to load in external data.

Ajax

As we saw in Chapter 8, Ajax—which is short for Asynchronous JavaScript And XML and is provided via the XMLHttpRequest (XHR) object—was one of the most significant recent innovations in JavaScript. It added the ability to add content to the client at run time without refreshing the browser. This opened up a world of complexity that you can introduce to websites; and for the first time, it let you really craft complex, client-facing web applications.

An Ajax transaction consists of the following steps:

1. Instantiate an XMLHttpRequest object.

2. Create a callback function that will fire whenever the network status of the XHR object changes.

3. Send a request for external data, either via an HTTP POST or GET.

4. When the network status changes, the callback function should check the readyState and HTTP status of the response.

See Figure 10-1 for a UML sequence diagram of an AJAX transaction.

Let's take a look at a code example!

First, we create and instantiate a new XMLHttpRequest object. In an earlier time, we had to check whether the browser supported the object natively or if we were dealing with IE 6, in which case we'd need to instantiate an XMLHttpRequest ActiveX object. But for our example, we'll keep the code pure and assume that our audience has followed Microsoft's advice and abandoned IE 6[3] in favor of something modern.

```
varxmlhttp;
xmlhttp=newXMLHttpRequest();
```

The open() method of the XHR object accepts five parameters:

■ The first parameter specifies the HTTP request method that our Ajax call will use, which is usually GET or POST). However, other methods are supported (e.g., HEAD or PUT), as long as the browser supports them and the server that we are hitting is configured to support them.

---

[3]www.ie6countdown.com

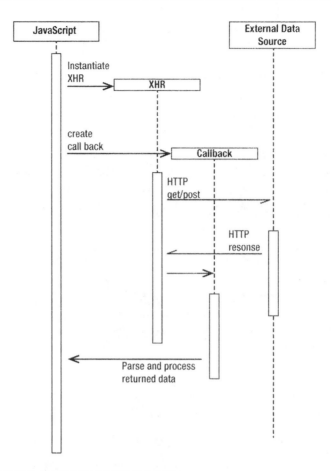

Figure 10-1. A UML sequence diagram of an AJAX transaction

- The second parameter is the URL of the remote data source.

- The rest of the parameters are optional. The third parameter is a boolean value that indicates whether the transaction is asynchronous (true) or synchronous (false). This is an important design decision. If your call is asynchronous, the page will continue to function normally and only react when the response is received. If the call is synchronous, all other functionality on the page will block until the response is received. If you leave this parameter off, it is assumed to be true (i.e., asynchronous).

- The fourth and fifth parameters are for the user name and password, if credentials are required.

Our next step is to call the XHR object's open() method:

```
xmlhttp.open("GET","",true);
```

Now we want to assign a callback function to the onreadystatechange property of the XHR object. In our example, we'll use an anonymous function, but you aren't limited to just using anonymous functions if you don't want to.

This callback function gets invoked every time the readyState property of the XHR object gets updated (because it is assigned to onreadystatechange). The readyState property has four potential values: 1, 2, 3, or 4. Here is what those values mean:

- 1: Indicates that the open() method of the XHR object has been called.
- 2: Indicates that the send() method of the XHR object has been called.
- 3: Indicates that the response from the remote server has started to load.
- 4: Indicates that the response has finished loading.

Our callback function needs to check the readyState property of the XHR object to make sure that the response has finished loading. It also needs to check the HTTP status code of the returned response, which is stored in the status property of the XHR object.

We want to make sure the HTTP status has a value of 200, which indicates a good response. We check this to make sure that we aren't reading in a 4xx or 5xx error message response. We may even want to trap 4xx or 5xx HTTP status codes and alert the user accordingly (or even include retry logic, depending on our business requirements):

```
xmlhttp.onreadystatechange=function(){
  if (xmlhttp.readyState==4 && xmlhttp.status==200)
  {
    //parse the response
  }
}
```

Finally, we call the send() method to send the request. We can also pass in any additional parameters that we would want to send with the request as a parameter to send():

```
xmlhttp.send();
}
```

We also want to make sure that we take into account any error that may occur during the transmission of the data. The XHR object has an onerror event handler that lets us to track when errors occur; we can either log the error for our own purposes, or, if the data was mission critical, alert the user of the error.

Let's look at a full example that assumes we have external data, formatted as JSON (JavaScript Object Notation) in a file named userData.js:

```
varuser={
 id: 21,
 uname: "tb4912x",
 playlist: [23343,1355,9303]
}
```

We load that data like this:

```
var xmlhttp;
xmlhttp=newXMLHttpRequest();
xmlhttp.onreadystatechange=function()
{
  if (xmlhttp.readyState==4 && xmlhttp.status==200)
```

```
  {
    user=eval(xmlhttp.responseText) // eval the JSON data in the responseText
                      // to convert the string to JavaScript
        alert(user.uname)
  }
}
xmlhttp.onerror=function(){
 alert("Sorry, we could not load your user data, please refresh and try again.");
}
xmlhttp.open("GET","userData.js",true);
xmlhttp.send();
```

But there are limitations to Ajax. The content that you load in must come from the same origin that your code lives on. Specifically, it must use the same domain, protocol, and port. So, a script served up via HTTP cannot call a remote file served up via HTTPS, even if it is at the same domain name. Also, a script that lives at the root domain cannot call a remote data source at a sub-domain of the main domain.

There are work-arounds to these limitations, which we'll look at in the next section.

Cross Origin Resource Sharing

Cross Origin Resource Sharing (CORS) is a new working draft from the W3C that allows for resources to be available across origins. The specification for CORS can be found at www.w3.org/TR/cors/.

The idea of CORS is that the remote server announces that content is accessible across origins by specifying Access-Control-Allow-Origin: * in the HTTP response headers. For most modern browsers, the XMLHttpRequest object will work with CORS—the notable exceptions to this are (of course!) IE8 and IE9. We can check for support of CORS proactively by using the withCredentials property of the XHR object.

Be warned: the withCredentials property is a symptom of CORS, not a direct indicator. It checks whether the XHR object supports credentialed HTTP requests, which are needed to set cookies with CORS (and thus indirectly implying support for CORS in the browser). However, this property does not actually indicate that the remote server supports CORS:

```
varxmlhttp;
xmlhttp=newXM LHttpRequest();
if(xmlhttp.wi thCredentials!==unde fined)
  {
  // make cross-site requests
  xmlhttp.onreadystatechange=function(){
  }
  xmlhttp.open("GET","userData.js",true);
  xmlhttp.send();
}
```

As noted previously, the major exception to this is Internet Explorer. IE8 and IE9 use a proprietary object that only those browsers implement, the XDomainRequest object. Trying to access CORS content using an XHR object in IE8 or IE9 will result in an error.

The syntax for using the XDR object is very similar to the syntax for using the XHR object:

```
xdr=newXDomai nRequest();
if(xdr)
{
    xdr.onprogress=XDRprogress; //callback function
    xdr.onload=XDRcomplete; //callback function
    xdr.open("get", url);
    xdr.send();
}
```

Tools

Arguably, the most important thing that differentiates a robust professional language from a hobbyist's toy is the toolset available for the language. Having good tools facilitates faster and higher quality development by allowing developers to, among other things, quickly and easily debug issues; create a suite of tests that assures the quality of the end product; profile (or measure) and track memory usage; and package up only the necessary bits for a faster delivery to the client. In recent years, the amount and quality of tools available for JavaScript has really blossomed as the language has come into its own.

Debugging with firebug

Web development turned a major corner in 2006 when Firebug came out. Firebug is a tool created by Joe Hewitt that allows, among many other things, real-time JavaScript debugging in the browser. Firebug started life as a Firefox extension; however, it has since expanded to other browsers. It also created the paradigm that most other browser debugging tools now follow.

Before Firebug, when web developers ran into an error in their JavaScript, the only real method of run-time debugging available was to put alerts in the source code to first try and identify where the error was happening (Does the alert fire here? OK, is the error is above this line? How about here?). And once the approximate location was determined, web developers used alerts to try and figure out the state of each variable when the error happened.

This was an imprecise process and took far too long.

Firebug allows JavaScript developers to enjoy a real debugging environment that previously was only available in compiled or object code languages.

Let's take a look at how we can use Firebug to debug our code. First, we have to make sure we have Firebug installed. It is available for download here: http://getfirebug.com/. Simply click the Install Firebug button and follow the instructions. When you have done this and your browser has restarted, you'll see the Firebug icon (usually) in the upper-right corner of your browser. Click it and open up the Firebug panel, which should look something like what you see in Figure 10-2.

The tabs that we will concern ourselves with right now are Console and Script.

Figure 10-2. The Firebug panel

Using the Console tab

The Console tab is split into two panels:

- The left panel is the console; it displays output-error messages from the page or explicit trace statements that you can embed in your JavaScript via console.log() calls.

- The right panel is the command line; it is an input box where you can enter JavaScript code that you want to run. All of the global variables on the current page are in scope here, and you can interact directly with your code in this window.

To see an example, type console.log(summerSlam) in the command line and click the Run button. You should see our entire namespace object serialized and displayed in the console (see Figure 10-3).

Figure 10-3. The serialized namespace object

This is a great way to invoke functions manually, to see potential issues, or to inspect the structure of objects. However, the real draw of Firebug is the debugger that is available in the Script tab.

Using the Script Tab

If we click the `Script` tab, we will be presented with the screen shown in Figure 10-4.

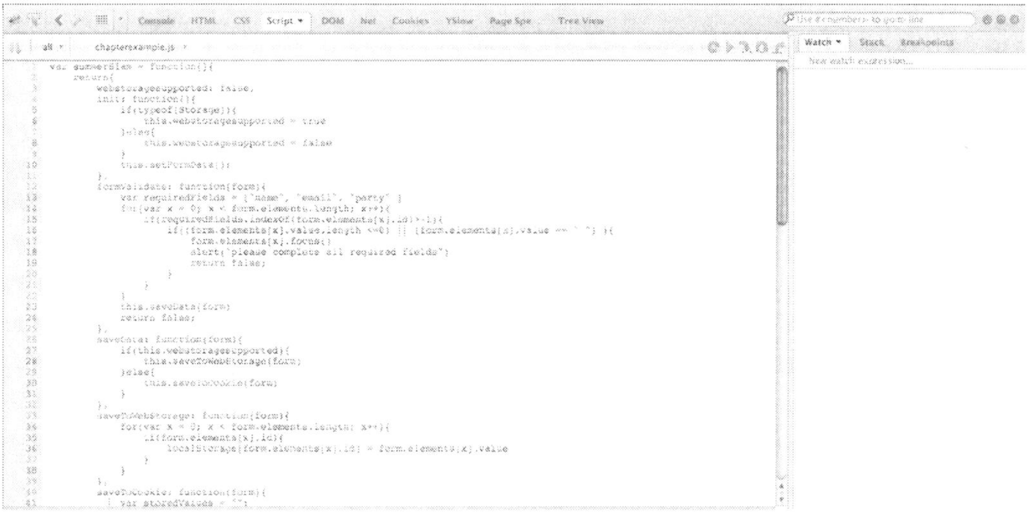

Figure 10-4. The Firebug debugger in the Script tab

The left panel shows our source code, while the right panel lets us keep track of watched expressions, the current stack, or a list of break points. Watched expressions are exactly that—expressions that we can see the current value of while the application is running. The current stack refers to the stack trace, which in JavaScript means the function we are currently in. The current stack shows what function called the current function, and you can use this to show the full chain of functions that were called to bring us to our current point.

In order to debug our application, we first need to create a break point, which is a point in the code where the interpreter will stop and allow the debugger to run the rest of the execution. When the debugger takes over execution, we can watch and step through the execution of the code and see what value each of our currently scoped variables holds. This will allow us to confirm that what is happening is what we expect to be happening. To create a break point, we simply click the left margin of a line of code, to the left of the line number. We will see a red circle where we clicked, which is the break point. Let's put a break point right in the `init()` function, so we can step through our JavaScript that populates the form data.

When we refresh the page, the debugger will jump to this break point and allow us to step through the code. Notice the buttons on the upper-right corner of Figure 10-5.

From left to right, these buttons allow us to re-run the code, continue to the next break point, step into a function line-by-line, step over a function so that it executes (but which we don't debug line-by-line), or step out to finish the current execution and return control to the original caller.

Also, notice that the current state of our application is represented in the Watch panel.

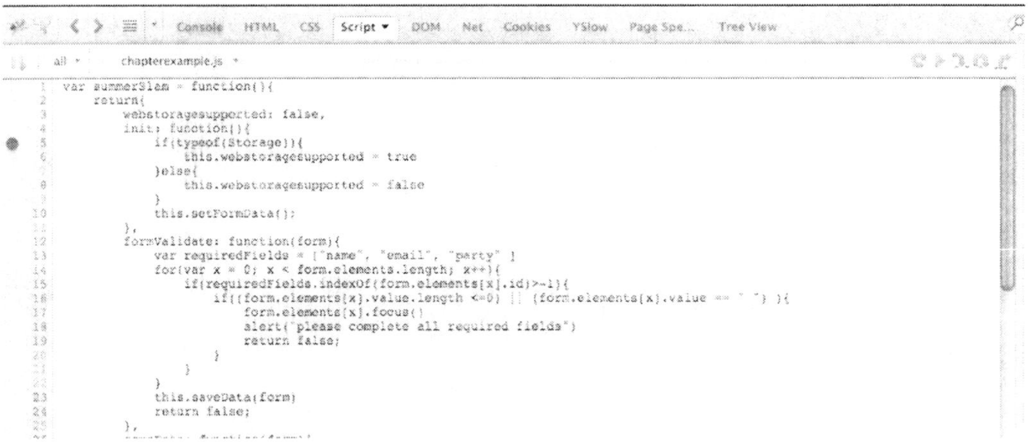

Figure 10-5. Placing a break point

Figure 10-6. We begin debugging at the break point

If we click the Step Into button, the debugger takes us to the next line of code that will be executed. If we continue to step through the code by clicking the Step Into button, we will see the complete execution of our code and the current state of each object as we go.

Minifying JavaScript

JavaScript does not acknowledge extra white space or line breaks. This means that we can pull out all extraneous spaces and new lines (as long as we properly end each expression with a semi-colon), and the JavaScript interpreter will read and execute our code normally.

We can take advantage of this by using a process known as minifying to strip out all of the white space and line breaks and serve up a compressed version of our code. Minification also involves using HTTP

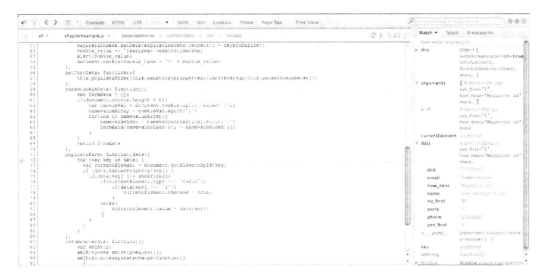

Figure 10-7. Stepping through the code

compression, which consists of setting the Content Encoding to gzip from the server end, and then combining multiple external JavaScript files into a single file.

Why would we want to minify? Well, when we view a web site, each page has a *payload*, which is the overall combined size of everything that makes up the page, including its images, CSS files, the mark up in the page itself, and the linked JavaScript files (see Figure 10-8).

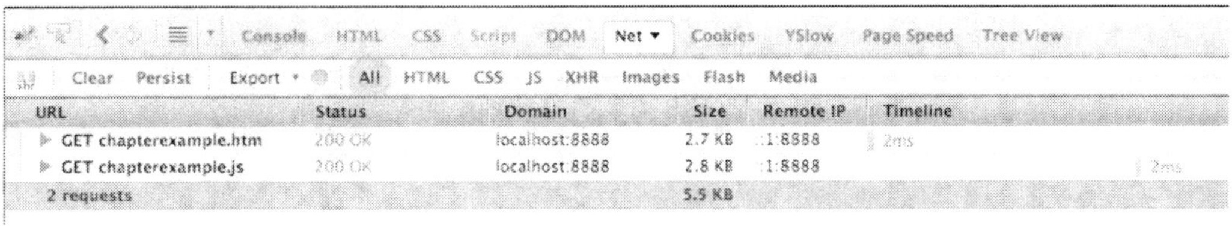

Figure 10-8. An app's payload as represented in Firebug

Stripping out extraneous characters from your JavaScript reduces the size of your JavaScript, which in turn reduces the size of the overall payload of the page, which in turn makes your pages load faster. Combining external files into one file reduces the amount of HTTP transactions needed to build your page, which also makes the page load faster. You see the trend; ultimately, these are optimizations that speed up the delivery of your content to your user.

So how do we minify? There are tons of great tools we can use to minify our apps—a simple Google search will turn up a huge amount of open source options. Google itself makes a minifier called Google Closure Compiler, and Yahoo has one called YUI Compressor. For our example, we'll use an open source tool called Minify. It is available here: http://code.google.com/p/minify/. Or, if you prefer, you can grab github here: https://github.com/mrclay/minify.

Minify can be downloaded as a zip file that you expand and put at the root of your web site. It has a web interface that you can access via this URL: http://[your%20site]/min/builder/. You can add all of the files you want to combine in the web interface, and Minify will generate a script tag that you can use in your web application to serve up the compressed JavaScript:

```
<script type="text/javascript" src="/min/f=chapterexample.js"></script>
```

Figure 10-9 highlights the improvement in page size that we get when we compress our external JavaScript file.

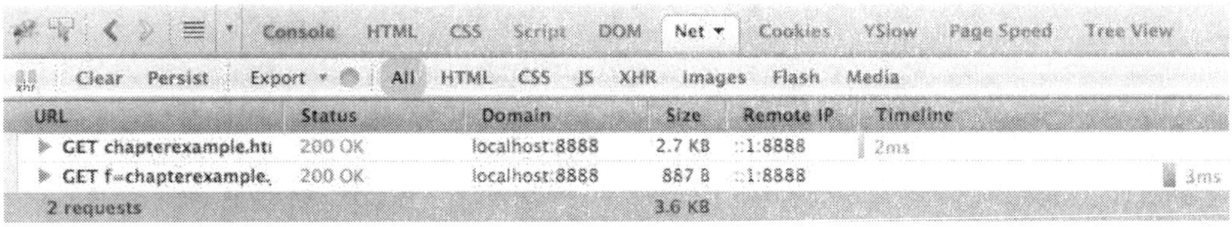

Figure 10-9. The improvement in page size achieved by compressing our JavaScript file

In this case, the file size fell from 2.8 kb to 887 bytes. The overall payload of the page went from 5.5 kb to 3.6 kb.

JavaScript Unit Tests with Jasmine

Test-driven development (TDD) is a formal methodology where you first write a test that describes a unit of functionality—ideally, the smallest piece of testable functionality—and then you write the functionality described by that test. These tests you write are called *unit tests*.

Your suite of unit tests for your application serves to describe its functionality to new developers coming onto a project. These tests also assure quality by throwing an error if any update changes the app's functionality, and they generally instill good programming practices by ensuring that you write code in small, modular—hence, testable—pieces.

With the release of unit testing frameworks, the idea of test-driven development is finally emerging in the JavaScript community. There are several frameworks available, but we'll focus on Jasmine, which is developed by Pivotal Labs and is available for download at http://pivotal.github.com/jasmine/.

For our example, we'll download the latest version of the standalone release, available here: http://pivotal.github.com/jasmine/download.html. The standalone release is a ZIP file that, when expanded, contains three folders (lib, spec, and src), as well as a single HTML file (SpecRunner.html).

SpecRunner is going to be our test harness. Traditionally, the test harness is the software that runs our tests and generates the report of their results. Viewing the source code of SpecRunner reveals that Pivotal was nice enough to include its own demonstration data—specifically, it included references to Player.js, Song.js, SpecHelper.js, and PlayerSpec.js. These files demonstrate how we will use SpecRunner; that is, we'll include our own external JavaScript file and craft a series of unit tests in a new file that we'll call SummerSlamSpec.js. But first, let's clear out all of the Pivotal data, so we can start fresh.

The source code of our test harness should now look like this:

```
<!DOCTYPE>
<html>
<head>
    <title>Jasmine Test Runner</title>
    <link rel="stylesheet" type="text/css" href="lib/jasmine-1.0.0/jasmine.css">
    <script type="text/javascript" src="lib/jasmine-1.0.0/jasmine.js"></script>
    <script type="text/javascript" src="lib/jasmine-1.0.0/jasmine-html.js"></script>
    <!--The below script tag should link out to our external js file .. -->
    <script type="text/javascript" src="chapterexample.js"></script>
    <!-- include spec files here… -->
    <script type="text/javascript" src="spec/SummerSlamSpec.js"></script>
</head>
<body>
 <script type="text/javascript">
    jasmine.getEnv().addReporter(new jasmine.TrivialReporter());
    jasmine.getEnv().execute();
</script>
</body>
</html>
```

Now let's add some tests to our spec file!

Adding Tests

At a high level, each test we will write is called a spec, and specs are grouped together into suites. We define suites using the describe() function, which takes two parameters:

- A string describing what the suite is for
- A function that returns the specs

The following snippet defines a suite for the Summer Slam website:

```
describe("summerSlam",function(){});
```

We add specs inside the function passed as the second parameter. Specs are calls to the it() function; these have the same signature as the describe() function:

- The first parameter is a string that describes what the spec will be testing.
- The second parameter is a function that can contain functionality, as well as a matcher.

And this code snippet shows the it() function in action:

```
 describe("summerSlam", function(){
    it("checks fields", function(){});
});
```

Matchers are functions that represent conditional logic with plain English descriptions. They are used to test the results of the functions that we are testing. A list of current native Jasmine matchers can be found here: `https://github.com/pivotal/jasmine/wiki/Matchers`.

OK, we have the preliminary concepts out of the way, so let's begin to write some tests for our `summerSlam` namespace object.

As noted previously, in actual professional development, you start out by writing tests that describe what you expect your application to do. It is not until you've written these tests that you begin to write the code to satisfy those expectations. You can even review your tests ahead of time with your business owner and QA team to make sure that everyone shares the same expectations for the app's functionality.

One of the nice things about following this workflow is that it encourages us to build our applications to be more modular from the get-go—if functionality is tightly coupled, we won't be able to test it. Since we are going back and adding tests for code that we've already written, we may need to refactor a little to make it more modular, so we can test efficiently.

Refactoring the Code

Let's look at our form validation function. The first thing that should jump out is that it is coupled to the DOM for the validation part. Let's refactor that a little to abstract that and to make what we are doing a little more readable.

We'll pull out the code that checks whether a form element is required and put it into its own function called `isRequired()`. We will also pull out the code that checks whether an element has a value and move it to its own function called `hasValue()`. So that we aren't referencing the passed in form variable directly, we'll store the name of the form and its value to local variables and pass them into the new functions:

```
isRequired: function(name, requiredList){
    if(requiredList.indexOf(name)>-1){
        return true;
}else{
        return false;
    }
},
 hasValue: function(data){
  if((data.length<=0) || (data == " ")) {
        return false;
    }else{
        return true;
    }
},
 formValidate: function(form){
    var requiredFields=["name", "email", "party" ]
    for(var x=0; x<form.elements.length; x++){
        var currentElementName=form.elements[x].id
        var currentElementValue=form.elements[x].value
        if(this.isRequired(currentElementName, requiredFields)){
            if(!this.hasValue(currentElementValue)){
                form.elements[x].focus()
                alert("please complete all required fields")
```

```
      return false;
    }
  }
}
  this.saveData(form)
  return false;
}
```

The resulting code is much more readable; it's obvious that the conditionals in `formValidate()` are now checking whether something is required and whether that something has a value.

Also, we have now exposed bits of functionality that we can create unit tests around, without tying directly to the DOM. Let's go back to our spec file and start a suite around our form validation.

Writing a Test Suite

Our first suite will test the `isRequired()` function:

```
describe("Summer Slam Check isRequired Function", function(){
});
```

We will add a spec to the suite that checks whether a name passed in is on the required list; if so, the function returns `true`:

```
it("given a list of required fields, returns true if the name passed in is in the list",
function(){
  expect(summerSlam.isRequired("name", ["name", "email", "party" ])).toEqual(true);
});
```

Next, let's add a spec that makes sure our `isRequired()` function returns `false` if the name passed in is not on the required list:

```
it("given a list of required fields, returns false if the name passed in is not in the list",
function(){
  expect(summerSlam.isRequired("first_name", ["name", "email", "party" ])).toEqual(false);
});
```

We can see our results by refreshing our test harness. If all of our tests pass, we see a screen like the one shown in Figure 10-10.

Figure 10-10. All our tests passed!

The beauty of unit testing our code is that, if our tests don't pass, we get a very explicit error message that tells us exactly why our code failed. To test this, we can change the value passed into the second spec to be one of the items in the required list; that should give us the result shown in Figure 10-11.

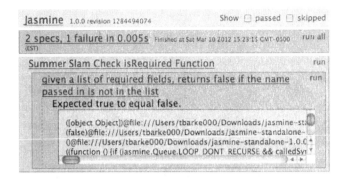

Figure 10-11. The unit test failed!

Now let's create a suite for hasValue(). We'll add a spec that tests passing in a string, passing in an empty string, and passing in null:

```
describe("Summer Slam Check hasValue Function", function(){
  it("given a parameter, returns true if the argument passed in has value",
    function(){
      expect(summerSlam.hasValue("test")).toEqual(true);
  });
  it("given a parameter, returns false if the argument passed in is an empty string",
    function(){
      expect(summerSlam.hasValue(" ")).toEqual(false);
  });
  it("given a parameter, returns false if the argument passed in is null",
    function(){
      expect(summerSlam.hasValue(null)).toEqual(false);
  });
});
```

Uh oh, what's this? When we run the preceding suite, we see that our spec to test null values fails, as shown in Figure 10-12.

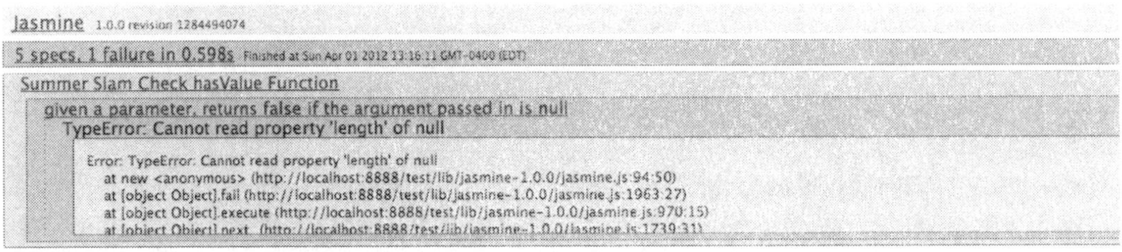

Jasmine 1.0.0 revision 1284494074

5 specs, 1 failure in 0.598s Finished at Sun Apr 01 2012 13:16:11 GMT-0400 (EDT)

Summer Slam Check hasValue Function

given a parameter, returns false if the argument passed in is null
  TypeError: Cannot read property 'length' of null

Error: TypeError: Cannot read property 'length' of null
  at new <anonymous> (http://localhost:8888/test/lib/jasmine-1.0.0/jasmine.js:94:50)
  at [object Object].fail (http://localhost:8888/test/lib/jasmine-1.0.0/jasmine.js:1963:27)
  at [object Object].execute (http://localhost:8888/test/lib/jasmine-1.0.0/jasmine.js:970:15)
  at [object Object].next_ (http://localhost:8888/test/lib/jasmine-1.0.0/jasmine.js:1739:31)

Figure 10-12. Our unit test for hasValue fails

Writing a test for this use case has uncovered an oversight in our logic; we never bothered to test whether anything is passed into the function at all. To address this, let's refactor the hasValue() function. We'll wrap the main logic in an if statement that tests whether the data variable has been initialized. While we're at it, let's refactor to use our own best practice of only having a single return in a function. Our new hasValue() function should now look like this:

```
hasValue:func tion(data){
retVal=false
if(data){
  if((data.length>0) && (data !=" ")) {
    retVal=true;
  }
}
 return retVal
}
```

And our full test suite should look like this:

```
describe("Summer Slam Check isRequired Function", function(){
 it("given a list of required fields, returns true if the name passed in is in the list",
    function(){
     expect(summerSlam.isRequired("name", ["name", "email", "party" ])).toEqual(true);
});
 it("given a list of required fields, returns false if the name passed in is not in the
list",
    function(){
     expect(summerSlam.isRequired("nme", ["name", "email", "party" ])).toEqual(false);
});
});
describe("Summer Slam Check hasValue Function", function(){
 it("given a parameter, returns true if the argument passed in has value",
    function(){
     expect(summerSlam.hasValue("test")).toEqual(true);
    });
 it("given a parameter, returns false if the argument passed in is an empty string",
    function(){
     expect(summerSlam.hasValue(" ")).toEqual(false);
});
 it("given a parameter, returns false if the argument passed in is null",
    function(){
     expect(summerSlam.hasValue(null)).toEqual(false);
});
});
```

Following this methodology, we can create a full suite of automated tests for our JavaScript functionality, so that we are confident our code works as we expect it to. And if we do make any changes that break functionality, our tests will alert us to that immediately, so that we can fix it.

This is just the tip of the iceberg for what is possible with unit testing. Once you are comfortable thinking about how you develop your code in this way, there are even more concepts to explore, from mocking up functionality to expand what you can test to using plug-ins that expose DOM-level interaction!

Summary

In this chapter, we created a framework for saving data on the client side. We took advantage of the new web storage capabilities of HTML5, but we also implemented fallback functionality to use an HTTP cookie if web storage was not supported. We also looked at Ajax and how to load data from remote data sources.

Next, we evaluated some tools available that have really raised the bar in the world of JavaScript development. For example, we looked at a tool that actually lets us debug our scripts in the browser and another that lets us use minification to optimize the delivery of our code. Finally, we learned how to do honest-to-goodness real unit testing with JavaScript!

Chapter 11

Using Server-Side Technologies

It's pretty hard to find a website these days that doesn't use some kind of server-side scripting and a database. So many different options are available, from commercial products to open source products, that it can be really daunting to decide which direction you want to go. In the case of web servers, web scripting languages, and databases, the open source alternatives are just as good as (and in some cases, even better than) the commercial options.

This chapter isn't going to walk you through the syntax of each of the various languages, and it isn't an instruction manual about how to set up and configure your servers. Rather, it is a guide to some of the different options available, as well as an explanation of the differences between the various products.

Occasionally, you'll have your choice of server technologies; and other times, you will be required to use what's already in place. A lot of web scripting languages are reasonably easy to pick up for technically minded individuals. The concepts that we covered when talking about JavaScript—from basic programming logic to branching and iterating—can all be transferred to these languages. It does take a while to master even the simplest of languages, however. Chances are, if you're asked to work on a project that is outside of your expertise, you should bring in a hired gun.

The server side removes barriers

In the early days of the World Wide Web, there was the saying that "content is king." Although that's still true today, visitors expect more from a website than just a passive reading experience. Putting up a static page with some interesting text and a pretty picture isn't enough anymore; end users expect interaction. They want to be able to search things. They want to add things to their wish lists and shopping carts, and they want to tie into social media websites like Twitter and Facebook. News websites are a prime example of this evolution: readers are encouraged to discuss topics inline with the stories, and they're asked to submit story ideas. Long gone are the days of the news editor sitting in her office deciding what is and isn't newsworthy. Client-side scripting (JavaScript) isn't enough anymore, either. To store input and interact with diverse data sources, websites have turned to server-side technologies.

JavaScript is limited in what it can accomplish, largely because of security concerns. Would you feel safe running an application on the Web that had free rein of your hard drive? How would you like a website that's capable of reading and writing any file on your hard drive? Some people think that JavaScript already has too much power, so the option exists within browsers to disable it. As a developer, you need to have confidence that what you've built will be able to run for all your users, regardless of whether they have something enabled.

Web servers: dishing out hypertext

Together, the web server and web browsers comprise the bare essentials of the World Wide Web. Web servers are computers that are constantly (we hope!) connected to the Internet, and they host websites. They respond to HTTP requests from browsers, serving a host of different types of files that reside online. Web servers are the front line in any website. They handle requests either by fulfilling them or by passing them off to a web application server to dish up dynamic content (we'll cover this in greater depth later in this chapter).

As with all the technologies we'll discuss in this chapter, you have a host of options available in web servers, and the best part is that most of them are free. Some servers are designed for specific purposes: for example, nginx is a speed demon that is great at serving static content, while Mongrel was developed specifically for serving Ruby on Rails applications. Others, like Apache, are generalists that can be easily extended through a series of modules.

Apache HTTP server

Apache is the reigning champion online and has been since 1996. It is an extremely popular web server that runs on virtually every operating system imaginable. (You can even run Apache on an iPhone!) There are a number of reasons for its success, but probably paramount among them is that it's reasonably fast, secure, and extensible.

Apache supports a module architecture where functionality can be added by loading new modules when the server starts. Because of this functionality, things like PHP are easy to add; instead of having to run a separate application server, PHP can be parsed directly through Apache, which makes things faster and easier to administer (we'll cover PHP in greater depth later in the chapter).

Apache has been losing a bit of market share in recent years, though. Because it's so flexible, it's neither as lean nor fast as it could be. That's not a big deal for your Aunt May's cat blog; but for a website like Amazon that serves up tens of thousands of visitors a second, the added bulk of Apache is a bit much. A relatively new contender is taking center stage here: nginx.

nginx

Pronounced engine-x, *nginx* is an extremely light, extremely fast web server that is gaining in popularity, particularly for serving up dynamic content. One of the most appealing things about nginx is that it requires far less horsepower to serve a single request. That means that more requests can be served using the same hardware (which is less expensive). In the past, folks would have to add servers to feed more power to Apache; but now some people are making the switch to nginx and discovering that their current machine is more than capable of handling their current level of requests. Nginx hasn't been around as long as Apache, and it doesn't have the same range of modules (or add-ons) available; nevertheless, it has enough flexibility for most situations.

Microsoft Internet Information Services (IIS)

Microsoft introduced its web server running on the Windows operating system in the mid-1990s. It gained popularity primarily because it was easy to configure and set up in comparison to Apache's command line and text file configuration mechanism (for some strange reason, people like their graphical user interfaces). IIS got quite a bad reputation in the beginning because early versions of the server were full of security holes, opening up the entire machine to an industrious hacker who could even launch self-propagating worms, which would then attack other IIS servers. One of the most notorious worms, Code Red, infected an estimated 360,000 IIS web servers at its peak and caused a noticeable degradation in network speed worldwide.

IIS was growing in popularity as it matured into a more secure and stable hosting environment; however, it too has recently seen a decline in market share. It would appear that more people are turning to open source technology, which offers a broader range of excellent, mature options. Microsoft has responded by bundling in its dynamic .NET languages into IIS, making it really easy to develop dynamic websites on the Windows platform.

Mongrel

A little later in this chapter, you'll read about frameworks and why they're taking off in popularity. Leading the framework pack is Ruby on Rails, and Mongrel is a web server developed specifically for dishing out Rails applications. Mongrel is the uncontested leader in terms of speed, scalability, and stability in serving Rails applications because it supports Ruby natively; other web servers deal with it via a module that executes Ruby code as a common gateway interface (CGI) script.

A wide range of hosting options

We're at a really great time for web development right now. The cost to host a website is falling, and it's easier than ever to outsource your hosting needs to a third party. If you're working for a big organization, chances are that it runs its own servers for web hosting or that it has at least a dedicated machine(s) at a third-party host. Smaller organizations and individuals will often opt for a hosting company and use shared hosting, where multiple websites are all run on the same server. Running a server takes a lot of skill and resources: it has to be connected to the Internet with a fast connection (that DSL line you have at home just won't cut it), it should be backed up regularly, and it should be kept in a secure place, especially if you're storing your customers' personal or financial information in a database. Not to mention, how many people have a backup generator in case of power failure?

You should look at a number of different factors when picking a company to host your website. Obviously, the features/application support will be a big one; if you've written a Ruby on Rails application, you'll need a server that supports Rails. Other considerations to take into account are bandwidth, disk space, machine specs, technical support, and an uptime guarantee.

Most hosting plans will give you a set amount of bandwidth every month. This is usually measured in the gigabytes of data transferred, but larger-capacity hosting plans may offer terabytes of bandwidth (1,000 gigabytes). You'll see a few different options in terms of types of plans offered, ranging from shared hosting to dedicated hosts. A shared host is exactly that: you're sharing the machine that hosts your website with other customers. If one of those other customers has a particularly high-traffic website or does something that locks up the server, your website will also be affected. Although that's not the end of the world for your personal weblog, a company that conducts business online may have a lower tolerance for frequent or extended outages.

The next step up from a shared host is a virtual machine. Virtualization software is special software that will let you run multiple operating systems, or multiple copies of the same operating system, on a single machine. If you're on a Mac and have ever used VMware Fusion or Parallels to run Windows, you're using virtualization software. The big advantage to a virtual machine over shared hosting is that each hosting account is housed within its own container. So, although all customers on a single machine are sharing that machine's resources, each container is isolated from all the others. If customer X does something that locks up his virtual machine, none of the other virtual machines on that computer will be affected. The added benefit of this is that, because customers are isolated from one another, hosting companies are often willing to let customers have more control over their own account. For example, hosting companies will often let their customers install software and reconfigure system and server settings to optimize performance (there's no way you'll get that level of control on a shared-hosting account).

Another option is dedicated hosting, where you get your own machine that is hosted by some other company. This has all the advantages of virtual machine hosting, but you don't have to worry about sharing resources (e.g., RAM, CPU, and bandwidth) with other customers. Shared hosting is by far the cheapest option, whereas dedicated hosting will cost you a few hundred dollars a month (or more).

Finally, there's cloud hosting. With cloud hosting, you pay for the processing, storage, and bandwidth you use with a hosting company, but there is no one machine that hosts your site. Cloud-hosting companies have a network of machines and are basically selling you the capacity you need to serve up your website on that network. The big advantage here is that you only pay for what you use, and this approach can scale up really quickly if you get a big spike in traffic. It is often argued that cloud hosting is more reliable because your hosting needs are spread among a number of machines; if one goes down, it doesn't take out your website. However, that isn't a certainty because there's a weakness in most hosting setups, and something can just as easily go wrong with a cloud host as with a traditional host.

Picking the level of hosting plan you need isn't that hard. Start with the least expensive that you think you can get away with and then upgrade as you go. Most hosting companies are more than happy to let you upgrade your plan at any time; it means they get to charge a higher monthly premium! There's no point buying dedicated hosting for that application you're developing if you're not sure whether you're ever going to have more than a dozen concurrent users.

Picking a host can be really difficult, though. If you just look at ratings and reviews online, you'll never be able to find one (online ratings are all heavily spammed, making it near impossible to identify what is a legitimate review and what is a review from the marketing department of host xyz). Every host has glowingly positive reviews and absolute horror stories posted about it. Your best bet is to ask around to friends, co-workers, and other professionals to see whether they have any recommendations for you.

Databases 101

We posted a question on a blog asking people how they would describe a database to somebody who has absolutely no knowledge of computers. The common consensus was that people would use the analogy of a file cabinet, with database tables being file folders and the individual papers within those folders being records. It's not a bad analogy until you try to explain all the other parts associated with a database setup—things such as primary keys, foreign keys, relationships, and, of course, Structured Query Language (SQL). Let's have a look at all this terminology.

Terminology

The field of database management systems is rife with all kinds of technical terms and acronyms. Here's a quick guide to some of the most common terms:

- A *relational database* is a database system in which the information stored in a table can be joined (or related) to information stored in another table. For example, you might use this kind of system if you are storing business contacts. Chances are that you know a few different people at a single company; instead of storing that company name 3, 10, or 50 different times in the record for each person, you could create a companies table and then just relate each person to the appropriate row in the companies table using the primary key from companies as a *foreign key* in people. The big advantage here is that, if the company gets bought out and changes its name from Acme Corp. to Wonderwhizz Inc., you would need to change that name in a single location only.

- A *relational database management system* (RDBMS) is an application such as MySQL or Oracle, and it is commonly (and incorrectly) referred to as a *database*. This kind of application is actually an RDBMS, the software that interacts with a database.

- A *database*) is a collection of data structured into records within tables. It might help to think of the difference between an RDBMS and a database in these terms: the RDBMS is similar to a web server, whereas a database is similar to all the pages available on that server (except in a far more structured way).

- A *schema* is the structure of the database, including the tables, fields, and any relationships between the tables.

- A *table* is a collection of records within a database. For example, you might have a table for "contact information" in which you list the addresses and phone numbers of a number of different people.

- A *record*, sometimes also referred to as a *row*, is a grouping of similar pieces of data. So for example, a set of contact information for your friend Mary would be a single record. All records within a single table are made up of the same fields.

- A *field*, sometimes also referred to as a *column*, is a single piece of information contained within a record. Mary's phone number would be stored in a field in a database.

- A *primary key* is a special field within a table that uniquely identifies a record. The reason tables have primary keys is so that each record can be uniquely addressed if changes need to be made to it. For example, I might have a table that contains a log of people buying things on a gift card. This log might list that "Ron" bought "1 cup coffee" every day for a month. If that's all it lists and (for some reason) you have to go in and say that he didn't in fact buy every seventh cup of coffee, then you would have no way of addressing those particular records. A primary key is often just a sequentially numbered field.

- A *foreign key* is the special piece of information that relates a record in one table to a record in another table. The foreign key in one table will refer to the primary key in another table.

- *Structured Query Language* (SQL) is a standardized language developed specifically for interacting with relational databases. SQL lets you add, remove, update, and query data. There are small variations in SQL syntax from one database system to the next; but for the most part, once you have the basics of SQL mastered, you'll be able to work with practically any database system out there.

The world outside relational databases

A lot of the terminology covered previously is specific to relational databases. Most DBMSs available today are relational because it's frequently advantageous to design your database schema in a relational manner to avoid the duplication of information. But RDBMSs aren't the only game in town, and there are a couple of other types of databases that you may run into online, so it's worth mentioning them here.

These DBMSs are frequently referred to using the broad grouping of "NoSQL" databases because they do not support and use structured query language for interacting with the information stored in the database. NoSQL databases are frequently used in very specific and unique circumstances (such as the Google BigTable—a compressed, proprietary database that powers the Google search index).

Object databases

Object databases aren't too common outside of very specific scientific applications. There is a very common and popular content-management framework called Zope that uses an object database, however. The Zope Object Database (ZODB) is ideal in its application because it supports versioning natively, allowing someone to undo a change made on the website.

XML databases

XML is widely used online for data exchange between websites/web applications, but it's also an effective way of storing data. Occasionally, this term will be used for referring to XML data stored within an RDBMS, but native XML databases also exist.

The biggest advantage to storing data in XML format is that XML is widely used for data exchange. Because of this, there is no need to convert data to/from XML, which saves on processing costs (that is, the server doesn't have a bunch of extra operations to perform). XML files can be copied from one machine to another and used immediately—there's no need to install additional software.

XML databases store data in nodes, which is the correct term for data arranged within a hierarchical structure of XML tags. Instead of using SQL to query an XML database, two forms of querying syntax are widely in use: XPath and XQuery (which is just an extension of XPath). Each provides a way to extract data from an XML database by providing a syntax for addressing the database's nodes.

Relational databases

A relational database simply means that data in one table can be joined (or related) to data in another table through the use of keys. Relational databases strive to normalize data; that is, they try to eliminate any duplication of data between records and tables. Normalized data is a good thing: if there is duplication of data within a database, the chance exists for there to be a data anomaly, which occurs when the two pieces of data become out of sync (think about our previous "company name" example).

For example, if you were developing an online store with a series of products, chances are you would have a table listing each of those products, along with their price and description. Occasionally, you might want to be able to offer certain items on sale by marking them down 15 percent. Instead of creating a table of sale items and duplicating the product names, descriptions, and prices there, you would simply relate to the original products table by referencing the primary key in that table and listing the discount. You might also include a field for terms and conditions of that item (e.g., the offer expires on the 15th of the month). That way, if a product's price changes, it needs to be updated in only one place.

Before we get started on how you interact with tables, do yourself a favor and find a good database client that makes it easy to create, delete, and alter tables. There are SQL statements you can use to do that, but it's way faster to just be able to create tables and columns with the click of a mouse.

Structured Query Language (SQL)

There are four main types of interactions you'll have with databases using SQL: SELECTs for getting data out of a database, INSERTs for adding data to a database, UPDATEs for changing data in a database, and DELETEs for removing data.

Getting data out

What good is creating a database of information if you can never get anything out of it? If you return to the original filing cabinet analogy, being able to find specific data within a database is the single biggest advantage over the old paper-based alternative.

How often have you looked at a big stack of papers and thought to yourself, "Gee, I wish I could just run Google on that"? (OK, so it might just be us.) If you boil it down, though, search engines are really just great big databases full of information about the information on the Web. Every time you run a search on Google, you're running a query on a database.

In SQL terms, that query looks something like this:

```
SELECTurl
FROMwebsites
WHERE content="that thing I'm looking for"
```

If you dissect this statement, it's actually pretty easy to read. You're asking for the url field from the websites table. Instead of just returning all the URLs stored in the table, you're narrowing the search down and getting only the URLs where the content field has "that thing I'm looking for" as a value.

There are a bunch of other options we could throw in here, such as an ORDER BY to sort the results or an INNER JOIN to relate the data from this table to the data stored in another table.

Putting data in

Your database would get stale pretty quickly if you couldn't add new information as it became available. SQL uses an INSERT to do this:

```
INSERT INTO websites (url, content) VALUES ("http://www.amazon.com/",
"A really big store that sells a bunch of stuff")
```

Again, breaking this down, you're adding a record to the websites table. We've specified two fields in this table, url and content, and given them both values. Depending on how the table is set up, there may be other fields in the table that you haven't specified. However, when you're creating a table, you have to go out of your way to specify that a field can have a NULL value; otherwise, running this SQL will give you an error.

Changing data

Shoot, that last addition we made makes it sound like Amazon is actually a store, located somewhere. We had better change the content field to clear that up:

```
UPDATEwebsites
SET content="An e-commerce website that sells a wide range of products"
WHEREurl="http://www.amazon.com/"
```

The first part of this SQL statement should speak for itself at this point. You're updating the websites table and setting the content field to have a better description. The last part (after WHERE) is the interesting part. You need to have some way to tell the RDBMS which record you want to update. In this case, you've done that with the url field, but this could backfire on you. If there were more than one record with http://www.amazon.com/ listed as the URL, all those records would be updated, as well. On the other hand, you may have specified that the URL is in fact the primary key in your table, in which case there could not be multiple Amazon.com records listed (recall that a primary key enforces unique values between records). You would get an error if you tried to insert another one.

Removing data

Websites come and go. Although it's not likely that you'll be removing Amazon from your database for that reason, you may at some point notice that your favorite store for buying lawn gnomes is now offline. You will need to keep things up-to-date:

```
DELETE FROM websites
WHEREurl="http://www.ultimatelawngnomes.c om/"
```

This snippet is a nice, simple statement to remove the ultimatelawngnomes.com site from the database. The same caution that applies to updating records also applies to deleting records; namely, you should try, whenever possible, to specify the primary key in the WHERE statement, so as to limit your deletes to the actual record you intend to delete. In this example, it would be OK because, even if you had multiple records for ultimatelawngnomes.com and the site really had gone offline, you would probably want to eliminate all such records. On the other hand, going into the HR database of a large company and running a DELETE on all records where the last name of the person is Smith may not be the best idea (that's why a lot of companies have employee ID numbers as the primary key; duplicates are not allowed).

Your best bet for learning more about SQL is to check out www.w3schools.com/sql/. The site has a pretty good set of introductory lessons to SQL. If you get further into databases, be sure to check out the documentation specific to your RDBMS because it might have some specific functions that can save you time and significantly speed up your queries.

A look at the RDBMS players

There are literally hundreds of different database systems, all great at different things. The ones listed in the following sections are the most common, so you're likely to run into them at some point when developing a website. We have limited the field here to database servers, so applications such as Microsoft Access didn't make the cut. Although you could use Microsoft Access as the back-end for a website (we have before), it doesn't scale really well because it doesn't handle concurrent users all that efficiently. If you're comfortable with Microsoft products, you're better off upgrading to Microsoft Access's big brother—Microsoft SQL Server.

Oracle

The longtime heavyweight in the database world and reigning RDBMS champ is definitely Oracle. Chances are really good that, if you have a large organization running a database, that database is Oracle. Having been around since the late 1970s, Oracle is a tested and proven solution for storing and retrieving large quantities of data (it's also the most expensive option available). Oracle is well known for its ability to handle extremely large data sets and to work with them in a fairly efficient manner (i.e., running a query on a million records isn't a daylong activity). However, it's definitely overkill for running that blog that your client has asked for.

Microsoft SQL Server

Microsoft introduced its own commercial RDBMS to try to compete with Oracle: Microsoft SQL Server (MSSQL). Early on, this database just wasn't up to snuff at handling large amounts of data, and it experienced a few security vulnerabilities. It's fair to say that, because of the database's rocky start, Microsoft hasn't really made a dent in the market that Oracle addresses (really big databases/applications); however, MSSQL is still a pretty big player in medium-sized applications. Those customers who need an Oracle-sized system will still buy Oracle. Those who think that Oracle would be overkill will generally either go with Microsoft or go with one of the open source alternatives.

Microsoft does offer an Express edition of its SQL server product, which is free, but it's generally not recommended for use in a live environment, and it certainly doesn't have the same performance as the full SQL Server product. Express is a great offering for building and testing against though!

MySQL

MySQL is the most popular open source database system available. It gained a great deal of popularity early on because it was really fast compared to PostgreSQL (see the next section), and it worked amazingly well for web applications. A number of large Internet companies have skipped the Oracle bandwagon altogether and have invested heavily in MySQL as their primary RDBMS.

Even though the software is open source, there is still a commercial company behind MySQL. This means that companies that want to use MySQL have someone to lean on for support. MySQL AB (the company behind MySQL) was purchased by Sun Microsystems, a hardware and software company that had been around for quite some time. In an interesting turn of events, in 2009 Sun was purchased by Oracle, so now MySQL is officially owned by the database giant. The world is getting smaller!

One of the big reasons for MySQL's popularity among open source RDBMSs is that a number of excellent front-ends are available. For example, phpMyAdmin is an interface written entirely in PHP, and it's hosted online, which allows developers to create, delete, and modify databases and tables within MySQL. It also allows developers to add, update, delete, and query data easily. MySQL AB has also released a number of GUI tools for Windows, Linux, and Mac OS X that ease development and server administration.

PostgreSQL

PostgreSQL is another excellent open source RDBMS that is completely driven and maintained by the user community. A couple of companies provide commercial support for PostgreSQL, but they are only peripherally involved in the continued development and evolution of the software (they're members of the user community, just like everybody else).

PostgreSQL's biggest selling point is that it's quite Oracle-like in the way it works and in its syntax subtleties. Therefore, companies looking for an open source alternative to Oracle's high licensing fees often turn to PostgreSQL because it provides the path of least resistance.

Other data sources

We talked a lot in the previous chapter about interoperability and the sharing data between different websites and web applications. This is generally accomplished using XML or JSON (JavaScript Object Notation); however, there are a handful of other terms and acronyms that you should probably be aware of when discussing data exchange:

- *Web services* are software systems that allow for computer-to-computer interaction over the Web (not necessarily involving the interaction of a person). It's a general term that can be used to refer to something as complex as an API or something as simple as an RSS feed from a weblog.

- *SOAP* is a protocol for exchanging XML messages over the Web (using HTTP or HTTPS).

- A *remote procedure call* (RPC) is a way of having one computer initiate a procedure on another computer without having the details of this interaction explicitly programmed. In other words, RPC is a way of getting another computer on the network to do something and return a result to your computer. On the World Wide Web, RPC will most commonly be used in conjunction with XML for data exchange between machines (XML-RPC).

- An *application programming interface* (API) is a series of *hooks* built into an application that allows external access to the application's data and functionality. An API is usually very similar to the four main database operations we discussed: GET (SELECT), DELETE (DELETE), POST (UPDATE) and PUT (INSERT).

One of the best things about developing applications for the Web is that there already exists a wide array of data repositories available to tie into your application. It's easy to integrate input from your users with map data available from Google and housing information stored in a database, as some realtors are now doing.

Web application languages

As with our look at databases, you'll find many applications available for programming on the Web. These are commonly called *scripting languages*, or *server-side scripting languages*, to be more precise. Each of these options uses a different syntax; but at the end of the day, they all pretty much do the same thing. While some may have certain strengths over others, when it comes to small- to medium-sized web applications, you really won't notice a huge difference in performance between any of the players.

If you're just starting out and you're not sure what language is best to pick up, we recommend sticking to PHP. It's free and is widely used, and PHP hosting plans are offered for next-to-nothing from a wide range of companies. Whatever you pick, don't sweat your decision too much. We have one friend who's a brilliant Python programmer and complains a great deal about the lack of job postings for Python developers. The fact of the matter is that, because he knows Python, he can easily pick up any number of other languages and be proficient in a matter of weeks (and he has for various projects).

PHP

By far the most popular scripting language on the Web among developers is PHP, which is free and is often installed with the Apache web server (the most common web server on the Web). PHP was designed to be a scripting language for the Web, so it focuses a great deal on the needs of web developers.

Chances are, if you've downloaded an open source web application (such as WordPress, Drupal, or PHPBB), that tool is written in PHP. PHP is widely used among open source web application developers because it is often self-contained; end users don't have to install a bunch of other software to get things working. To install a PHP application, it's usually as easy as uploading the files to your web host, creating a database, and editing a configuration file (of course, depending on the application, your mileage may vary). Organizations of all sizes have rolled out PHP-based applications in some capacity.

PHP is a great starting point for people wanting to learn web application development. Because it's free, you can download a copy and install it on your own web server (if you don't feel like spending a few bucks for a hosting plan). PHP got a bit of a reputation for having security problems early on, which has prevented its adoption in a lot of large organizations; however, that's definitely changed. Organizations we know that had previously never touched PHP are rolling out redesigns of their corporate websites using PHP-based content-management systems.

Ruby

Ruby is a computer language that has been around since 1993, but it previously was not considered a strong contender for developing web applications. It's only with the introduction of the Ruby on Rails framework (which we'll discuss in a moment) that Ruby has joined the mainstream for web application development. Since the introduction of Rails, many other Ruby-based frameworks have been introduced, as well (e.g., Sinatra is a great place to start if you want to learn Ruby).

Developers are tired of having to repeatedly develop the same "type" of application, and they have turned to Ruby on Rails to streamline the process. Rails is an "opinionated" framework; that is, if you surrender to a few conventions offered in the framework, it can significantly speed up your development projects. Rails has seen a huge uptake among technology startup companies, and it is now (and has been for some time) accepted as a stable, well supported framework. Today, it powers some extremely popular web applications.

Python

Python, similar to Ruby, has been in existence since the early 1990s. However, it was not until recently that it has been adopted as a mainstream web application language. Python has gained a lot of steam because it has been used extensively by Google. It scales extremely well, is a high-performance language, and has a reasonably strong community. It's not as widely used as some other options.

ASP.NET

ASP.NET (once upon a time ASP stood for Active Server Pages) is the Microsoft-centric solution to web application development. The biggest advantage of ASP.NET is that it integrates well with other Microsoft offerings; users can be authenticated off Active Directory servers easily, for example. ASP.NET has been around for quite some time, but it is available only on Microsoft IIS servers. You'll find ASP.NET used primarily at large Microsoft-centric organizations, but there are a few stand-alone applications written in ASP. NET, as well. .NET developers are an interesting breed. A solid .NET developer can do anything—the sky's the limit. However, there is a barrier to entry because .NET hosting can be more expensive than choosing an open source route.

Java/JSP

Java/JavaServer Pages (JSP) were quite popular during the first web boom in the 1990s, but they have somewhat died off since. Java was a quite common skill for developers during the dot-com boom, but today it is pretty onerous to use for developing web applications. JSP didn't die out because it lacked functionality or because it was an inferior technology, but because development cycles took too long. We don't mean for it to sound like we're ringing the death bell for JSP—it's still used in a number of enterprises—but you don't see many startups choosing JSP for their applications these days.

In all honesty, the previous paragraph is as true today as it was five years ago, and Java is still hanging in there. It hasn't gained tremendously in market share, but it hasn't lost much, either. So we're going to go out on a limb and say that Java is just going to hang in there for the foreseeable future.

Frameworks

A framework is one step above a web application language in terms of functionality. Frameworks are a collection of functions and libraries that make web development easier by automating some of the common (and tedious) tasks in developing a website. Things such as user login/logout and access control are used in a lot of different web applications, so why would you want to write code to manage that function over and over again? Similarly, a lot of web applications use a database on the back-end to do adds, updates, deletes, and listings; but wouldn't it be nice if there were a simple way to build a basic page to add a record to the database, without having to rewrite that code in SQL repeatedly?

Why bother with frameworks?

Frameworks aren't a new idea, but they really seem to have taken off in popularity recently. Everyone seems to have an idea about how best to implement a framework: some people prefer flexibility to efficiency; others just want to keep things simple. Most of the major frameworks support similar features; they just take a different approach to how they do it. Most frameworks are language-specific; however, there are a few that have been ported between languages.

For the most part, you need to learn the language before you become proficient with a framework. Once you do reach that point, however, frameworks can save you a great deal of time and really allow you to focus on the big picture instead of worrying about writing code to interact with your database (to list one example). There is no right or wrong time to use a framework; if you are comfortable working in a particular language, it might be a good time to branch out and explore the frameworks available to you. Whether you're creating a big project or a small one, frameworks will save you time.

A few popular candidates

Frameworks are available for every language and every purpose. We've limited the discussion to three here, all based on popular open source languages. If you're not into Ruby, PHP, or Python, however, just run a search for *<language> framework,* and we guarantee you'll get at least two or three solid results.

Ruby on Rails

Ruby on Rails (RoR) is a great example of a web-development framework. An enterprising developer, David Heinemeier Hansson, created Ruby on Rails when he was working on a project-management web application. He grew bored of always having to rewrite the same code over and over again and realized that some of the process could be automated.

Frameworks can be great boosts to productivity, but they can also impose constraints on your development process. For example, Ruby on Rails applies a *convention over configuration* philosophy to development: if you follow certain conventions, the code will almost write itself; otherwise, you'll end up rewriting a bunch of stuff by hand. One example of this occurs if you create a class called product (i.e., it is meant to add/delete/edit products in your database). Ruby on Rails will assume that the table in your database storing product information will be called products. It's not a big deal, but some organizations may have a strict naming scheme in place for database tables—for example, they may require that you put the name of the department before your table name. In cases like that, you're going to have to do a little extra legwork (you can still use Rails, but you'll need to spend a little extra time configuring things instead of using some of the framework's built-in convention over configuration functionality).

Another feature of Rails (and several other frameworks for that matter) that's worth mentioning is its extensive implementation of the Model-View-Controller (MVC) architecture. We've talked about separating content from function when using HTML5, CSS, and JavaScript. MVC is sort of like an implementation of this in server-side development:

- The *model* handles all the data and logic in an application. It isn't directly responsible for data storage. Although we've focused on databases in this chapter, there are certainly other ways of storing data, such as a flat-text file or as an XML file. The model is more interested in "working data"—such as the total for a person's cart is $99.95 or that Friday is three days from today.

- The *view* is the presentation layer. Any sort of user interface rendering is handled through the view, from the colors used on a page to the placement of check boxes and input fields in a form. The view will often generate the UI on the fly based on information from the model.

- The *controller* is responsible for handling input, interacting with the model, and returning output back to the view. All of the application legwork is done in the controller.

CakePHP

If Ruby on Rails isn't your thing—or if you're already a whiz at PHP, but you love the idea of what a framework has to offer—then you're in luck. There is a long list of frameworks available for PHP, and most of them implement MVC architecture. CakePHP is one such framework for PHP that has grown in popularity since its creation in 2005. Although it shares a number of features with Ruby on Rails, it's been written from the ground up as its own distinct and powerful framework.

One of the big advantages of CakePHP is its ease of use and excellent documentation. If you're new to PHP, you may just want to skip all the groundwork and dive right into CakePHP—chances are you'll be able to accomplish 95 percent of what you set out to do with it right out of the box.

Django

Python developers out there need not feel left out (nor should ASP.NET developers nor pretty much anyone else—there is a framework for just about any popular web application language). For example, Django offers Python developers features similar to the other frameworks we've covered, and it has been used on a few high-profile web applications (such as Revver and Pownce).

Of special note, Python developers might want to consider Google's Google App Engine application platform, which essentially lets you host your web application with Google. The Google App Engine has built-in Python support, and developers were using Django quite extensively in the early applications that were built to run on this platform. It's definitely a great boost for the Python programming language and the Django framework.

Summary

As we mentioned in throughout this chapter, it doesn't really matter what application server, language, or framework you choose (assuming you even have a choice). They're all mature enough products that they are equally capable in their feature sets. If you're new to the area, pick something open source because those products are the easiest and least expensive to learn on.

It's easy to get bogged down in language/database/framework discussions on projects. If you're going to be doing the technical development, you should ultimately be the one making the decision on what to use. Developers have to be confident in the tools they use; if the back-end architecture is being dictated to you, but it's something you've never worked with, then be sure to either get some help or to allow extra time for learning the technology. End users can tell whether there are problems in a site's construction.

Chapter 12

Using WordPress to Jumpstart Development

Up to this point in the book, we've covered a lot of the bases for building a website from scratch. We've talked about the most fundamental building blocks of the web and how to combine those together to get up and running with a website. We've covered using JavaScript to add some interactivity to our pages and to make things dynamic. We've even briefly looked at various server-side languages and systems that can help to make a website a truly dynamic system.

It's all quite daunting and overwhelming, isn't it? This chapter is going to let you in on a little trick that will give you everything that we've talked about, but also have you up and running in a matter of minutes (give yourself quite a few of those minutes the first time around—you're still learning, after all). In this chapter, we're going to take a look at an excellent open source blogging and content-management system called WordPress.

This chapter builds on our knowledge up to this point. We don't have the time or space dive into the details of using PHP and database in this book, yet that is exactly what we're going to use to leverage WordPress in this chapter. We still won't be diving into all the gritty details; but by the end of this chapter, you will have a completely functional database-driven website.

Introducing WordPress

WordPress is a really great piece of software that was built using many of the technologies that we've already discussed. The current version has valid HTML and CSS, and it is written using PHP and powered by a MySQL database. You might not have keyed in on the best part of those last two sentences, though: WordPress has already been built! You don't have to spend hours (or days) reinventing the wheel and writing code that will let you build a database-powered website; you just have to install WordPress, adjust some settings, and customize it as much or as little as you see fit.

This chapter will run through downloading and installing WordPress locally, on the desktop machine. This is always a good starting place—you always want to have a place to test your website before uploading it to the web host you've selected.

Installing WordPress

Before we get on with installing anything, we've got to make sure that we have the required software available to run things. It would take an entire chapter to run through how to manually install PHP, MySQL, and a web server, so we're going to take a shortcut here.

Whether you're on Windows or a Mac, there's an extremely easy way to run all three of these components:

- www.mamp.info/en/index.html: MAMP (and its big brother, MAMP Pro) on the Mac gives you a one-click download and setup of Apache, MySQL, and PHP. It even bundles a nice graphical user interface for configuring your servers. MAMP is free, while MAMP Pro has a small licensing fee (for our purposes, all we need is MAMP).

- www.wampserver.com/en/: WampServer provides similar functionality for Windows users. It provides one-click downloading and installation, and you're up and running.

The authors are on a Mac, so we'll be describing the MAMP setup process. However, WampServer is just as easy to download and install, so all these instructions broadly apply to that software, as well. With MAMP, once you've completed your installation, head over to your /Applications folder, open up the MAMP folder, and double-click MAMP.app. You should see something similar to what's shown in Figure 12-1.

The green lights in the Status window on the left indicate that Apache Server (with PHP) and MySQL Server are up and running. Take a minute to go brag to your friends that you just set up a complete website testing environment. Done? Okay, onward! Chances are that when you started up MAMP, it also started up your web browser and took you to the MAMP Start page. Click the phpInfo link along the top of that page.

Hey, that's great news! It means that you've now got PHP up and running properly. Next, click phpMyAdmin. You might remember that we mentioned phpMyAdmin in Chapter 11 of this book. phpMyAdmin is a piece of software, written entirely in PHP, that allows you to interact with your MySQL database server. You're going to need this in order to create the database needed by WordPress—in fact, let's take care of that right now.

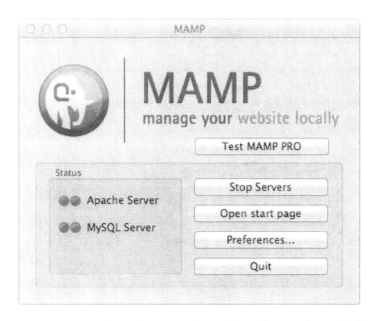

Figure 12-1. MAMP is up and running, and it provides a complete testing environment for developing PHP- and MySQL-based websites.

Creating a database and user

Follow these steps to create the database and user profile:

1. Click the Databases tab and, at the bottom of the page under create new database, type in wordpress. When you eventually host this website live on the Internet, you'll want to use something more descriptive than what you've got here, but this will do for now.

2. Select utf8_bin as the collation (that creates our database with Unicode support) and click the Create button. You'll see a message saying that the database was created successfully.

3. You're ready to create a user who can access that database—click the Privileges tab, and then click the Add a new User link.

4. It's time to add a username (the authors used the extremely creative "wordpress" as our username). For the host, select local. The authors let phpMyAdmin generate a password, but feel free to set up your own.

5. Note the username and password you select; you're going to need them when installing WordPress.

6. Under the Database for user section, select the Grant all privileges on database "wordpress" option, and then click the Go button. Your settings should look something like what is shown in Figure 12-2.

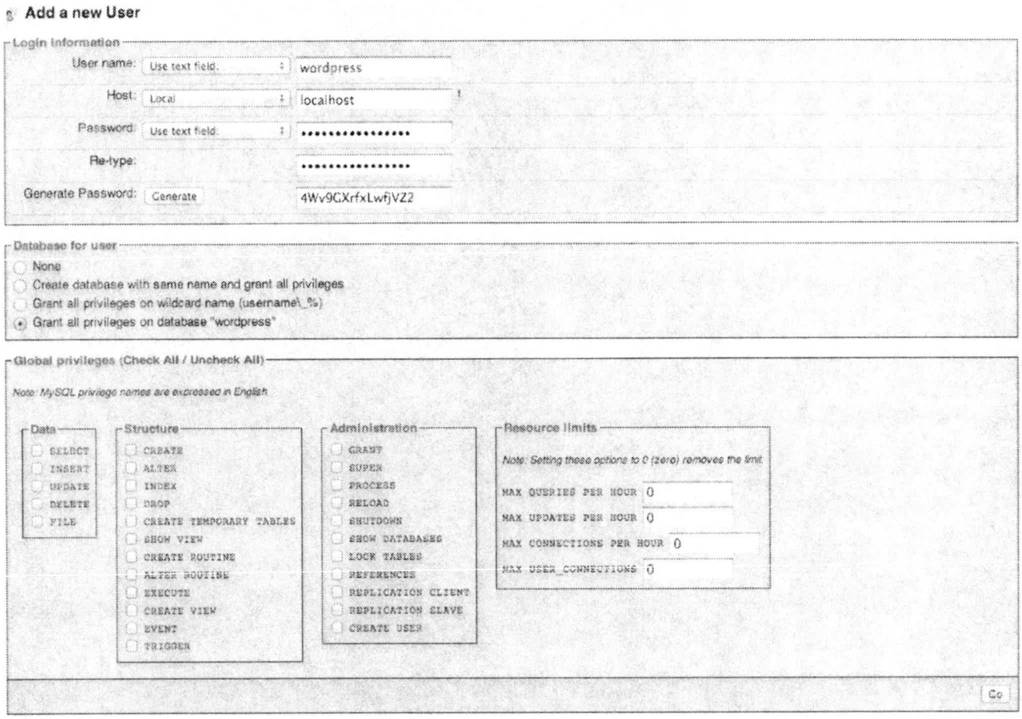

Figure 12-2. Database settings for out testing environment

Grab a copy of WordPress

You've got your preliminary setup done. Now it's time to grab a copy of WordPress and get that set up and running:

7. Head over to `http://wordpress.org/download/` and download the latest version.

8. Download the zip file and uncompress it. MAMP keeps its website files (i.e., its document root) at `/Applications/MAMP/htdocs/` by default. Copy the entire contents of your wordpress zip file into that folder.

9. Now, if you load `http://localhost:8888` (again, that's the default for MAMP, but you can specify a different port number), you should see something like what's displayed in Figure 12-3. This is perfect; it means that you have WordPress installed and that it's being processed by PHP and served to you by Apache (have you broken a sweat, yet?). It is also telling you that you have some configuring to do, so it's time to get started on that.

10. Click the Create Configuration File button.

11. The next screen says that WordPress needs some information about your database (see Figure 12-4). No problem: You set that up earlier and noted of all of the relevant information! Click the Let's go! button.

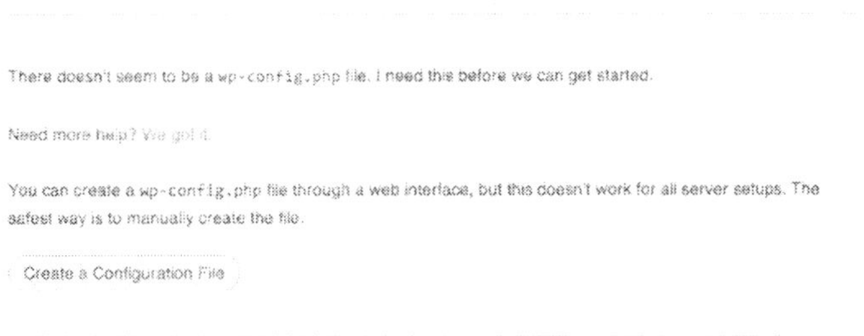

There doesn't seem to be a wp-config.php file. I need this before we can get started.

Need more help? We got it.

You can create a wp-config.php file through a web interface, but this doesn't work for all server setups. The safest way is to manually create the file.

Create a Configuration File

Figure 12-3. The newly installed, but not yet configured WordPress

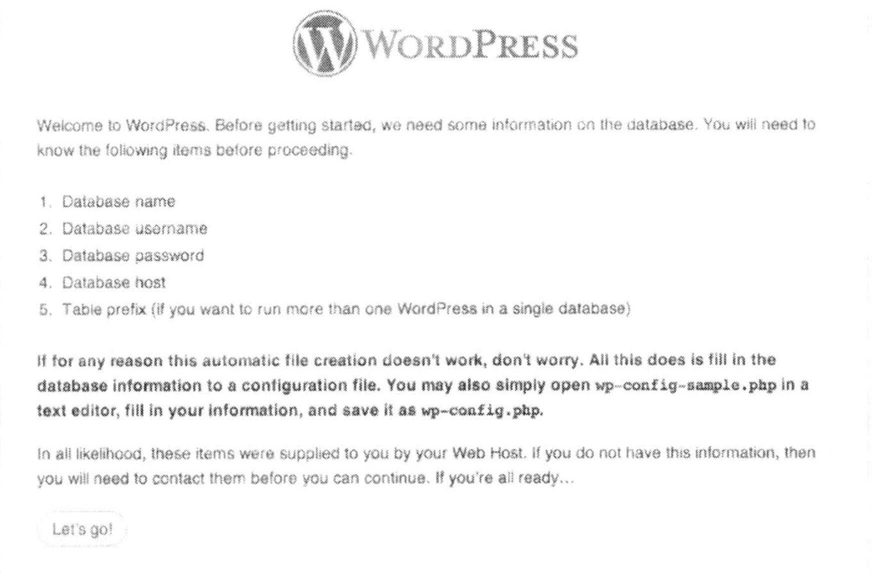

Welcome to WordPress. Before getting started, we need some information on the database. You will need to know the following items before proceeding.

1. Database name
2. Database username
3. Database password
4. Database host
5. Table prefix (if you want to run more than one WordPress in a single database)

If for any reason this automatic file creation doesn't work, don't worry. All this does is fill in the database information to a configuration file. You may also simply open wp-config-sample.php in a text editor, fill in your information, and save it as wp-config.php.

In all likelihood, these items were supplied to you by your Web Host. If you do not have this information, then you will need to contact them before you can continue. If you're all ready...

Let's go!

Figure 12-4. The WordPress Welcome screen

12. Enter your database name (again, the authors used wordpress, but you might have used something else), the username (again, we just used "wordpress"), and your password. The database host in this case will be localhost (i.e., the same machine you're working on), and you can just leave the table prefix as-is. In the end, you should end up with something like Figure 12-5. Click the Submit button.

Figure 12-5. The WordPress Database settings—this screen looks daunting, but this is all information you provided in the previous section, so it's all readily available.

13. If all goes according to plan, you'll get a friendly message saying that you were able to connect to the database and that this part of the installation is done (if you didn't get that, go back and double-check your username, password, and database name). Click the Run the install button.

14. You're on the last step now, which involves setting up a few settings and creating an account on WordPress (see Figure 12-6). Your site title is just that—it's what will appear on your website when people visit. For the sake of this chapter, let's carry on with the Summer Smash example used in previous chapters. For a username, select something other than "admin" (for security reasons) and then select a good, strong password. Setting up good security here is important because anybody with administrative access to your WordPress website will be able to change anything he wants on the website—an ounce of prevention is worth a pound of cure! Enter your e-mail address (this is so that you can reset your password, not to sign you up for any mailing lists), and then click the Install WordPress button.

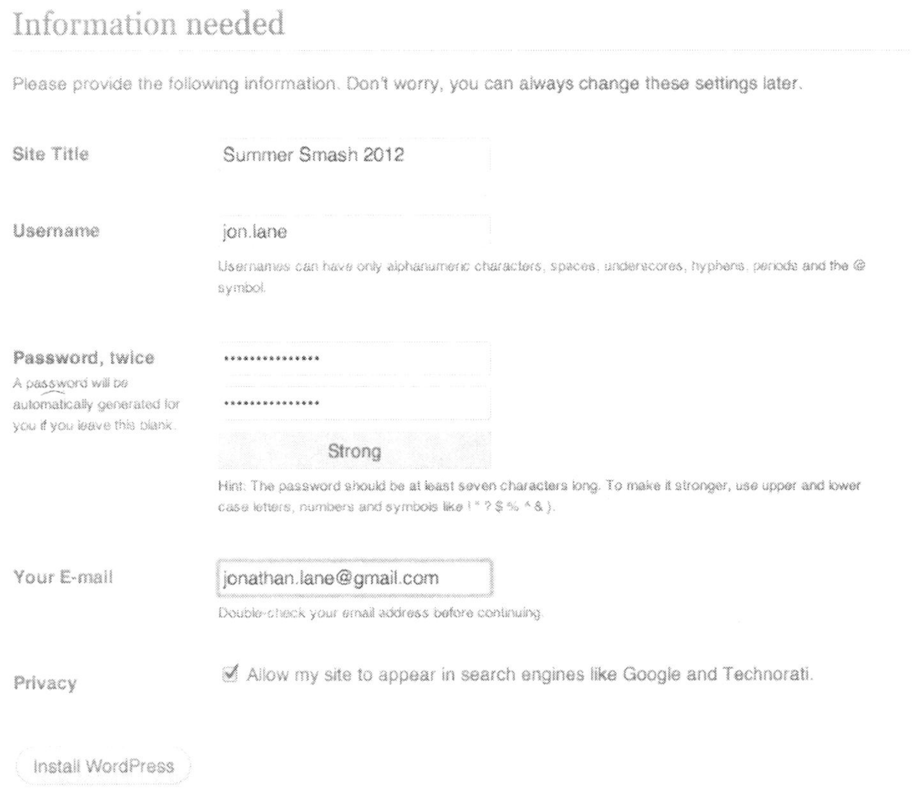

Information needed

Please provide the following information. Don't worry, you can always change these settings later.

Site Title	Summer Smash 2012
Username	jon.lane
	Usernames can have only alphanumeric characters, spaces, underscores, hyphens, periods and the @ symbol.
Password, twice	••••••••••••••
A password will be automatically generated for you if you leave this blank.	••••••••••••••
	Strong
	Hint: The password should be at least seven characters long. To make it stronger, use upper and lower case letters, numbers and symbols like ! " ? $ % ^ &).
Your E-mail	jonathan.lane@gmail.com
	Double-check your email address before continuing.
Privacy	☑ Allow my site to appear in search engines like Google and Technorati.

Install WordPress

Figure 12-6. Setting up a WordPress administrator account and selecting a good password

Again, you'll receive a friendly confirmation that everything is set up and ready to go. Click the Log in button.

A little customization

By this point, you've come a long way. You've set up a web server, an application server, and a relational database management system (or a database server, if you prefer). You've also created a database, installed one of the world's most popular content-management systems, and performed some basic configuration. That's not bad for a few minutes of work!

If you're following along, you're probably looking at a WordPress login box that is asking for your username and password. Let's delay logging in for a minute, though, and instead go take a look at the website as it sits right now. Click the link at the bottom of the page that reads, Back to Summer Smash 2012.

Not bad, right? Figure 12-7 shows your default WordPress website without any additional customization or styling. Do you want to be further impressed? Try resizing your browser window down, so that it's really tall and narrow. Notice how the page format changes, depending on your viewport. What you have here is a responsive website! The default theme in WordPress is, in fact, a responsive theme, and it provides a ton of customization options (as you'll see in a second).

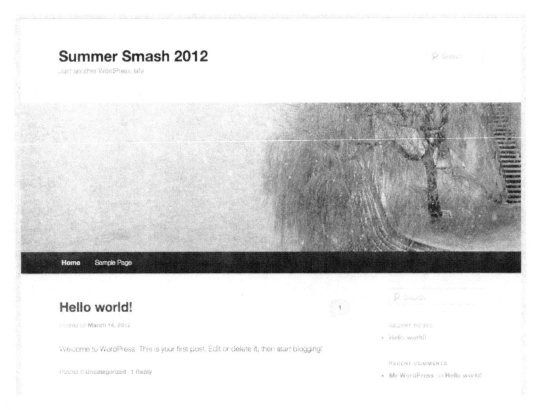

Figure 12-7. The default Wordpress theme is a completely responsive design. It's not very smashing, but it's a great place to start.

Feel free to click around and look at a few of the pages. By default, WordPress is set up to be a weblog. What you're seeing on the home page is a listing of posts made. Posts support comments, so that visitors to the website can respond to what they read. These posts are also searchable, and they are automatically organized by category and chronologically by month (you can see links for all of this in the sidebar of the page).

Finally, WordPress provides an RSS feed of your entries and comments. This means that visitors to the website can subscribe to your news feed using a news reader. Click the Log in link in the sidebar and head back to the Login page. Enter your username and password, so you can check out some of the options available.

The Dashboard

Once logged in, you're presented with the WordPress Dashboard (see Figure 12-8) and a nice getting started message. This message is a relatively recent addition to WordPress, but it is super helpful because a lot of the links listed here walk you through exactly what you'll need to do for the site. Let's start in the left column by clicking the Select your tagline and timezone link.

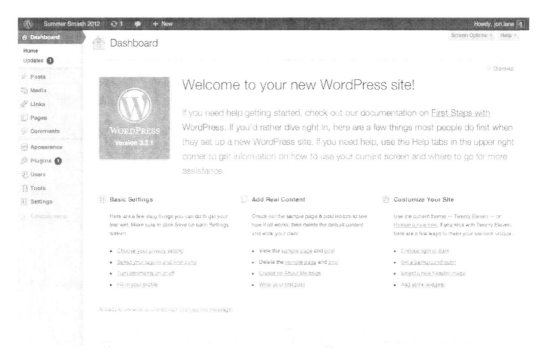

Figure 12-8. The WordPress Dashboard: This is the perfect place to start customizing your website.

You may recall that in earlier chapters we used "This Summer's Most Smashing Event" as the site's tagline. Let's put that in here. Select your timezone and set any date and time formatting options you want. Click the Save Changes button when you're done and head back to the Dashboard. Next, click the Turn comments on or off link.

This screen is largely about customizing blog-type settings. If you don't plan on running a blog (or using the blog functionality for a "news" section on your website), then you can safely skip over this section. If you are going to use WordPress' blogging abilities, then it's worthwhile to take a couple of seconds to set up how you'd like to deal with comments.

Most of the settings on this page are pretty self-explanatory. You can be as easy going or as strict as you'd like with who can post a comment on your site. The top section, Default article settings, requires a little explanation. This section will allow WordPress to automatically "notify" websites (usually other blogs) that you've linked to them. Also, it will automatically create a link on the other weblog leading back to your particular post (it's a bit like magic). This can be great for generating inbound traffic from other websites; however, it is also a mechanism that can be used to *spam* your website with links to other websites (just a heads up). The basic rule of online communities is that, if you're going to have one (i.e., allowing folks to comment on your site is implicitly taking steps to build a community), then you have to participate and moderate it.

Tweak any other settings you like, and then head back to the Dashboard! Your next step is to create a few pages for your website, and then change your home page over to something other than the default.

1. Click the Pages link in the sidebar, and then click the Add New button. WordPress provides some basic editing tools to put together your page.

2. You're not going to bother authoring anything too wonderful at this stage, so just enter "Summer Smash Home" as your page title and leave the body blank for the time being.

3. If you left comments on in the previous step, you'll probably want to turn them off for this page (who wants to have a bunch of anonymous comments on her home page?). Click the Screen Options link in the upper-right corner and put a check in the box next to Discussion.

4. Uncheck the Allow comments and Allow trackbacks & pingbacks options. All of the other settings on the page can be left as-is, so click Publish. You should receive a confirmation that the page is published, as shown in Figure 12-9.

5. Click the All Pages link in the sidebar.

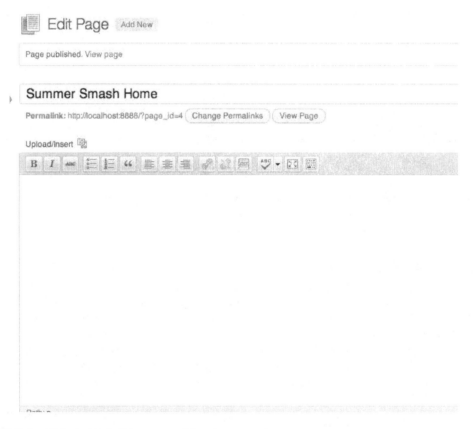

Figure 12-9. A published page (in this case, our future home page)

You've now got two pages on your website, the sample page that was created by default by WordPress, and the home page you just created. Hover over the sample page and click the Trash link (you won't be needing that page). At the top of the screen, you can see that the page was moved to the trash and that you can undo that last action (that's reassuring, just in case you delete something you'd rather keep).

You are going to use WordPress' blog functionality; you just don't want it to be your home page. To that end, you want to create a second page called "Summer Smash News" that you can use for posting updates (see if you can create the page yourself!).

Next up is another Settings page: the Reading Settings page. Click Settings and then Reading in the sidebar. Under the Front Page Displays section, select the second option, and then assign your Home page as the home page and set your News page to handle posts. Remember to click the Save Changes button!

Let's pause for a second and take a quick look at what you've got. Click the words "Summer Smash 2012" in the bar at the top of the page, and you'll be taken to a preview of what your website looks like. You'll see a masthead graphic with a navigation menu below it (it currently contains two links: Home and Summer Smash News). Things are coming along, but you've got a few more things you need to do.

Extending WordPress

WordPress gets used in a lot of places for a lot of different things. The built-in functionality is pretty great, but when you need to take things a step further, you'll need to call in a little help. The following features can really help you get the most out of WordPress:

- *Plugins*: These allow you to add additional functionality to your website (e.g., a members' area, a discussion forum, or a registration form).

- *Themes*: These are pre-packaged styles for WordPress websites that allow you to completely change the look of your site with just a few clicks.

We're already using a theme in WordPress; by default, WordPress comes with a great, responsive, standards-compliant theme called Twenty Eleven (this changes from time to time, but at the time of writing, Twenty Eleven is the default). You can buy additional themes, install free ones, develop your own, or just tweak/customize an existing theme (this is what you'll do for Summer Smash).

Changing the look of WordPress

It's easy to change the look-and-feel of WordPress. Follow these steps to do so:

1. Click Summer Smash 2012 in the top bar to get back to the Dashboard. For now, you should focus your attention on the last column in the top section. Click the Choose light or darklink.

2. Summer Smash, despite being a smashing event, is a little bit darker. You're looking for an edgier feel with the site, so start by changing your theme over to dark.

3. The default link color for dark is a great orange color, but that's a little too Halloween-y for this site. Instead, change it to a nice, deep (but still contrasting) red. Click the orange color, and you'll get a handy color picker (the authors went with #e4211f, but feel free to pick whatever color you like). Also, leave your default layout with the content on the left, just as you did when developing with the form in previous chapters.

4. Save those changes and preview the site again (see Figure 12-10). We should have mentioned this earlier, but don't be dismayed if your screens have different masthead images than the screenshots in this book—Twenty Eleven rotates through a series of images.

5. Next, it's time to tweak the background a bit. Head back to the Dashboard and click the next link in the last column. You're going to use a background image to give the page a little texture. Subtlepatterns.com is a great online resource of really tasteful background textures (that are free to use). We grabbed one called "Vertical cloth" (http://subtlepatterns.com/patterns/vertical_cloth.png), but feel free to get a little creative if you like!

6. Those masthead images just aren't quite right. Head back to the dashboard and click Select a new header image.

7. The masthead is a place where you can really reinforce what this site is about. You need an image that just screams *smash*. Here's one (www.sxc.hu/photo/1181196) from a website called stock. xchng that is a great source for free stock images. That source image is a little big (WordPress indicates that the image should be 1000 pixels by 288 pixels, but it's easy enough to do a little resizing and cropping. If you don't have an image editor on your computer, don't fret. WordPress has you covered there, as well. Just upload the image, and you'll be able to crop it right on screen.

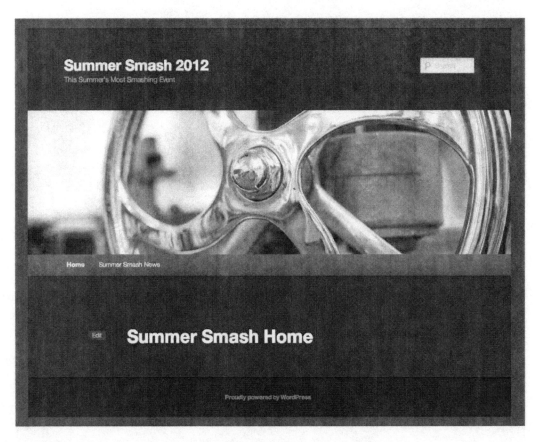

Figure 12-10. After switching to the dark variant of the default theme, your website is starting to take shape.

Going beyond

OK, the site you have now looks much different than what you started with—but what if you'd like to go further still? For example, assume you want to flex your CSS muscles and make some changes of your own. WordPress is more than happy to let you have at the source files. Click the Appearance link in the sidebar, and then click Editor.

The first file that opens up is exactly what you're looking for: the style sheet. It's quite big already; there is a lot of style information in Twenty Eleven (the current theme). The question is, where on earth should you start?

You're already familiar with what style declarations look like; you just need to know what you're applying your style to, as well as any corresponding class names/ids. Let's begin with a simple goal: to give the "content area" a bit of a glow to set it apart from the background of the page. We should mention that this chapter is just a starting point. You could delete everything and start over from scratch, writing your own custom style declarations for the various elements on your pages. However, working with what's already here provides you with a shortcut and gives you a chance to make use of your skills from the preceding chapters.

One way to approach this would be to scroll through the style sheet looking for a likely suspect (div#content, perhaps?). You can't be sure that the page author used an id of content though, or that he even used a div. Therefore, you need to use a tool called that is built-in to most browsers these days: the *Web Inspector*. Firefox, Safari, and Chrome all have this tool built-in. It can also be installed optionally with the developer tools for IE, but don't use IE—seriously.

Now load up the preview site for Summer Smash 2012. Next, right-click the content area and select the Inspect Element option (that's what the menu says in Chrome, it might be a little different in your browser of choice). You should see something similar to what is shown in Figure 12-11 (depending on where you clicked).

You'll see a preview of your page up top and the markup for your page in the bottom section. If you scroll your mouse over the various elements in the bottom of the page, they'll be highlighted in the top of the page. The Web Inspector is a ridiculously useful tool for checking out a page's structure and identifying what styles are applied to a particular element.

In this case, you're trying to find the outer-most element that encases your content. The div with an id of page looks like a good suspect. There is a trick you should be aware of when using WordPress, though; different pages may have different structures, so you should check this across a few of your pages. Begin by clicking the News page. The div#page is still there. You should also check one more thing: click "Hello World" (the sample post) just to make sure that post isn't div#post or something like that.

Everything looks good so far. Use div#page to apply your glow, and then head back to Appearance ➤ Editor and look for #page in the style sheet. You're going to put a box shadow on this element to give it a bit of a glow, so look for the following (remember to click Update File after you make your changes):

```
#page{
  margin: 2em auto;
  max-width: 1000px;
}
```

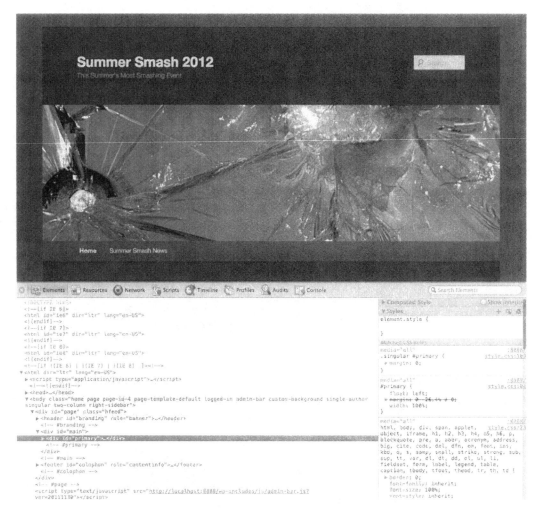

Figure 12-11. The Web Inspector tool in Chrome helps you to quickly identify various elements on a page, so that you can know what to target in your style sheet.

Now incorporate the following additions:

```
#page{
  margin: 2em auto;
  max-width: 1000px;
  -moz-box-shadow: 0 0 20px rgba(255,255,255,0.3);
  -webkit-box-shadow: 0 2 20px rgba(255,255,255,0.3);
  box-shadow: 0 0 20px rgba(255,255,255,0.3);
}
```

Box shadow is a new CSS3 property, so you need to use some of those vendor-specific prefixes for the time being. Let's make one more edit and change the header font to the one that was picked out in the earlier chapter: Frijole. First, you have to include the style sheet for Frijole, which goes in the Header of the page. To do this, go to Appearance ➤ Editor, click Header (header.php), and paste in this line:

```
<link href="http://fonts.googleapis.com/css?family=Frijole" rel="stylesheet">
```

You want this line to come before the main style sheet, so paste it in immediately above it. Click Update File when you're done. Now you need to hop back to the style sheet, so click Stylesheet (style.css) in the right column. Again, you need to figure out what the title and tagline elements are, so head back and inspect them (it might be helpful if you just open a second browser window to save yourself the trouble of jumping back and forth so often). It looks like your main header is an <h1> with an id of site-title, and your tagline is an <h2> with an id of site-description. They're both enclosed within an hgroup, albeit within a div with the id of branding. You can use the cascade to apply your font to both of these elements with a single declaration. Look for the declaration #branding hgroup in the style sheet to see some existing margin declarations. Now add your font-family declaration:

```
#branding hgroup {
  margin: 0 7.6%;
  font-family: "Frijole", Arial, sans-serif;
}
```

Next, click "Update File" and head over to take a look at your page. The nice smashing font is back.

Go beyond with plugins

Previously, we spent a few chapters designing a great registration form for our event—wouldn't it be great if we could use that and make it submit somewhere? WordPress itself doesn't have baked-in support for form handling (aside from letting visitors submit comments on a page, but we don't want that for our Registration form!). However, let's see if we can add something to WordPress that will help us out in that department.

The first order of business is to create a page for the Registration form. Follow these steps to do so:

1. Go to the Admin page, click Pages, and then choose Add New. Title this page "Registration" and, as before, turn off comments and trackbacks/pingbacks.

2. Grab the completed markup for the form from Chapter 4 and paste it in. By default, you'll be looking at the Visual editor, so toggle over to the HTML editor (in the upper-right corner) before pasting. Click Publish.

3. Next, click Plugins. You can see that there are already two plugins installed in WordPress (neither of which is active, though). The Akismet plugin will protect your blog against spammers. If you're going to be opening up comments or trackbacks on any page of your website, we highly recommend that you take a few moments to configure the Akismet plugin for your site. Hello Dolly is just a test plugin, and you can delete it.

4. Neither of these plugins does what you need in terms of forms processing though, so you need to find something to fill that role. Click Add New under Plugins in the left bar. You're looking for a *form processor*, so try doing a search for that. This search returns a lot of results, but after a quick scan of the search results, it looks like a plugin called Filled In might just fit the bill. Click the Install Now link below this plugin, and then click the Activate link.

5. Chances are that you'll have to do a little configuring before this plugin works, so click Tools and then `Filled In` in the sidebar. OK, it looks like you will have to create a new form. Call it `Registration` and click Create. You can also see a pile of other configuration options (feel free to check those out on your own); for now, you're just going to do the bare minimum to get things working. Click `Registration` in the list of forms.

You want to accomplish a couple of things with this form:

- You want the results of this form to be e-mailed to you.

- You want the registrant to see a nice "Thank You" message after clicking the Register button.

Follow these steps to set up this form:

1. Under the Post Processors section, select Send as email and click Add. Next, click the link that appears, enter your e-mail address, and click the Save button.

2. Under the Result Processor section, click the Display a 'thank-you' message option and click Add. Next, click the link that appears and enter your thank you message.

3. Check the box for "Auto Formatting" and "Replace entire page, and then click the Save button.

OK, it's great that our form will do all of that, but how do we link this up with the form we put together in previous chapters? The answer lies in the Help pages.

If you click the `Help` link in the upper-right corner and read over the Filled In Documentation, then you can easily link a form to this form processor just by giving the form an id of (in this case) `Registration`. Follow these steps to finish linking this new form up with the form we created in previous chapters:

1. Head back to your Registration page (i.e., click `Pages` and then `Registration` from the list).

2. If you did a straight copy of the form code, remove the `action=…` attribute from the form, and replace it with `id="Registration"`.

3. Click the Update button and then look at your form. You'll notice that the formatting is a bit funny because you haven't copied over any of the style information from Chapters 5 and 6; however, you can do that in a second. For now try filling it in and then clicking the Register now! button.

You'll notice a couple of things In Figure 12-12, you can see a nice Confirmation page with your thank you message displayed; it looks as though everything worked properly. However, chances are that you didn't receive an e-mail message with the registration information. That's OK; on our desktop computers, we don't have a mail server set up to handle sending those messages. Once the website is uploaded to a real web host, however, that part will work just fine. In the meantime, how can you be sure that something actually happened?

Now head back to our Admin page, click "Tools" and then the `Filled In` link. Next to your `Registration` form, you should see a 1 under the Succeeded column. Click that 1, and you'll be able to access the entry.

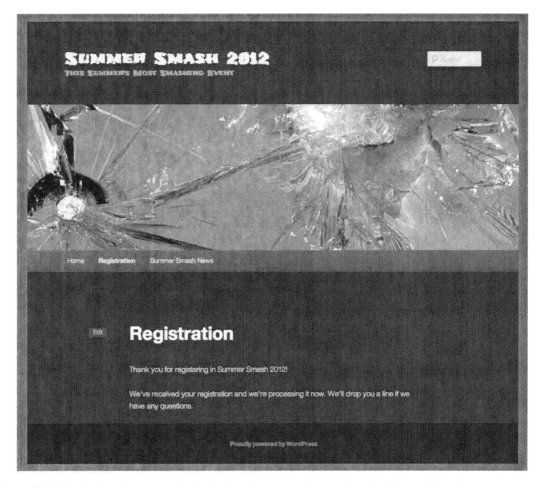

Figure 12-12. The Confirmation screen that is displayed once somebody registers for Summer Smash.

Wrapping things up

In just a few short pages, you've gone from zero to having a fully functional, database-driven website. You've taken the form that was created in previous chapters and added processing capabilities (remember to add the style declarations, as well, so that the form is properly formatted!). You've customized your WordPress theme and given it the personality that you developed in previous chapters.

Our next steps will be to work out the content of the other pages on our website, to test them out, and then to move our site over to a proper host, so that it's available 24/7.

Chapter 13

Afterword: The Business of the Web

This afterword will look at a few different areas on how to best conduct business as it relates to the Web. We've known brilliant designers who weren't very adept at billing. We've known excellent developers who have had trouble getting paid because they didn't work out the terms of an agreement before starting work. Freelancing is a very popular option among people working on the Web. We don't know whether it's the nature of the industry or just the personality type of the people who work online, but based on conversations we've had at conferences with others working in the field, there seems to be a really high occurrence of people doing side work for themselves among those employed at larger organizations. It's not uncommon to find individuals who work in completely different fields such as print design or photography (we've even met a couple of licensed electricians!) to occasionally work in web development.

This afterword will most apply to *freelancers*, or people in business for themselves. If you're working for a company, you will likely have other people who will handle things such as invoicing, setting your rates, and collecting payment (consider yourself lucky there). From time to time, everyone will have to find a little help though, so the section on hiring is fairly universal.

Basic needs of the freelance web professional

You have skills and a love for what you do. In order to turn that into a business, however, you're going to need a little bit more. If all you want is to build websites for the love of creating something, best wishes to you, and feel free to skip this chapter. If, on the other hand, you want to make a living at what you're doing, you will need to handle the business side of things too. The good news is that, as far as businesses go, web design/development is one of the easier ones to be in. You don't have to worry about inventory, shipping, or accepting returns; and you can outsource things like web hosting to any number of commercial web hosts. The risk factors are really limited because all you need in terms of equipment is a computer, and most folks have one of those already.

If this is going to be a viable business though, you'll need to have a way to find clients, convince them that they should have you do the work for them, and then ensure that you get paid for the work you do. It's only intimidating when you put it in terms like "accounts receivable," "nondisclosure agreement," and "payment schedule." These terms all translate to plain English just as HTML, CSS, and JavaScript do for you now.

We think that the biggest shift you need to make is to get into the mind-set that you're running a business. Even if your livelihood doesn't depend on the income you're getting from contract work, pretend that it does (it's not as easy as it sounds). Your attitude and approach toward watching your finances and interacting with clients/prospective clients will completely change. While it's great that you love what you do professionally, given the option, would you rather spent that chunk of time developing a web site or enjoying the outdoors with family and friends?

Being legally well informed

We'll preface this section with the common Internet disclaimer of "we are not lawyers." Even if we were, it would be impossible for us to write legal advice that would be common across all countries, states, provinces, or even cities. If you're in doubt about anything, we encourage you to seek competent legal advice. With that in mind, there are some basics that we can talk about, such as types of businesses, and we will describe some of the current best practices in the industry.

Freelancing on the side

We can't think of a single designer or developer we know employed full-time who doesn't freelance. Most employers are completely fine with it, as long as it isn't done on company time or using company resources (equipment, bandwidth, server space, and so on). Freelancing on the side is a great way to get started if you're eventually planning on going solo; it allows you to build a client base while still having the security of a salary and medical benefits.

The flip side is that if you become successful, you could find yourself with very little free time. It's pretty difficult to find motivation to work on client projects after having spent eight hours at the office, especially if your full-time job is working with the Web, too. When we were working in this situation, we would always be up-front with new clients about the lay of the land. We wouldn't try to pretend that we were working full-time on their project; we told them that it was a side business. If your client really wants to work with you, and they're somewhat flexible, things will be fine.

So how do you find the motivation? Love for what you're doing is a big part of it. Only accept projects that interest you and that you know you'll be successful at. Also, set reasonable expectations for yourself; you won't be able to put in four hours every day after work, and then spend 10 hours each day of the weekend working on projects. Allow yourself some leisure time, or you're sure to burn out.

Making the transition

One of the most common questions is, "How do I know when to quit my full-time job and freelance full-time?"— assuming that's your ultimate goal. There is no hard-and-fast rule on when you're safe to leave a regular paycheck, but you definitely need to start thinking about some savings if that's the direction you're headed.

Every case is different; if you already have a defined client base that you're working for and you're earning a good, consistent monthly income from your side work, you're probably safe to drop out of full-time work with three or four months worth of living expenses saved up. If you're starting from scratch and need to build up your client base, you shouldn't even consider going solo until you have at least six months worth of living expenses tucked away. Reaching a break-even point isn't that glamorous, but it's the single greatest feeling you'll experience early on in your freelancing career.

Think of it this way: even if you have a number of big jobs lined up, it may be months before you start seeing payment on any of them (depending on the terms you've worked out with your client). One of the things we'll look at later in this chapter is the concept of cash flow—having enough money to live on now. You may have contracts that are promising to pay you thousands of dollars when they're finished; but if your account balance is zero, and you still have weeks worth of work to do on each, then you'd better start asking your friends for dinner invitations.

One idea to consider, if you're moving in the full-time freelance direction, is to see whether your current employer will let you drop down to working part-time. That way, you'll still have the security of a regular paycheck (although diminished), but with more free time, especially within regular business hours, to build your client base and spend with existing clients.

More information

One of the best resources we found when making the switch ourselves is the Freelance Switch website (http://freelanceswitch.com). This site is a great source of information for everything from pricing your services to advertising and finding clients.

Business types

In Canada, there are three routes you can go for setting up a business; the United States adds one other option that's worth exploring. We're listing them in order of simplicity from what you can do today with no paperwork/setup to the most complex setup involving setting up a board and figuring out shareholders.

The good news is that, no matter what route you decide to go, you can handle most of your incorporation/ business setup needs from the comfort of your own home. The final filing of the papers (depending on where you live) may have to be done in person, but all of the forms and name searches (if you want to use a cool trade name like Google—wait, that's taken!) can all be done online.

Sole proprietorship

The first (and simplest) option is a sole proprietorship—going into business for yourself. The majority of people we know who do "side work" operate a sole proprietorship in which they are the only owner and operator and they get paid directly for any work they do. Come tax time, any income you've made freelancing is included on your tax return (no need to file separately for the company). Customers pay you directly, and payments can be deposited directly into your personal bank account. Any legal agreements, such as contracts or nondisclosure agreements, are between you and the client directly. If you decide to try for a bank loan to grow your operation, you'll be using your own personal assets as collateral.

The major benefit to this arrangement is that it's simple; there's really nothing special to set up. You can (in certain places) file paperwork with the government in order to secure a trade name (or "doing business as" name, sometimes abbreviated to DBA name). The drawback is that, if something goes sideways with a client or with the bank, your personal assets are on the hook. For example, if you're contracted to build an e-commerce website that subsequently gets hacked and ends up costing your client its business (don't get scared; although it's a possibility, we're talking worst case scenario here), then that client could choose to sue you. If you lose in court because you left some major security hole in the code, you will be personally responsible to pay what the court awards.

Partnership

A partnership is similar to a sole proprietorship in that the profits don't go to a company and then get paid to employees; the profits flow directly through to the partners of a company according to the division identified in a partnership agreement. There is no need to file a separate tax return for the company; any income is reported directly by the partners on their individual returns.

So, let's say you and a friend of yours decide to start a company. She's brilliant with HTML and CSS, whereas you've always been a killer designer and can produce graphics like nobody's business. You're working part-time for the local newspaper, though, and don't want to give that up at this point, so you decide that you'll be able to devote only 50 percent of your time to the company. It wouldn't be fair to split the profits 50/50 in a case like this, so you opt for a 75/25 split because your friend will be devoting all of her time to running the business, selling to potential clients, handling the accounting, and doing all the coding on website projects.

Being friends and all, you may be tempted to just start working together based on this verbal agreement. It's probably a good idea to go one step further, though, and put some things in writing. In certain places, partnerships are required to register a partnership agreement with a government office; other jurisdictions are far more lax (this is something you'll want to check on). Regardless of whether you need to have a formal partnership agreement in place and registered, you should probably draft up something that answers a few basic questions:

- Who are the partners?

- How will money be divided amongst partners?

- Who will look after what parts of the business?

- How will decisions be made about the business (vote, certain people handle certain decisions, one person has authority)? What happens when there's a tie vote?

- What happens if one of the partners wants to leave the partnership? What if one of the partners dies?

- What happens if one of the partners wants to increase their stake (such as if you decide to quit your job with the newspaper and go full-time)?

- What happens to any assets if you decide to end the partnership (dissolve the company)?

It doesn't have to be complicated and written in heavy legalese. Just put something in writing that everyone agrees to and signs off on, so that you have something to reference in case any of these situations arises. We're not trying to say that lawyers are useless here; in fact, if you have the money (usually a few hundred dollars), have a lawyer write up your partnership agreement for you; it could remove any ambiguity in future interpretations. But even if it's just a friendly document you write up over drinks one night, it will help you to have something to reference in times of trouble.

Limited Liability Company (in the United States)

An LLC isn't unique to the United States; it's also available in certain European countries (usually under a different name). The gist of an LLC is that it gives you all the simplicity of a sole proprietorship/partnership in terms of taxation, with some of the legal protection of a corporation. An LLC's profits can "flow through" to its owner/partners, so there is no need to file a separate tax return. LLCs can have shareholders, but they aren't required to hold annual shareholder meetings.

Corporation

Strictly speaking, an LLC is a form of a corporation. We mentioned it separately, though, because it's not available in all places, and it's probably your best bet if it is available to you. The most complicated route to forming a business is incorporating. In the United States (not in Canada), you have the option of either forming an S corporation (which has a lot of similar benefits to an LLC) or forming a C corporation, which is what most big companies are (like Microsoft or Dell). The differences between S and C corporations are pretty complex and have mostly to do with structure and taxation—so if this is the route you're going to go, talk to an accountant.

The single biggest benefit to incorporating, instead of going any of the other routes, is that you have a tremendous amount of flexibility in how many/what types of shares you can offer. In general, if you plan on trying to raise investment money later or if your plan is to grow your business and then sell it off, incorporating may be the best route for you. This is not to say that you can't sell any of the other types of businesses, but a corporation is the most formal of business structures.

Contracts

Contracts are a funny thing. Depending on whom you talk to, the answer will be either "never start work without a signed contract in hand" or "don't worry about contracts; a verbal agreement is fine." We take the middle road in this discussion: sometimes you need a contract, sometimes you don't.

Let us qualify that a bit: if it's a repeat customer or someone we're really familiar with, we're usually OK with just a verbal agreement (unless they have a history of not paying us!). If push ever comes to shove and you need to collect for some work you've done, having a contract in hand will make things a lot easier on you, especially in court. Chances are that you won't sue your Uncle Mort if he stiffs you for part of the bill (or maybe you will, that jerk!). Standard payment terms are to accept a deposit up front for new work, get another payment at the 50 percent point, and then get final payment on completion (25-50-25 or 50-25-25 percent are common splits). Occasionally, we'll waive this practice if it's a serial-repeat customer (we have a few of those). On the other hand, there's nothing wrong with asking a client to sign a contract or being asked to sign a contract by a client. Call it an "agreement" if you want to soften things a bit. What's important, after all, is that you both agree on the terms.

In most cases, a contract will cover a lot of the things we talked about in Chapter 2: time, money, and scope. If that sentence made you sit up a little straighter, thanks for having read and bought into what we said about project management: how can you define scope in the contract when you're not sure what the project will look like?

You can define it generally (you're going to be doing the website, but not a logo, business card, and three-panel brochure for the company), and then put in a statement about how things will be revised as the project progresses. This informal, up-front contract can sometimes be called a statement of work (SOW); it just provides a written record of some of the things that both you and your client understand about the project. It doesn't hurt to describe the way you work, too; for example, if you're only going to present a single design option, say so. If you're only delivering completed files and none of the working files (for whatever reason), say that too. The less surprises, the better. Don't get exhaustive, though; a 30 page contract for a two-week project is overkill.

Your contract/agreement/statement of work should contain a price and payment terms. It should also include any penalties for late payment (including the interest rate you charge). Finally, if your client has a "drop-dead" date, be sure to include that. If it doesn't, feel free to include a launch date of your own—it can really help to keep a project on track if you've got a set end date written down and agreed to.

Do you need a lawyer?

The short answer is maybe/eventually. When you're just starting out, lawyer fees can be a bit daunting. Most lawyers charge hundreds of dollars per hour, which usually translates to a lot of billable hours for a new freelancer. Chances are that most of your clients when you're starting out will be reasonably small, and you'll be able to work really closely with them. That goes a long way toward avoiding potential the legal hassles that lead to one person suing the other. For the work you're doing in the beginning, the costs to sue/defend a lawsuit will be way higher than just completely refunding your client (not that you should immediately offer that option if there is some disagreement).

What we're getting at is that you should, in the beginning, skip the lawyer. You can find contract templates and other legal forms online or offline in a lot of business-supply stores and bookstores. You can then customize these templates to your own needs. It really isn't until you start to get into projects that are worth tens of thousands of dollars that you should get concerned about the legal system. Even then, keep your head down, do good work, and everything will work out in your favor. Nobody is going to stiff you if they're ridiculously happy with the work you've done (okay, somebody will, like that jerk Uncle Mort).

Resources?

Here are some resources to keep in mind:

- `www.designerstoolbox.com/`: Let's you buy individual templates that you can then customize.

- `www.nolo.com/`: Provides good, general legal advice on all kinds of things.

- `www.mynewcompany.com/`: Serves as a good resource for new businesses, providing information on how to incorporate, and so on.

Nondisclosure/noncompete

You're not likely to have to deal with either of these early on (we have yet to see one from a client); but in the event that you do, it's good to know what you're getting into. Normally, a nondisclosure agreement is pretty harmless; it's just there to make sure you keep anything you learn from your client to yourself. Your client/employer may ask you to sign one of these if you're going to be exposed to some sensitive company material. Generally, these agreements are there to prevent you from learning everything about a client's business and then taking that and marketing it to one of its competitors.

The only thing to watch out for is if the nondisclosure you're asked to sign also has a noncompete clause. What that means is that you may be legally prevented from taking on certain clients for a period of time. So, if you went to work for Pepsi and were asked to sign an NDA with a noncompete that had a five-year term, you couldn't then, two years later, go and work for Coca-Cola.

The two factors to look at are the length of the term and how general the clause is. We're not saying to refuse to ever sign an NDA with a noncompete clause. You just need to be sure to read it before signing and to decide whether the benefits outweigh the costs. If you take the Pepsi/Coke example, add in the fact that your practice specializes in food and beverage manufacturer websites, and then also add in a clause that actually applies to all beverage manufacturers (not just Coca-Cola), then you're effectively reducing your potential client base for the next five years.

If the contract with Pepsi is profitable enough (either financially or in terms of prestige) and if your practice is general enough that you'll have no trouble finding clients outside of the industry, then go for it. The terms of these agreements are usually not written in stone though, so feel free to give it a thorough read and suggest revisions.

Making money: financial survival

You're probably not in this just for the glamor of sitting at a computer for hours a day, and you probably want to make a little money. Thus, looking after your finances is a good idea. There are a few terms and concepts you should be familiar with in order to ensure your financial well-being. Although you hear a great deal about revenue and profits when you're watching business news, a more important concept for new business people to learn is about cash flow.

Staying in business

Yes, it's important to make money (revenue). And yes, it's important to turn a profit (bring in more money than you spend). But both of these concepts are secondary in the early stages as you're just struggling to survive. Cash flow is more of a big-picture concept where you look at how much money you're starting out with (savings), how much you're going to make every month (revenue), and what your expenses are every month. In the early stages of starting your freelancing career, don't expect to be pulling in profits hand-over-fist. In fact, if you're making enough money to cover your own living expenses, you're doing great!

Let's look at a quick example of cash flow. We'll assume that you're starting out with some savings and that you're the only source of income for your household (you aren't, for example, living rent-free in your parent's basement). You've just quit your job and are starting up your own freelancing practice. You've managed to put away $5,000 in savings, in addition to already owning your own equipment.

You've also sat down with a spreadsheet and determined that you need $2,000 per month to cover rent, utilities, and to eat. It's easy to see that, if you don't get a single paying job for the next 60 days, you're going to be out of business. You need to pull in at least $1000 over the next 60 days just to stay in business, and then you'd need to double that in the following 30 days. That's not an impossible proposition, but taking a two-week holiday somewhere in the middle probably isn't in the cards.

Getting paid (aka accounts receivable)

Standard practice in the web design and development world is to accept a down payment at the start of any work, another payment at the halfway point, and then a final payment that covers the remaining balance upon completion of the project. If you're doing fixed-price work (quoting a total for the project up front as opposed to working hourly), then normal practice is to divide your payments into 50:25:25 or 25:50:25 percent (feel free to adjust these terms however you like; these are just guidelines).

The reasoning behind taking a majority payment up front is that it commits your client to the project. Although that might seem like a silly statement to make, it's not uncommon to get hired by a client asking to have a project developed, for you to put in a bunch of work in developing a prototype or design for them, and then have that client drop off the face of the earth because the client gets busy with other things. If the client isn't committed enough to pay you half of the total contract up front, then chances are the client isn't committed enough to follow through until completion. We'll reiterate here what's been said a million times in this book: developing a website is a collaborative process; you are going to need your client to work with you throughout the process.

As with everything, take things on a case-by-case basis; but with new clients that you've never worked with before, a substantial deposit is your only insurance they'll stay engaged.

Tracking time and invoicing

Regardless of how you're billing (flat rate or hourly), keeping track of the time you spend on individual projects is essential. It's completely within your clients' rights to ask to see an accounting of the time you've spent on their project, and it will help you down the road at estimating (quoting) a job. It's the only source of data that you'll have if you get into financial trouble and need to try to figure out why you aren't making money. It might not always be obvious, but if you have a log of the time you spent over the past few months, you'll at least be able to see whether the problem is that you haven't been putting in enough billable hours or whether your rate is set too low.)

Thousands of different applications will run on a Mac, a Windows machine, or even a number of really good, web-based products that will let you track your hours. A lot of these products are integrated with some type of invoicing software, so once you've tracked the number of hours you put in on a project, you can then automatically generate an invoice to send off to your client. Speaking from experience, a client is far less likely to question the hours on an invoice if it contains a good amount of detail. Handing someone a piece of paper that says "10 hours: $300" just won't cut it. Break it out into individual work periods (Mar. 2: two hours, Mar. 5: two hours, and so on), and be sure to provide a short description of what you were working on during that time.

We use an excellent web-based product called Harvest (www.getharvest.com) for all of our time tracking and invoicing (full disclosure: Jonathan also works for Harvest). Harvest makes it really easy to run timers for the work you're doing (whether that's billable or unbillable work) and then report on your time and invoice your client based on those hours.

Do you need an accountant?

Although we stayed pretty noncommittal about the need for a lawyer, we will highly recommend that you talk to an accountant early on in your freelancing career. An accountant will tell you what you need to keep track of come tax time and will be able to help you immensely (save you money) if you decide to set up a corporation.

If you're really determined to save the expense, you can forego getting things set up professionally. Just bear in mind that it may end up costing you a little extra come tax time. Either hire yourself an accountant or save a little extra money from every invoice (just in case). Taxation varies a great deal from country to country, state to state, province to province, and in some cases, from city to city. If you decide to go it alone, without seeking the advice of a professional, then at least look for information that's specific to your locale. Assuming that advice from the United States will apply in Canada (and vice versa) is foolish.

Resources

Here are some resources:

- http://cpadirectory.com/: A directory of certified public accountants (in the United States)
- www.accountants-4u.ca/: A directory of Canadian accountants

Advertising and promotion

The best (and least expensive) way to gain exposure is to do really good work. If you build up a solid reputation as someone who produces high-quality work and is reliable in meeting time and budgets, then you'll receive a ton of business through word-of-mouth referrals. What better way could there be to find more good clients than to have your current good clients recommend you to their associates?

If your specialty is in design, build up a great portfolio (and show it off). If you're having trouble landing those first few clients because you have nothing to show them, make some stuff up. Just because the "Bank of Steve" doesn't actually exist doesn't mean that it doesn't need a website. Similarly, the "Antarctic Beach Resort" is just crying out for a solid online presence; it's way more fun making up your own clients with their own bizarre requirements than to have to explain real-life examples most of the time, anyway.

No client is too big or too small to be showcased, and no client is too real or too imaginary.

A word of caution, especially when you're starting out: some folks will offer to "let you" do their web site for free in order to build up your portfolio. Under no circumstances should you ever accept these gigs. If you want to build your portfolio, do it on your own terms. If you work for people free, they won't respect you, and they won't respect your time. The project will end badly. It will. We're serious.

Getting the word out

But hey, producing a great product is not enough. You have to shout it from the rooftops once it's done. The best way to do that is to build up your reputation online. The only way to build a reputation is to get out there and communicate. It's just like you'll be telling your clients: it's not enough to have a really great website; people have to know about it and visit it, too.

There are a few ways you can drive traffic to your website. You could go out and buy some advertising, but if money is tight, it might be more useful to look at some free alternatives:

- *Participate*: Comment on blogs, join threads in discussion groups, and write your own blog; do anything to get your name out there. It used to be said that there's no such thing as bad publicity. That's certainly not true online. If you're out there stating your opinion and joining the discussion, don't be a jerk. Nobody wants to work with a jerk.

- *Write*: Write and submit an article or two for an industry-specific website. Websites like A List Apart (alistapart.com) take submissions from their readers all the time. Your article will need to be well thought out and pretty innovative; but if you manage to get published, you'll get an instant jump in prestige out of it.

- *Design*: Developers have it rough. It's really hard to get anyone (other than another developer) excited about code you've written. We have yet to hear anyone exclaim: "Wow! Look how efficiently it parses that text string!" Designers, on the other hand, are constantly producing beautiful work that's easy to show off. Similar to A List Apart, if you're a designer, get your work featured on CSS Zen Garden (www.csszengarden.com), and a number of other people in the industry will get to see it. Publish your own beautiful portfolio of work, as well.

- *Develop*: Join an open source project and get involved in the community. If you're pretty good with PHP, Ruby on Rails, Python, or any number of other languages, there are all kinds of open source projects to choose from. Pick one and start looking at the code. Fix up/improve on it, and submit it; it won't be long until other developers start noticing your work. Designers, this works for you, too. Many open source projects suffer from very poor visual design; pick one and clean it up.

All of these activities will give you name recognition, and chances are people will start to link to your website. Although you're making your mark primarily within the community (you're not really getting exposure with potential clients), when you're starting out, a lot of your work may come as a subcontractor to someone else or as a referral from someone who's just too busy and was really impressed with your work. That's a great way to land clients, make new contacts, and even secure yourself a mentor.

Finding work to pay the bills

Following the steps in advertising and promotion (discussed earlier) will eventually get you the clients that you've always dreamed of. It's really a wonderful feeling once clients start coming to you in sufficient quantities that you can pick and choose who you want to work for. However, that doesn't happen overnight. Sometimes, you'll just need to pay the bills.

You have two options for finding work right out of the gate. You can go local and try to drum up work in your city or town, or you can go online to a number of job sites that post contract jobs. There are advantages and disadvantages to each approach; let's look at each individually.

Working locally

Depending on your locale, this may be a viable option for you. If you're in an urban center, flush with businesses looking to build an online identity, then you have a viable source of work. If you live in a rural setting, where you have to drive an hour to the nearest supermarket, chances are lower (but not nonexistent). The biggest single advantage to working with local clients is that you have access to them. If you're developing a website for Acme Hotels down the street, and you want feedback on what you've done, all you need to do is go for a short walk.

Recruiting local clients can be much easier, as well (at least we've found this to be the case). It's hard to convince someone that you're the right person for the job using only e-mail and phone calls. Meeting with someone in person to discuss their needs and expectations and talking with them about work you've done is often a far easier way to sell yourself. In general, people will first look at whether you'll be good/easy to work with before they will look extensively through your portfolio of work. That doesn't mean you don't have to produce quality projects; but small-business owners, in particular, like working with other small-business owners.

Working locally also has its challenges. The same advantage that access to people gives you during development can turn into a challenge if you land a client who is needy and believes that every problem is a disaster (you know the type). Other disadvantages—again, depending on your locale—are that local projects may be smaller (in terms of budget) and the local mind-set may be that web development services are worth little.

We previously lived in a primarily agricultural center. Although there was work to be had locally, the budgets for local projects were often no higher than a couple of thousand dollars (and that was for fairly complex projects). People in this center just didn't realize the amount of work that goes into certain things, and they truly believed that technical skills are a very cheap commodity. Your mileage may definitely vary on this factor, however.

Be innovative in this space. Small businesses can be quite concerned with the costs of a website getting out of control and "hidden costs" in a web project. We've seen some really great approaches to addressing this issue, such as offering package pricing for a web site: the scope is very clearly defined, and a fixed price is set. Businesses know what they'll be paying, and you can rest assured that a project will only hit a certain size and timeframe.

Finding work online

Finding work online has become increasingly difficult. There are a huge variety of job sites allowing employers to post contract gigs. You aren't limited by geography; assuming the client is comfortable working at a distance, you can bid on projects nationally or even internationally. It can take some practice to produce projects completely online; for example, not being able to schedule a face-to-face meeting if something goes wrong is a bit of a detriment. Also, it can make it harder to enforce contracts/collect payment, especially from clients in other countries. If you do decide to go this route, be diligent about getting a deposit up front.

The major downside, of course, is that your competition isn't limited by geography either. You'll often find yourself bidding against folks from countries where the cost of living is significantly lower than it is in North America. Some clients won't care and will simply go for the lowest bidder. Others will be hesitant to work with individuals where language may be a barrier to success. The only thing you can do here is stand behind your work; if you have a great portfolio, you'll win over those clients who have a large enough budget to pay you. Just make sure you're not cutting your rate to compete with individuals in India or Vietnam; that's not a sustainable set up.

Finding good resources: people

You've survived the startup, and your client base and the corresponding workload have increased to the point where you need some help. It's time to hire, subcontract, or partner. There's a bunch of options here, and they're all appropriate in various circumstances.

Hiring: finding the right skills and personality

Hiring is one of the most intimidating and difficult decisions for a new freelancer (or business owner) to make. It's the point where you decide that you are making enough money to not only support yourself, but also to support someone else. You have to be sure that you're not just enjoying a temporary spike in business, but that you've seen enough steady growth that you can now sustain two (or more) people.

All of that aside, you have to make sure you find the right person(s) for your business. Not only do potential employees need the right mix of skills and interests, but they also need to be able to fit in culturally. As the only employee up until this point, you've set the culture of the company. If you value alone time and being able to work through a problem on your own from start to finish, hiring people who need to constantly collaborate to solve problems may not be the best bet (or maybe it is, and you can offload all your client-facing work to them, which leaves you to work behind the scenes). Hiring someone who believes in a strict development cycle will certainly go crazy working for a firm that practices agile development.

We've sat through countless interviews and hired quite a few people to join our team in the past. Hands down, the people who have worked out best were those individuals who fit in culturally, well above those individuals who looked really good "on paper." Skills can be learned, but the right attitude toward the work you do is something that only certain people will bring to the table.

Where do you find candidates?

The best hires we've ever made have been people we found out about through referrals. If a friend of a friend is looking for a job, we're usually very interested. The main reason is that it's difficult to recommend someone for a job. If a friend of ours refers somebody and that person is a complete disaster, we won't even consider going to that friend for a referral ever again. Likewise, if we're ever asked to refer somebody, we will draw upon only the very small pool of individuals we've worked with, people we know will be able to accomplish what needs to get done.

If you're having trouble finding candidates for what you're looking for, rethink what you're looking for. We live on an island with 1000 other people. The chances of us finding someone local who can develop websites, configure web servers, and work directly with clients on projects is slim. Expecting a local candidate—or even expecting that someone be willing to relocate here to work for us—would severely limit our pool of candidates.

Likewise, you shrink that pool considerably when you advertise a job using the shotgun approach. Monster. com is horrible for job ads that request candidates be expert PHP programmers, Photoshop masters, Flash developers, and certified project managers. Although it may be true that what you really need is a generalist, most people don't categorize themselves as such. Most people will say that they are a really strong designer, so listing "PHP expert" will immediately have them self-disqualify.

If you have to resort to posting a job ad, try Craigslist first. We're not sure what it is; it's probably just the type of person who frequents Craigslist, but in general, applicants to well-written Craigslist ads seem to be of a higher quality. The only real drawback is that you do have to target the ad geographically; if local/remote work doesn't bother you, then you will have a difficult time reaching all potential candidates using Craigslist.

Finding temporary help: subcontracting

Subcontracting is pretty common in the web industry. The major advantage to hiring subcontractors is that the labor is available to pick up the slack when you're busy, but you don't have an ongoing commitment to feed those individuals work. The biggest drawback to subcontracting is that the people you're working with aren't your employees, so they may be busy when you need them. Also, identifying reliable individuals who are easy to work with can be difficult.

There are some key things to keep in mind when subcontracting work:

- *Subcontractors work for you.* They are not partners, and they don't work for your client. If your client decides he isn't going to pay you for a project that you've already completed with the help of subcontractor(s), you're still on the hook to pay your subcontractor(s). This is another great reason why you should get partial payment up front on a job.

- *Subcontractors are responsible for their own equipment.* You aren't required to buy them a computer or a piece of software to complete a job. The price they quote you to do a job is just like the price you quote your client: all-inclusive.

- *You don't need to deduct taxes or provide benefits to a subcontractor.* They'll take care of their own taxes when they report their income at tax time. They aren't employees, so they get treated differently. Depending on the amount of work you throw their way though, you may still have some tax hoops to jump through, so check with your accountant on that front.

- *In essence, you're the client when using a subcontractor.* All of the rules that apply to your clients may apply to you (depending on the contractor), and they may require partial payment upfront. They may also want you to sign a contract for their services.

Expect to pay a higher hourly rate for a subcontractor than you would an employee (of the same quality). Subcontractors are just like you; they're trying to make a living. They need to provide for themselves all the overhead (e.g., office space, Internet connection, and computer equipment) that you would normally provide for an employee. As such, contractors will typically charge a premium for their services over what you would pay an employee with a similar skill set/level of experience.

Partnering with others to complement skill sets

We talked about partnerships earlier; but in a different sense, you may encounter people or organizations with which you want to partner. This makes complete sense if you each have a set of skills that is unique or if you both address a similar market. Joining forces will allow you to do more while sharing all the risks and benefits that go with that partnership.

Similar to hiring, however, make sure there is compatibility in company culture if you plan on working closely. A number of web designers and developers will either officially or unofficially partner with a hosting provider. It's difficult and expensive to run a server and to keep it online 24/7. Usually, freelancers don't have the resources to do it themselves (your home DSL line just won't cut it for bandwidth).

A simple example of partnering is that most hosting companies will offer a reseller discount. So if you sign one of your clients up for web hosting with them, they will charge you 10 percent less than the normal rate. You can then turn around and charge your client the full rate and pocket that profit. There's an advantage to the hosting company because you're bringing it business, and it's happy to reciprocate by throwing a little money your way in return. It sure beats buying a really expensive server, high-quality bandwidth, and better backups; hiring a systems administrator; and possibly even colocating your server depending on your needed uptime.

You may partner, on an ad hoc basis, with other individuals from time to time, as well. If you're working on a job and need to bring in some expertise; or, if you're brought in on a job because of your expertise; then make sure that you establish the relationship up front. If it's a partnership, you're entitled to a part of the profits (and you're entitled to know what those profits are). You're also at risk though: if the client doesn't pay, you don't get paid.

Growing your practice and increasing capacity

Don't fear growth, but at the same time don't rush toward it foolishly. If you need additional people or equipment or servers to host your clients, then get them; however, don't do this in response to a "what if" scenario. What if your hosting plan doesn't have enough disk space to accommodate this new website? Wait and see; soon enough, you'll find out whether you need more disk space. Don't upgrade to the next most expensive hosting plan in advance out of fear that you'll run out of space. Don't hire that new employee now because you think you'll have enough work for them to do in the future. If you have enough for them to do now, hire them; if not, subcontract it or just juggle your schedule.

Growth is the single greatest thing and, at the same time, the biggest challenge to any team. You'll hear that you need to grow to survive; that's hogwash. If you have a good, diverse client base, you're making enough money to cover your expenses (and feel free to increase those expenses as you become more successful), and you're happy with what you're currently doing, then you have no obligation to grow beyond where you're at currently. For some bizarre reason, there is a mentality in the business world that you have to constantly grow and expand, turning higher profits every year and hiring more employees. Why?

Bear in mind that there will be additional overhead in growing your team. This means that, if your workload doubles overnight for some strange reason, and you have enough work for two of you to do, then hiring someone will not automatically solve the problem. Generally, when new people come on, they will need some time to get up to speed with company policies and practices; they will need to become familiar with your clients; and more than likely, you will have to be the one to bring them up to speed. So although you shouldn't hire early to deal with an anticipated workload, you shouldn't wait until the last minute either, expecting a new hire to come in and save the day.

Training to stay current and competitive

The last topic we'll cover is training. As a web professional, you have an obligation to yourself and to your clients to keep your skills up-to-date. Thankfully, the very medium you work in is also one of the greatest sources of information about your profession. It's really easy to keep up on things by reading various online sources of information.

Books are another good option, but the thing with books is that the information goes out-of-date at some point (we appreciate the irony of you reading this in a book!). That's not to say that books don't have their place; books are generally highly concentrated sources of information that are professionally organized and presented. A good book can really give you a leg up and jump-start your understanding of a particular topic.

There are also a number of really good industry conferences that take place every year at various locations. The cost to attend these conferences can be quite high, but we have never regretted a decision to attend one because of the great information and networking opportunities offered. Without fail, when we return from a conference, we always have a flood of new ideas and creative energy, even if the actual speakers contributed little actual new knowledge.

The bottom line is that training consumes resources, both in time and in money—but it's also essential. If you don't keep current on industry trends, you will lose your competitive edge in this business because clients look for designers and developers who can provide the latest solutions.

Index

D

other applications, 26
Trac application, 24–25
traditional Waterfall model, 13
  communications management, 14
  cost management, 14
  human resource management, 14
  integration management, 14
  procurement management, 14
  quality management, 14
  risk management, 14
  scope management, 14
  time management, 14
Project planning. *See* Planning
Prototype of product, 41–42
Pseudo-class selectors, 100
  adjacent sibling selectors, 102
  child selectors, 102
  descendant selectors, 101
  simple selectors, 99
Python, 229, 230, 232

R

RDBMS. *See* Relational database
  management system (RDBMS)
Record, 223–227, 231
Relational database, 223, 225. *See also*
  Structured Query Language (SQL)
Relational database management system
  (RDBMS)
  definition, 223
  MSSQL, 227
  MySQL, 228
  Oracle, 227, 228
  PostgreSQL, 228
Relative link, 61–62
Remote procedure call (RPC), 228
Resident memory, 164, 165
Responsive design
  @media query, 149–152
    phone-specific rules, 152–155
    source code, 156
    tablet-specific rules, 155–156
  mobile-friendly website, 148
  responsive website, 147, 148
  screen size, bandwidth and speed, 148
    website in range of resolutions, 149

Responsive website, 147, 148
RoR. *See* Ruby on Rails
  (RoR) framework
RPC. *See* Remote procedure call (RPC)
Ruby, 220–222, 229–232
Ruby on Rails (RoR) framework, 229–232

S

Schema, 223, 224
Scripting languages. *See* Web application
  languages
Self-invoking functions, 184–186
Server-side scripting languages. *See* Web
  application languages
Server-side technologies
  database, 219, 221, 223–229, 231–233
  data sources, 220, 228–229
  field/column, 223
  foreign key, 223, 224
  frameworks
    CakePHP, 232
    Django, 232
    Ruby on Rails (RoR), 220–222,
    229–232
  interaction and security concerns, 218
  primary key, 223–227
  record, 223–227, 231
  relational database, 223, 225
  relational database management
    system (RDBMS)
  definition, 223
  MSSQL, 227
  MySQL, 228
  Oracle, 227, 228
  PostgreSQL, 228
  schem, 223, 224
  Structured Query Language (SQL), 223,
    225–227
  table, 223–226, 228, 231
  web application languages
    ASP.NET, 230
    Java/JavaServer Pages (JSP), 230
    PHP, 229
    Python, 230
    Ruby, 229–230
  web hosting

X, Y

Z

CPSIA information can be obtained at www.ICGtesting.com
Printed in the USA
LVOW110742041112

305742LV00003B/62/P